Suzane Piela, R.N.

You Are So Beautiful Without Your Hair
A Daughter's Journey
with the Death of her Parents

Suzane Piela, R.N.

You Are So Beautiful Without Your Hair

A Daughter's Journey
with the Death of her Parents

Bluestar
Communications®
Woodside, California

© 2000 Suzane Piela

Published by:
Bluestar Communications
44 Bear Glenn
Woodside, CA 94062
Tel: 800-6-Bluestar

Edited by Jude Berman

Cover design:Petra Michel
Layout: Petra Michel
Cover photograph: © 2000 Suzane Piela
All other photographs: Mary C. Bowlin

First printing 2000
ISBN: 1-885394-37-3

Library of Congress Cataloging-in-Publication Data

Piela, Suzane, 1952-
    You are so beautiful without your hair : a daughter's journey with
the death of her parents / Suzane Piela.
        p. cm.
    ISBN 1-885394-37-3
    1. Death--Psychological aspects. 2. Parents--Death--Psychological as-
pects. 3. Cancer--Patients--United States. 4. Terminally ill-
-Family relationships. 5. Loss (Psychology) 6. Grief. I. Title.
BF789.D4P54   1999
155.9'37'092--dc21   99-21686
[B]   CIP

All rights reserved. No part of this book may be reproduced in any form without the
written permission of the publishers, except for brief quotations embodied in critical articles
and reviews.

Printed in USA

Dedication

To my parents, John and Edna Piela,
for whom I've become.
"Z" and Solano, for their counsel of wisdom,
love and support.
And to God, for whom I am.

To Inge —
May your life be rich
with abundant blessings.

Love,
Suzane

Suzane Piela and her family
(Top row from the left: Vernon, Ron, Johnny, Mark, Mary.
Bottom row from the left: Ann, Edna, John, Suzane)

Contents

Foreword

It was a cool, clear night as I ventured out into Topanga Canyon State Park in Los Angeles to do my New Year's Eve blessing. The stars in the sky looked like millions of vibrant sparkling diamonds as I made my way in the darkness to the place I had chosen for my annual ceremony. The moon in its glorious fullness lit the dirt path, eliminating my need for a flashlight. In the distance I heard coyotes baying, as if they, too, desired to have their prayers heard on the wind. The multi-colored Peruvian bag on my back carried my Native American ceremonial pipe and treasures from the altar in my home. It had become a ritual for me to bless the new year outside in nature, where I felt the greatest connection to God and in harmony with the earth.

There was something different about my ceremony that particular year. I felt the winds of change stirring inside, the way an autumn breeze swirls falling leaves before they touch the ground. I sat on a blanket on the damp, hard earth with my holy objects in front of me on a red, flannel cloth. I wrapped another blanket around my shoulders to keep me warm from the crisp chill of the night. A magical stillness echoed through the canyon, as if to sing silent thanks for blessings of the past year and to offer up hope for the new one.

As I sat with my legs crossed in a yoga position, I gently placed the alabaster bowl of my pipe on the ground with the stem resting on my lap. I blessed the naturally grown tobacco, pressing it to my forehead and asked that the smoke offer my sincere prayers to the Creator. I reverently placed the tobacco in the pipe bowl and felt a quiet wind sweetly nudge my face. A peaceful feeling washed over me and I smiled to myself.

Taking a breath, I drew the naked silence deep inside. My eyes were drawn to the full moon positioned in front of me. It was huge and possessed a seductive quality I had never felt before. An aura of golden blue surrounded it, creating rays of light that radiated a magical glow. Before I could light the pipe with my first prayer, I felt myself mysteriously pulled upward, my face fixated on the brilliant ball of light. And I was drawn into the loving embrace of its energy, like a mother's arms around her newborn babe. I heard my voice speak into the silence, "Beloved Creator of all life, thank you for the gift of who I am and the privilege of being on this earth. Transform my life that my vocation and my dedication to being in service to God be one and the same. Guide me in my greatest potential to express my gifts for the highest good of my soul and all of humankind. I proclaim my love to you and commit my life … always … to you."

As these words vibrated like a hum through my body, I felt a mystical force surround me. I heard a strong, gentle voice outside my head say, "Blessings, sweet child of the Light. You have the grace and strength to soar like an eagle in your unwavering love of God. You are asked to take on the challenge presented before you, if you so choose. You have the capacity and will reap great rewards. Be in joy and walk always in the love and power of God."

All of a sudden, I found myself standing with my arms outstretched to the heavens and I heard myself speak in a strong, clear tone: "I accept this challenge. Provide me the courage to walk forward."

I heard no reply. Unable to move, I was riveted to the ground. I felt as if I were in a dream-like state and everything seemed surreal. A peacefulness pervaded inside and I hungered for it to last forever. Many moments passed and then I felt the mystical energy slowly release around me. As I looked into the sky, it took a minute for my eyes to focus. The moon had lost its golden-blue hue and looked like a small, white ball far off in the distance.

I sat back down on my blanket and stared out into the night. My mind was blank and all I felt was great euphoria. I had no idea how late it was, nor how much time had passed since the mysterious voice had spoken to me. I knew something profound had just happened in a place deep inside me. My body began to gently rock back and forth as I gathered my pipe in my hands to continue the ceremony. It suddenly became apparent that it was complete.

Little did I realize, as I walked in humbleness down that canyon path in the early morning hours of 1993, that I was being prepared for a mission that would change my life dramatically. It would occur two years later and result in the death of both of my parents a little more than a year apart.

I was guided to write *You Are So Beautiful Without Your Hair* as a book about hope and the possibility of experiencing death and the dying process in a new way. Both my parents were diagnosed with cancer in 1995. My father passed away five months after his diagnosis. I returned to my childhood roots, uprooting from a busy metropolitan lifestyle, and cared for my mother. She passed away at home one year later.

The reality of their terminal illnesses was devastating and I was faced with a choice. I could view the circumstances before me as unfair and tragic, or trust in my spiritual understanding about death. I chose to embrace it as a sacred event and look for the magnificent pearls interwoven throughout the experience. What resulted was an extraordinary journey into the miracles, mystery and grace within the dying process.

We all face the death of our parents. No one is immune. It affects people from all walks of life and every spiritual perspective. What makes it unique is how each person walks through it. For most people, just talking about death or dying is extremely uncomfortable and overwhelming. The mere thought casts a dark cloud of fear and trepidation. Whether we are the person facing death or a family member, the experience penetrates the very core of our existence. Individuals feel lost, confused, helpless and conflicted about how to be with each other. A vast array of emotions emerges and lives are forever changed. We are left harboring ashes of pain, loss, incompletion, regret and sorrow.

Death need not be this way. It can be a time of renewal and intimacy—an uplifting experience of coming together, as profound and blessed as the miracle of birth. As we gently tender a new life into this world, it seems only natural to gently tender a tired and weary life out—to cradle that same life who brought us into this world and embrace the exquisite nature of that one's soul.

In the seeming adversity that was before my family, this was my experience. I have shared my intimate story to present the possibility for a higher creed in living the holiness of death. It is my hope that hearts find strength, comfort, courage and freedom within its words and be blessed to know the beauty of this path.

You Are So Beautiful Without Your Hair is a testimonial to the resilience and mystery of the human spirit.

Chapter One

A Past Experience Connects the Future

I awoke with an uneasy feeling in my stomach that lingered all day. It was not the first time I had felt that way—and, each time it occurred, something dramatic happened. One of my most vivid memories of a similar sensation was on my thirtieth birthday. Living in Seattle at the time, I had been working the night shift as an R.N. at University Hospital, near the Washington campus. The queasy feeling began while I was getting ready to leave the Cardiac Unit on the third floor. Changing out of my nursing uniform into jeans, a fleeting thought signaled to be careful that day.

It was October and a light drizzle was falling as I left the hospital around quarter to eight that morning. While unchaining my bicycle from the bike rack, I breathed in the freshness of the autumn air and the unique fragrance fall weather brings. This had always been my favorite time of year. It stimulated an excitement that made me feel very alive, and a yearning to spend time alone in the inner sanctuary of myself.

On that particular morning, the tiredness from working all night was overshadowed by anticipation of taking a three-day trip to the Oregon coast to celebrate my birthday. The mixture of the uneasy feeling coupled with the excitement of turning thirty left me feeling a little perplexed. I wondered if maybe I wasn't supposed to go on the trip. Adjusting the straps of the green canvas backpack, I found myself saying a prayer while waiting at the curb for the traffic light to turn green. "Dear God, please watch over me today. If I'm not supposed to go to the coast, give me a clear sign."

As the light turned yellow, I glanced both ways at the traffic. Seeing no cars in either direction, I swung my leg over the bar of my brand new, black bicycle. With my right foot pushing down on the pedal, I began to ride slowly across the intersection. One rotation of the pedals and something told me to look toward the left. Out of nowhere, a blue car appeared and began to skid on the wet pavement as the driver slammed on her brakes. Through the sound of squealing tires, I heard a voice inside my head: "Turn your bike to the right." As I did, the tail end of the car smashed into the left side of my body. I was thrown from the bicycle and landed on the green backpack, preventing the back of my head from directly hitting the pavement. In that moment, I was keenly aware my life had just been spared.

For some reason I felt calm lying on the wet asphalt. A moist, light rain was falling on my face as my eyes glanced upward to the gray sky. I was conscious of a hysterical woman and a policeman hovering over me. My mind thought, "Okay, God, I get it. I'm not taking this trip. Thank you for saving my life and having the hospital right across the street." In spite of the severity of the impact, I had no broken bones and only a few minor lacerations to my right hand, elbow and knee. Within two days, my entire body was black and blue, making it almost impossible to move for a week. Consequently my birthday trip to the Oregon coast never materialized.

The experience left me with two important insights.

Life is not about random events that have no purpose. Everything happens for a reason. Each experience affords us an opportunity to grow and change, rather than see ourselves as victims of situations. Instead of feeling powerless over what happens, we always have a choice to take a new action or shift our perspective to see something in a new way. Being physically unable to take the trip forced me to stop and look intimately at my life.

The second lesson was to listen and honor my gut instincts. In the day-to-day activity of doing, it is easy to believe the mind is in control and knows the best course of action. Somehow I wasn't hearing an inner guidance trying to get my attention. It took a bike accident to literally knock me off my feet and open my ears internally. There was no question a voice was saying loud and clear, "Hey, wake up. Look at where your life is headed." The accident definitely made an impact, not only physically but also emotionally and spiritually. I began to reassess many things in my life, especially the manner in which God communicated with me and how I wasn't listening.

Years had passed since the bike accident and my world had changed dramatically. I now worked in the entertainment industry for a dear friend of mine, Sabrina. She had her own small production company that created inspiring and uplifting projects, and was also writing her first book. Her office was in her home in Beverly Hills and my responsibilities entailed marketing and development.

On this particular morning, as I went to work, there was a difference in the precariousness of my feeling. I could sense something was going to happen, but I was not especially concerned for myself. It reminded me of when a farmer says he can smell change in the wind, but can't pinpoint what it is.

Being a very intuitive person, Sabrina sensed something was going on almost the minute I walked in the front door. "Good morning Suzane." She greeted me with her usual hug. "Are you okay?"

There was a concerned look on her face and her eyes pierced through mine as if she could see deep into my soul. For some reason I felt vulnerable and did not care to share the uneasiness inside. I was a little surprised my feelings were so readable. Normally we were very open with each other, which had created a strong bond in our working together. She was like a sister to me and I treasured her unique, strong German upbringing and passion for life. A beautiful, blond woman, she had been a successful television talk-show host in Germany. She was not conceited by her fame and was down-to-earth and unassuming with it all. Originally we had met through a circle of spiritual friends and felt a powerful connection. We shared a mutual love of God.

"Good morning, Sabrina. I'm okay, just a little quiet." Smiling with reassurance that I really was all right, I sat down at my desk.

Each morning we started the day by doing a five-minute meditation and I was especially eager to begin, in order to take the focus off me. In my inner silence, my prayers asked God, "Bless the day and make us fruitful with our labors, guide us to the appropriate people to contact and let us be in receivership of all that is to come." Then in my inner thoughts I heard, "Especially watch over my family." These last words created a shiver in my body and a momentary curiosity.

Obliging my need to be quiet, Sabrina did not ask again if something were wrong.

It was a warm, sunny January in Los Angeles. From the office windows, I could see several large pine trees overlooking the canyon. Sabrina, her husband Richard and their daughter Julia lived on a secluded, dead-end street. It almost felt as though they lived in the woods because there were no houses across from them. Instead, they had an open view of the surrounding canyon, outlining its vastness. One afternoon while glancing out the window, I had been surprised to see a deer walk across the street and disappear into the trees. Usually, however, it was hawks, squirrels and blue jays that caught my attention as they graced the canyon with their presence.

On this morning the sky was a cloudless, aqua blue, evoking a mesmerizing peacefulness. Thankful for the constant pace of activity, my mind stayed focused on the tasks at hand. Every now and then I became aware of a haunting ache deep inside, but refused to focus on it. Late in the afternoon, a lone eagle soaring overhead caused me to notice a large cluster of clouds beginning to encase the hillside. There was a stillness to the air that felt like the calm before a storm, and triggered an intensity to my uneasiness.

It was dark leaving Sabrina's to travel to my apartment twenty minutes away. Usually I loved this drive because the streets meandered through an exclusive section of L.A., peppered with beautiful homes and finely manicured lawns. The wealth that abounded in this city always amazed me, a drastic contrast to my simple farm roots. But that night I did not feel soothed. The queasiness in my stomach became more pronounced the further I drove and my thoughts pon-

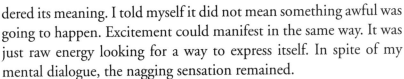

dered its meaning. I told myself it did not mean something awful was going to happen. Excitement could manifest in the same way. It was just raw energy looking for a way to express itself. In spite of my mental dialogue, the nagging sensation remained.

I lived in a small apartment complex in Brentwood protected by iron gates. The walkway was filled with an assortment of fresh blooming flowers and diverse green shrubbery. It felt like being in a cocoon hidden from the hustle and bustle of busy streets. I checked my mail to see if, perhaps, there was a letter that would shed some light on this perplexing feeling. There was none. Walking up the cement steps to my second floor studio, I faintly heard a television in the unit next to me. The quiet darkness of my apartment greeted me with welcome relief and I sighed deeply, glad to be in my own space. After fixing a cup of tea, I sat on the sofa bed with my bare feet wrapped underneath me. Something told me to light the pink candle sitting on the corner of my altar behind the couch. Placing my teacup on the desk to the left of the altar, I knelt down. The uneasiness tightened in my stomach. It was around 6:30. I lit the candle, and its flame drew me in as its light danced upward like a swirling ballerina. A soft breeze coming in through the open window caressed my face.

The phone rang, startling me out of silence. I took a deep breath and hesitantly walked to it. On the third ring, I picked up the receiver and heard my mother's strained and tired voice: "Susie, your father has cancer." Her voice broke and she began to sob.

The uneasy feeling moved up to my throat, causing difficulty swallowing. I took another deep breath and noticed a calmness to my voice. "Mom … Mom, tell me what's happened." I waited nervously at the other end of the line until she calmed down. The feeling in the pit of my stomach began to gnaw at my insides.

The last time I had seen my father had been the previous fall when I'd flown back to Wisconsin to participate in filming a white buffalo calf that had been born on a farm outside of Madison. I rented a car and drove three hours to spend the weekend with my parents. Upon seeing my Dad, I asked if he felt okay because there was a certain look in his eyes that caught my attention. He told me he was feeling great and danced a little jig to prove it. He was his usual outrageous self, and nothing about his appearance reflected anything different. Except the look I saw in his eyes.

My dad was a retired dairy farmer. During the winter he worked in the woods, cutting hardwood trees and hauling them to a nearby pulp mill. He had done this for years, even before my parents sold their cows, and I was used to hearing about his various cuts and bruises. He had always been a robust, energetic man who thrived on a love of the outdoors. His life revolved around hunting and fishing, and even a broken leg could not keep him from being active.

At the time, I questioned whether I had really seen anything at all in his eyes. Perhaps I was just sensing something else that had nothing to do with his health. Later, when Mom mentioned a soreness in his back after Thanksgiving, I thought he had just pulled a muscle. Dad was not the type to ignore persistent aches and pains, and was actually very in tune with his body. When the pain continued, he went to his local MD. A chest x-ray was taken and the results were negative. The doctor dismissed his complaint as bruised ribs or Dad's arthritis acting up, prescribed pain medication and sent him on his way. When I spoke to my parents over Christmas, there was no mention about Dad's back pain. I didn't really give the incident more thought—which was surprising for me because I am usually quite intuitive.

Years ago, my brother Vernon and his fiancée Margaret were planning their wedding. They were married in Seattle and a week later flew back to Wisconsin for a reception and dance. My maternal grandmother, who was eighty-two at the time, attended the festivities. At one point during the evening, I turned to Vernon and said, "Make sure you spend some time with Granny before you fly back." He looked at me and said, "Why?" Out of my mouth flew the words, "Because she isn't going to be around through next year." He looked at me with a shocked expression on his face and said, "What are you talking about? You're crazy." My grandmother died in July the following year.

As I spoke with my mother, I realized the fleeting look in my father's eyes during our last visit hadn't been my imagination. It had been a sign of dramatic change that was soon to come.

Dad had smoked cigarettes when I was younger and later substituted a pipe for them. Eventually he had given up the pipe altogether. As a child, his smoking had been a trademark for the way he made decisions. When something bothered him, he would light his pipe and puff on it as he gazed off in the distance. Shortly thereafter he would seem to have an answer. It had been many years since he had quit smoking entirely.

Through my mother's crying, I was able to piece together events leading to her shocking call. When Dad's back pain had persisted after Christmas, he had returned to his doctor, insisting they do more tests because he felt something was wrong. They did a bone scan and took another chest x-ray. The scan was negative. The x-ray detected some kind of shadow on the lung. Unclear about what that meant, Dad's doctor gave the x-ray to a cancer specialist who consulted at their local hospital once a week. Mom was calling me on the day they had met with him. Upon learning about Dad's history of smoking and reviewing the questionable x-ray, the specialist had told Dad he had lung cancer, nothing more could medically be done and he should go home and prepare to die.

Disbelief thundered through my body. I was not sure what was more upsetting: hearing Mom say Dad had cancer, or the outrageousness of this doctor shredding their lives of any hope with his unproven diagnosis. My heart ached at the thought of what my parents must be feeling. It had always been Mom's greatest fear that she or Dad would get cancer. To her, the word meant death.

Struggling to push aside my own emotions, I tried to remain objective. "Mom, does this doctor know for sure Dad has cancer? The shadow on the x-ray could be anything. You know how doctors are, they always tell you the worst case scenario and most of the time are wrong. First of all, is he a lung specialist?"

"No."

I asked if she had talked with my sister Mary. "Yes," she replied. "I called her from the doctor's office. I told her what he said. She called him and he claimed he never told us your father has cancer and should go home and prepare to die."

Mary lived in Florida and was a nurse for several doctors who specialized in treating cancer. Throughout the years, Mom and Dad had come to rely upon her medical expertise. Established in the profession long before me, she had earned a reputation as the nurse in our family.

Quickly I found myself sorting for the truth in what Mom was saying. Did Dad definitely have cancer or did the doctor just suspect he might have it? Had Mom overreacted when she heard the word and it was not as serious as she implied? It didn't matter because the cancer seed had been planted in their conscious minds and fear had already taken root. It was going to be difficult to overcome their initial reaction—especially Mom. She had a tendency to selectively listen for what supported a certain belief and would now filter all information through the reference point of cancer. Worry and fear would constantly occupy her thoughts. Dad was just the opposite. I had rarely seen him express worry. If a situation arose, he looked for a solution and moved on. He believed that everything always has a way of working out and he trusted in that.

Mom was no longer crying. I sensed she was desperate to hear any words of encouragement. "Mom, I'm so sorry about what the doctor said, especially when they have nothing to confirm it. God is the only one who knows, and that is where you need to turn right now. Light your candle tonight and pray, and I'll do the same. When you go to bed, just imagine God's arms around you. And we'll just take it one step at a time. Promise me you'll do that."

"I promise," she responded quietly.

I asked to talk to Dad. "Hey, Pops, how are you doing?"

His voice was strong, but anxious. "I'm feeling great except for this pain in my ribs. They tell me I might have cancer, but the doctor doesn't really know. I have to go for more tests. Could be nothing. Don't worry, your old Pops still has his zip and I'm not ready to throw in the towel yet. I've weathered the storm before, and I'll weather it again."

His voice didn't sound convincing, which was unusual. I could tell he was worried but trying to hide it. I asked if there was anything I could do and he replied, "Just pray for me."

His request left me quiet for a moment because he had never asked this before. I told him I would and that I loved him. He replied, "Me, too." A sense of awkwardness came over me and I didn't know what else to say, so I asked to put Mom back on the phone.

She was calmer now. "I always feel better after talking with you. Keep calling me. I need that right now."

I told her to think positively and stay in touch. "I love you Mom."

"I love you too, Susie," she said and we both hung up the phone.

In the stark silence of my apartment, I felt very alone as I rested my head against the back of the sofa. Staring up at the ceiling, the conversation with Mom played over and over in my mind. My body started to shake. Closing my eyes, I slowly took a deep breath, then gently blew the air out, asking that any anxiety and fear leave my body. I repeated this process three times. The trembling stopped.

Inside my head I heard, "Don't confuse your own feelings with your mother's." My nervous system was very sensitive and could absorb other people's emotions easily. In the past, I had taken on their worry and fear, causing me to feel as though I were on an emotional roller coaster. I had learned that everyone has an energy field with which we constantly interact. It is like being hugged. When we are hugged by someone who is happy, we feel their happiness. The same is true about sadness. When we walk away, remnants of the particular emotion still linger with us. Experience had taught me the importance of keeping my energy field balanced and of allowing my emotions to remain intact.

I sat for a long time lost in thought—about my parents, my brothers and sisters and what was important. Then I began to feel angry. Anger at the audacity of the doctor telling my father to go home and prepare to die. Anger about not having any control over what might happen. Memories of working as a nurse resurfaced, rekindling old frustrations of interacting with the medical profession in similar situations. Now it was happening in my own family. What a way to begin the new year.

Realizing my thoughts could drive me crazy with any number of scenarios, I made a choice to stay in the present. If the doctor were right, there was a bigger hand at play and all I could do was to trust in the outcome. The only things I had any control over were my thoughts and my response to them. As Dad had said, if it turned out he really did have cancer, we'd "cross that bridge when we get to it." It wouldn't do me or my family any good to go into a place of fear or to be unable to function because of worry. Mom had been a good teacher about that one. My reasoning brought some solace inside, yet I had a foreboding about what the doctor had said. I could feel it in my bones. Part of me wanted to call Mary to find out what he had told her, but I realized one conversation about cancer was all I could handle that night.

The evening had left me exhausted. Deciding not to unfold the couch into a bed, I gathered my quilt and pillow from the closet. Sleeping on a full mattress seemed too empty that night. What I really wanted was to be snuggled in someone's arms. I knelt before my altar and prayed to God. "Please give my family and me strength and courage in the days ahead. May I hold what is to come in the highest good and trust in your love. Especially watch over my parents and provide them comfort. Guide my thoughts to always see a greater perspective."

Blowing out the pink candle that had been burning for hours, I lay down in a fetal position with my spine against the back of the sofa. Pulling the quilt around my shoulders, I gently rocked myself back and forth. Praying the doctor was wrong, I fell asleep.

The next morning, I awoke early to the sounds of birds singing in the courtyard. My thoughts immediately went to Dad and I remembered that it was his birthday. Although he was turning seventy-four, he always bragged he would live to be a hundred. My ritual was to call him in the morning before he went into the woods, sing "Happy Birthday" and tease him about getting younger. But what could I say to him this morning? "Hey Pops, it's going to be your best year ever? This summer let's go fishing at Turtle Lake and I can watch you catch that big northern you claim has been hanging around there all these years."

The thoughts chattered back and forth in my mind as if I were engaged in a dialogue with a friend. Finally I heard one that made sense: "Just be real with him. Focus on what's great about him. Inspire him and make him laugh. That's what he most needs. It's what you most need, too."

My stomach had nervous jitters as I called half an hour later and caught Dad walking out the door to haul a load of logs to the mill. He was in a chipper mood. "Heeelllooo!" I heard him practically yodel the word as he picked up the phone.

I started my rendition: "Happy Birthday to you, Haappy Biirthday too yoou, Haaaaapppy Biiirthdaaay, dear Pooopppps, Haaappy Biirthdaay, tooooo you."

"Thank you, thank you. I've been waiting for your call to wish your dear old Dad a happy birthday. Gotta make it special, you know. Only comes once a year." He sounded more like his usual, normal self this morning.

"You know I wouldn't miss our yearly ritual, Dad. I'm sure my singing is what makes it so special." We laughed together and I continued, "At least it comes on time, that's more than I can say about my presents."

He chuckled. "Yeah, that's for sure."

We bantered back and forth in a teasing way with no mention about his possible illness. I was relieved.

Dad's birthday had always been special to him and he was never shy about reminding anyone not to forget it. Either Mom or my sister Ann usually cooked him a special evening meal and some sort of celebration always took place. He was so different from Mom—who would just as soon forget her birthday. While Dad loved all the attention, she shied away from it.

"Pops, make sure you save up extra wind to blow out all those candles tonight and eat a piece of cake for me," I teased him.

"Your Dad may be getting older, but he still has a lot of spunk left in him. I can still go one-on-one with you any day," he quipped back. "Well, I gotta get going. That pulp is waiting for me and I gotta keep one step ahead of Johnny. Don't want him to think his old man is slowing down." He chuckled.

"Have a great one, Dad. I love you."

"Me, too. Thanks for the call." He hung up the phone.

I felt lighter inside. This part of our relationship, the teasing and bantering, I had always loved. In spite of everything else that might be occurring, I trusted this would never change. I felt uplifted and hoped he did too.

Two weeks passed before the next jolting phone call. A doctor Mary worked with arranged for Dad to see one of his colleagues at a hospital two hours away from my parent's home. In the process of further testing to detect what was wrong, fluid began to build up in one of Dad's lungs. It was removed and sent to a lab to be tested for cancer. We waited for the results.

One evening I heard the phone ringing as I turned the key to unlock my apartment. It was Mom. She was crying. The test results had come back positive. Dad had been diagnosed with adenocarcinoma, cancer of the lungs. The first doctor had been right!

I felt numb. No amount of mental preparation could have softened the impact of knowing what was wrong with Dad. I was unable to imagine what he must be feeling. I thought of Mom calling all seven of us kids with the news and pain stabbed at my heart. I wondered where she would find the strength. It felt so unfair. I wept in my aloneness and thought to myself, "Dad is

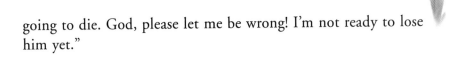

going to die. God, please let me be wrong! I'm not ready to lose him yet."

Chapter Two
A Long Journey Home

As my plane waited for takeoff at the Los Angeles airport, I sat wrapped in a blue airline blanket and stared out the window. I was thankful no one was sitting next to me. I was flying back to Wisconsin to visit my parents. It would be my first time seeing them since Dad had been diagnosed. It had been an intense two months for everyone in my family as we had all come to grips with his illness. The initial shock had passed through me and I had been focusing my energy on exploring options for treating Dad's cancer. I had not been alone. Through dialogues with various siblings, I had found they, too, had been researching possible therapies that might be acceptable to Dad. My brother Vernon and I were opposed to chemotherapy. Mary was an advocate of it. I was not sure where the rest stood. I just knew we all wanted what was best for Dad. But what did that really mean? Did "best" mean maintaining a quality of life that allowed him to live with the cancer and not be sick and miserable? Or did "best" mean having treatments that made him sick and miserable in the hope he would live longer? Much to my disappointment, Dad had chosen the more traditional route and undergone his first round of chemotherapy.

My four brothers and two sisters were spread throughout the United States. Every one was married except my sister Mary and myself. She was the oldest and had no children. Johnny, a truck driver, had one college-age son and lived a few miles from Mom and Dad. Ann, also living a few miles from the homestead, had three children—two sons in college and a daughter in high school. She was an assistant treasurer in the county court courthouse. Vernon lived in Seattle and was the president of his own construction company. He had three boys in grade school. Mark lived in Madison, had two boys and a girl all below the age of ten and was a manager with a medical equipment manufacturing company. Ron, the youngest, lived in Minneapolis, had no children and was a business executive with a large home health-care organization.

Five of us had college educations. Although there were three nurses in the family, Mary was the only one who currently worked in the profession. My sister and I differed in our basic thoughts about orthodox medicine, even though our nursing careers reflected similar paths. She had remained active in a more traditional approach, while I had left nursing because of it.

My training as an R.N. started out at the University of Wisconsin, in Madison, where I received a bachelor's degree. I was initially drawn into the profession because of my sister and her ex-husband. Both were nurses and I loved listening to them share about their patients and hospital experiences. Their stories had a certain excitement and intrigue that were fascinating to me. My marriage was on rocky ground and I felt stagnant working as an administrative aide in the Wisconsin legislature. I wanted a change and it was easier to start a new career than address the major issues in my relationship. So I enrolled in school full-time, while maintaining my job on a part-time basis.

Along with graduation four and a half years later, came my divorce. I moved alone to Seattle and began working as a nurse. The hospital where I interviewed hired me to work on their cancer unit. Arriving for my first day on the job, however, I learned the unit had been closed for remodeling and I had been placed on a cardiac floor instead. Initially I loved the work. University Hospital was a teaching facility similar to the one in Madison where my training had occurred, with a constant flux of new residents rotating every couple of months. Their eagerness kept the floor feeling young and exciting, and I enjoyed the challenge of learning and growing professionally. The unit felt like family. It was on this floor that I met Margaret, an assistant head nurse, who became my best friend and later married my brother Vernon.

I worked for six years as a nurse, both in a hospital setting and out in the private sector. I cared for cancer, burn, cardiac, newborn, maternity, rehab and surgical patients. The conclusion to my nursing career was treating individuals who had severe eating disorders. Upon quitting that job, I vowed never again to return to nursing. I was finished with caring for "sick" people and everything that went along with it.

My disillusion with the medical profession started gradually and grew in intensity. It finally reached the point where stepping into a hospital made me sick to my stomach. Several key factors brought about my decision to leave nursing. I felt restricted and unchallenged and slowly lost passion for being a nurse. For me, passion was essential. It stirred my creativity and made me feel expansive and inspired. It was one way I could feel really attuned with God.

The other reason had to do with the predominant philosophy of the medical profession. The myopic perspective of treating symptoms rather than the whole person was frustrating. Patients were their diseases. There was little or no focus on their emotional, mental or spiritual well-being. They weren't seen as "Mr. Jones a single father, divorced husband or the president of a company who was having financial problems." It was rare to hear a doctor ask patients if they were happy or loved their work. These factors didn't seem to play a role in helping them get "well." The goal was to alleviate symptoms— using pills, surgery or whatever it took. Little or no attention was focused on identifying patterns contributing to the physical imbalance in order to prevent the ailment from reoccurring. It was like finding a weed in your garden and pulling the top off instead of the roots. Many times I felt we were just applying Band-Aids to what could be seen or described, and thus we lost sight of the deeper causes. It was uncommon to watch a physician sit at the bedside of a patient, hold the person's hand and talk in an intimate way. Usually they came into a patient's room, advised about the scheduled procedures, gave results of completed tests, asked how the person was doing, said they'd return the next day and left. The visit would take all of five minutes.

I became a strong patient advocate and was not afraid to share my opinions and beliefs. Many times it got me in trouble. I became tired of relating to doctors who thought they were God and who were challenged or insulted by suggestions about incorporating a holistic approach into treatment plans. I was frustrated that patients had to endure endless tests to explore what was wrong with them, only to learn the results were inconclusive. Added to that was the constant prescription of drugs to fix complaints. I cared for patients who were taking ten to fifteen different types of pills. There was a pill to help them sleep at night, one to make their bowels move, one for indigestion, one for pain and on and on. The pills that could be prescribed for any sort of ailment were literally countless. And all in the name of making someone "well."

Working with cancer had a greater impact on me than any other illness. Emotionally it was more challenging. The rewards came from the intimacy of engaging with patients and their loved ones. You rallied with them on good days and shed tears with them during their setbacks. It was easy to become attached. Whole families had their lives turned upside down based on what information a doctor would share and the manner in which it was given. Most doctors had a purely clinical approach. They gave statistics on the effect chemotherapy or radiation might have, but the bottom line was always that their days were numbered. Rarely did I hear a physician speak with them about hope. Many times patients shared that their doctor had said they had six months or a year to live. It was incredibly painful seeing sorrow in their eyes and seeing the wind knocked out of them because the length of their lives had been predetermined. What was equally disheartening were the words, "I'm sorry. There is nothing more that can be done for you." No one should ever have to hear these words. They eliminate hope and can be destructive to the human spirit.

What was most difficult was watching lives deteriorate. Most people do not realize the effects chemotherapy drugs or even radiation will have on their bodies, even though they have been told. To hear what will happen and to experience the reality of it are two different things. They would vomit; lose their hair, their appetites and their energy and become depressed. Their quality of life would be greatly diminished. It was easy to understand what—given the choice of living or dying—a person would endure to survive. Fear is a powerful motivator and most people who are ill make choices from that place.

I finally reached a point when administering chemotherapy felt like giving a patient poison. Not only were cancer cells being destroyed, but so were healthy ones. Yet no supplements were given to nourish and strengthen the immune system that had been weakened. When my personal views started affecting my ability to effectively care for patients, it was time to explore other avenues. Little did I know at the time how valuable those experiences would be later in my life.

I had always been a progressive thinker and had been criticized many times for being too idealistic. A friend of mine once told me, "You look at life through rose-colored glasses. The amazing thing is that it seems to work for you." My nursing background and frustration with traditional medicine turned out to be an incredible gift. It forced me to look at the body and healing in a whole new way. In watching what did not seem to work, I started to search for what did. It had always made sense to me that our body has brilliant healing capabilities—if we only listen to the messages it sends us. For healthcare providers, I turned to homeopathic, naturopathic and Chinese medicine practitioners. I experienced acupuncture, acupressure, Jin Shin Shiatsu, rolfing, massage, aromatherapy, psychic surgery and healing by touch. Each enlightened me to innate knowledge about my body and changed my thinking. For example, I perceived a person who had a disease as one simply out-of-balance. I realized that, when I was truly happy, I rarely became sick.

In spite of the shortcomings of Western medicine, I recognized the incredible role it played—and continues to play—in advancing the health of humankind. Cancer patients have been cured. People live longer and healthier. Trauma units in hospitals save hundreds of lives a day from gunshot wounds, severe automobile accidents and drug overdoses. Yet we are a society rapidly changing and expanding in our wisdom and awareness of the intricacies of the human body. Traditional medicine no longer holds all the answers. By joining hands with the growing movement of holistic perspectives, greater possibilities exist to maximize and compliment the best both worlds have to offer.

We had been in the air an hour when I heard a flight attendant pushing a beverage cart down the aisle. Closing my eyes, I could hear the couple behind me. They were returning from a vacation in Hawaii and were laughing. They sounded as though they had been on their honeymoon and were excited about going home. I wished I felt the same way. My heart felt sad and heavy and there was nervous anticipation about seeing the change in Dad's physical appearance after getting chemotherapy.

He had always looked younger than his age and been full of energy. He was strong and muscular, yet lean and fit. His physical appearance was important to him. He was especially proud of the thick hair he combed to the back of his head. When he was young, it was black and wavy. As the years went by, it became peppered with gray. Now his hair reminded me of the color of a beautiful silver fox. He had always been handsome and having gray hair hadn't changed that. He had started to wear glasses for reading when he was around forty-five and carried them in his shirt pocket. He usually misplaced them so he kept a spare set in his bedroom dresser. When I was little, I thought Dad was tall at five foot eight inches. Over the last couple of years he seemed to have shrunk—or else my perception of tall had changed. When he smiled, his grin lit up his whole face. When he laughed, he slapped his knee and you could hear his laughter echo through the house. He had a great sense of humor and was merciless with his teasing. I had called him 'Pops" ever since I could remember.

A chill went through me at the thought of seeing the detrimental effects of chemo on his body. I was all too aware of how he might look. I found my emotions vacillating between feeling like a little girl and an adult woman. The little girl wanted to curl up safe and secure in the arms of her father, knowing he would be in her life for a long time—whereas the compassionate, adult woman desired to wrap her arms around her father to offer support and comfort. At moments I became overwhelmed. This was not one of my usual trips to go home and play, tease Dad or be spoiled by Mom's cooking. But, oh, how I hungered for simplicity and normalcy.

What I really desired was to see Dad healthy and to make peace with the probability of him dying. Although intellectually I had been grasping what lay ahead, seeing Dad face-to-face would be a whole different experience. It always was like that. No matter how much I intellectualized about something, when confronted with an actual situation, my physical response still surprised me. I heard myself say, "Just be yourself. That's what they want and need from you. And don't be afraid to be vulnerable. Then they will feel like they can, too. Let them know how much you love them." My body relaxed as my own words became soothing and reassuring.

I reflected on the past two months and the series of events surrounding Dad's illness. His normal routine during this time of year was to get up around seven in the morning, have his morning cup of coffee and the breakfast Mom had prepared, gas up his red pulp truck and spend hours in the woods working with my oldest brother, Johnny. During the day, he hauled one or two loads of logs to a nearby pulp mill. At five o'clock, he returned home, where Mom had supper waiting for him. In the evening they usually watched television. Sometimes they read. Normally they were in bed by ten o'clock.

All that had changed. There were no more carefree days. The past weeks had consisted of being shuffled from one physician to the next and going through a battery of tests to finally diagnose his cancer. It had entailed driving two hours each way in rural Wisconsin during the winter to see specialists at Marshfield Clinic where he was being treated. That had required them to rise at four thirty in the morning to arrive on time for scheduled appointments. Because he was experiencing difficulty breathing, needles were stuck in Dad's chest to remove the fluid building in his lungs. Powerful, foreign chemicals had been injected into his cells, causing his beautiful hair to fall out and making him too weak to haul his pulp trees. Conversations with his children who normally called to say "hello," were now inquiries about how he was doing and constant reminders to him that he was sick. He was having to be strong not only for himself, but also for Mom, who had never been good at handling a crisis. Added to that were his own struggles with declining health and with the fear of dying and losing control over his life. I thought I knew what feeling overwhelmed was like. He was dealing with far more than I could imagine. I wondered how he and Mom were coping. Tears began to stream down my face as I searched in my purse for Kleenex.

I had prepared well for this trip. In my suitcase were several videotapes to share with my parents. Two about angels had played on television during the past year. They explored the presence and meaning of angels in our present-day existence and related true stories about individuals who had experienced them. Mom was a strong believer in angels, but I didn't know about Dad. I had never discussed it with him. Having found the tapes inspirational and uplifting, I hoped they would do the same for Mom and Dad. I had also packed a video by Dr. Norman Cousins, an M.D. who cured himself of cancer through laughter. Since my parents placed a lot of trust in physicians, they could relate to him because of his credibility as a medical doctor. I had explored his approach of using humor to raise the body to a higher vibration to facilitate healing and I valued his work. The beauty of his video was that he talked in layman's terms about his journey with cancer and shared in an inspirational way how he had cured himself.

Another video nestled among my clothes was *What Your Doctor Won't Tell You About Cancer*. I hadn't had time to look at this, but thought Mom and I might watch it to assess whether Dad would like it. He was a down-to-earth man and had a difficult time with information or shows that were too complicated or intellectual. The tape's

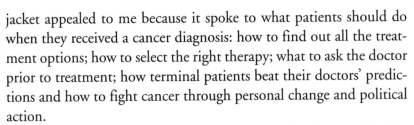

jacket appealed to me because it spoke to what patients should do when they received a cancer diagnosis: how to find out all the treatment options; how to select the right therapy; what to ask the doctor prior to treatment; how terminal patients beat their doctors' predictions and how to fight cancer through personal change and political action.

As an extra bonus, I was led to buy a series of videos on *The Best Years of Johnny Carson*. When I was growing up, Dad would watch him every night and loved his show. Many a night I would go to bed hearing him laughing as he sat amused by the antics of Johnny. For some reason, Johnny Carson reminded me of Dad and I knew he would enjoy these because they would take him to happier times.

In addition to the videotapes, I had brought two audio tapes. One was by Dr. Bernie Segal, *Love, Medicine and Miracles* and the other was by Dr. Norman Cousins, *The Anatomy of an Illness*. Even if Dad were too overwhelmed to listen, or was not open to their message, I knew Mom would explore them. She always seemed more curious about fresh, innovative ideas than did Dad. She was a conduit for him and understood his ways well enough to interject ideas he could hear. She also needed a lot of support and encouragement now because she was in a lot of fear.

My main preparation for the trip had been emotional. I had a tendency to fall back into old patterns when I went home, causing me to resort to childhood feelings when I was there. It didn't happen right away—usually it took a couple of days. It reminded me of looking through an old photo album and seeing pictures that transported me back to past experiences. The memory seemed as real in that moment as it did when it first happened. Old patterns were usually triggered subtly at first, perhaps by a certain tone of voice or look on one of my parent's faces. For just a moment, old feelings of helplessness would come back. When a door was opened in this way, the challenge was to change the familiar reaction. It was easier said than done. If my parents got into an argument or Dad started talking about entrenched beliefs, I shielded myself by hiding my emotions or becoming silent. Many times I escaped by going for a walk in the woods. It had taken me years to identify these patterns and develop tools so I would not respond in an old way. Occasionally I faltered, but I no longer felt controlled by a particular situation. It was amazing how the minute I walked in their front door I could feel tested. This happened to me even when things were fairly normal at home. It was very different this time. Dad wasn't the rock in the family now. He was more vulnerable. We all were. It was bound to be a challenging trip.

My parents lived in northern Wisconsin outside a small town called Antigo, with a population of nine thousand. It had stayed this size since my birth. The area was composed of dairy and potato farmers and small business operations. The only mall consisted of KMart, Copps, a video store and a small clothing boutique. Normally I flew into a small airport that accommodated commuter planes, about an hour from my parents' house. On this trip my destination was Minneapolis. I was borrowing a car from my brother Ron. The drive to my folks would take four hours. I wanted time to acclimate to my childhood environment and gently ease into familiar feelings, rather than just get off the plane and face seeing Dad so quickly.

The plane landed and I made my way through the terminal to the baggage claim area. As I waited for my luggage, I could feel the winter cold and zipped up my jacket. Loading my two suitcases on a metal push cart, I made my way to the parking ramp across the street. The freezing ten-degree weather bit at my face and fingers, causing me to wish I had brought gloves. Throwing my luggage into the trunk of the car, I felt chilled to the bone and knew it was not just from the bitter cold. I drove the car out of the parking ramp and began the first of what were to be three major trips back home.

It was four o'clock in the afternoon, and I had been driving for two hours. The sky was a stormy gray and occasional gusts of wind rocked the car with their force. There was a light dusting of snow on the road, cautioning me to be careful driving. It had been several years since I had driven in winter weather. I had long since left the freeway in Minnesota and was driving on a two-lane highway in rural Wisconsin. My soul breathed in the snowy landscape. The country side was beautiful—even with the winter starkness. Small, quaint towns were interspersed through long, isolated stretches of nature and a few farm houses. There was such a dramatic contrast with the fast pace of Los Angeles, where houses, office buildings and traffic went on forever. Here the rolling hills of agriculture and dense forests slowed the body into a tranquillity that made driving a joyous treat. It reminded me of the peaceful space inside when meditating. I had made a wise choice to fly into Minneapolis. I could feel myself becoming more relaxed the further I drove, helping me forget momentarily the reason for this trip.

The clock on the dashboard told me I would be driving into the yard of my parent's farm in forty-five minutes. "What do you want to accomplish with Dad?" The question thundered through my mind. Taking a deep breath, tightness formed in my stomach. "What is it I want to accomplish with Dad?" I asked myself again. The thought riveted my body. A dull ache stabbed my heart and my shoulders became tense. I was drawn back to a conversation a few weeks earlier with Solano, one of my spiritual teachers. Having known him for nine years, I had come to love and trust his wisdom and insight.

"Solano, I desire some direction on how to walk through my father's illness and support him." It was a relief to finally get input about my concerns and I listened beyond his words to grasp the full meaning.

In a gentle but strong voice he replied, "How best to support your Dad? First and foremost is to simply express love, in whatever way you can. Don't give him empty platitudes. An example of an empty platitude is, 'You're going to beat this, I know you are.' For you don't know that. Rather you can speak from your own experience and say you have witnessed people who took their life-threatening diseases and put them into remission by having more fun in their lives. For you have seen that. You have seen in your existence that, when you are about to fall ill or are ill, what it takes for you to turn the tide on the illness is a shift in your perspective of the body. Likewise, there are innumerable people who possess knowledge your father would respect. You can put them in front of him in the form of tapes or books. These will support what you say in such a way as to expand his knowledge. You have a degree of credibility with your father based on what you have experienced in your life."

He paused and I could feel his eyes pierce mine as he continued, "Make sure you establish a rapport with your father. Spend time together, tease him, make him feel safe. Right now he is being showered with a lot of attention. Some people express sorrow and pity for him, some express fear looking at him, some project upon him healing energies in the hope he can grow greater and stronger again. Therefore, in this particular phase, do not be too strident; do not be too much of a difficult coach. It is rare in his life for so much focus and energy to be gifted him. In many ways it gives him strength. He wants to be the strong head of the family, yet he yearns to be loved and nurtured like a little boy. When you engage him in conversation about his health, do it from the place of wanting to explore together routes he may want to take. In this way, you provide him the sense that you are shoulder-to-shoulder with him as he goes through a process of becoming comfortable and confident with what he chooses. Then you do not sound like the teacher and he an ignorant man. He will feel more open to listening. Remember, the route of therapy he chooses is not as important as what makes him feel confident. This is because any reservations he has will prevent the approach from working. In all of this, recognize that there is not only his fear about this disease, but fear about death as well."

I felt his message resonate inside me as if he were awakening seeds of courage that would enable me to have such an interaction with Dad. It was clear I was being nudged to find the strength to do this. Thoughts of "but what if" fell to the wayside. They only reinforced my own doubts and negativity. I knew better than to share them. Instead I asked, "Could you suggest a way in which to say these things that doesn't sound overbearing?"

"It can be as simple as, 'There is much help in the world. There is much known about cancer and about stemming its effects and putting it into remission. All the ways are different and each is appropriate for a different person. Let us together examine all the means that are available. And after examining them, let's come up with one that you are most comfortable with and confident in.' But it is also important for him to know that the single most influential factor for anything to work is a shift in his attitude. You can open the door for this shift to occur by saying, 'You can spend the remainder of your days not only sick but also miserable. Or you can spend the rest of your days sick but enjoying good humor—and perhaps, as a result, not spend the rest of your days sick'. He knows how he feels when he laughs and how much he likes being around other people having a good time. You can tell him these things in a loving way that will soften the words that are vital for him to hear."

I was really being stretched by Solano's words, and by the mere thought of having a dialogue like this with my father. Dad had always been the strong one in the family and rarely, if ever, asked for advice. I had felt intimidated by him for most of my life and it had been difficult to talk about sensitive issues with him. Teasing had been my safety valve for slipping in something I wanted to say. There was discomfort inside just thinking about a conversation of that nature. Any hesitation I felt was overshadowed by what Solano said next.

"Imagine this is the last time you are going to see your father. What would you want him to know? What would you regret if you didn't tell him? What would you dare yourself to say if you felt it might make a difference in his choosing to live or die? Use this as a gauge for being with him. It doesn't matter if he doesn't say what you want to hear. Don't expect that because of his illness he will all of a sudden express his feelings differently. He may not be able to. By your doing this, it will allow you to feel complete should he choose to pass quickly. His process may be very different."

Tears welled up in my eyes at the thought of telling Dad face-to-face that I loved him. Whenever I spoke with him on the phone I always said, "I love you, Pops" as we ended the conversation. His reply was usually, "Me, too." Only once had he actually said to me, "I love you." That was over the phone a year ago, on Easter. It had surprised me in the middle of a conversation. It was interesting how my interpretation based on not hearing the exact words implied they had not been said.

Could something I said make a difference in Dad's life now? Could it affect his choosing to live or die? Did I have more credibility in my father's eyes than I gave myself credit for? Perhaps wisdom learned throughout my adult years could be valuable in lessening his pain. All I really knew was that my love for Dad and the possibility of him dying were enough to make me willing to take the risk to share my feelings. If I didn't do it soon, there might not be another opportunity.

As my hour with Solano drew to a close, I was thankful to receive some wonderful insight and powerful guidance. Everything he said rang a tone of truth inside. Now all that was required was the courage to do it.

I asked Solano if there was anything further that would be valuable for me to know. He took a long pause before responding. "Remember to shield yourself from any negativity. Emotions will be running high. Fear has a way of evoking the best and worst in people, so shield yourself from being sucked into others' emotions. Keep your ability for listening, feeling and receiving completely in attention and balanced. In that way you can move from room to room, conversation to conversation, from your bed to your father's bedside, and take with you all that you know and all that you are. This will prevent you from going into your own place of fear and catching the contingent of fear that exists there. Instead you will be able to exude the confidence in yourself of knowing that no matter whether your father lives long or dies soon, what is important is the process in which you all are engaged."

There were two miles left as my mind finished reliving the conversation with Solano. Recapturing his words in my mind created a stabilizing and peaceful sensation inside. It did not, however, take away

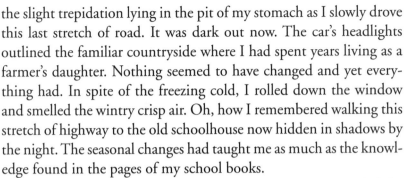

the slight trepidation lying in the pit of my stomach as I slowly drove this last stretch of road. It was dark out now. The car's headlights outlined the familiar countryside where I had spent years living as a farmer's daughter. Nothing seemed to have changed and yet everything had. In spite of the freezing cold, I rolled down the window and smelled the wintry crisp air. Oh, how I remembered walking this stretch of highway to the old schoolhouse now hidden in shadows by the night. The seasonal changes had taught me as much as the knowledge found in the pages of my school books.

Lights from the house appeared in the distance as I rounded the curve in the road. My heart started pounding. There were no more thoughts to prepare me for what lay ahead. It was time to step into whatever feelings awaited me. I turned into the gravel driveway and saw Mom's face peeking out from the large picture window in the living room. A moment later a floodlight illuminated the side of the house. I turned off the ignition in the car and sat quietly for a moment. A hanging basket that held Mom's geranium flowers swung empty in the breeze by the back door. Ginger, their golden retriever, barked loudly by his doghouse as I opened the car door. Stepping into the chilly night, I heard the words, "The truth will set you free."

Chapter Three

The Unknown Through the Kitchen Door

The lingering aroma from Mom's cooking greeted me as I opened the back door and stepped into the porch. The smell of venison tantalized my senses and I realized I was hungry. Peeking through the small window on the door leading into the kitchen, I grinned at Mom standing by the maple kitchen table. Teasingly I knocked and walked in.

"Hi, Mom, I'm finally here."

She smiled as she came to hug me. "You made it. I'm so glad you're home, Susie," she said in a relieved voice. Her arms were tight around my back and we held each other for a long time. Sensing a heaviness in her body from the strain of what she had been through, I stepped back from our embrace and saw a weariness on her face. Through her glasses, her brown eyes were sad. Considering what she had been through the past couple of months, she looked remarkably well and her spirit felt strong. "You must be tired after all that flying and driving," she said in a concerned mother's voice. "I bet you're hungry. Have you eaten?"

"No, Mom. I'm a little hungry, but I'll catch a bite to eat later. It's just good to be home. Smells like you fixed Dad venison for supper. I bet he loved that. How's he doing?" I began to talk in a quickened pace, indicating my nervousness. It was much easier to be calm talking to her on the phone. I was beginning to pick up the tension in the house from the last couple of months and could feel my shoulders tighten.

"He's lying down. He wanted to be up when you got here but he said, knowing you, it could be awhile." She smiled. "He said to wake him when you arrived if it wasn't too late. He gets tired so easily now. And he's lost most of his hair. His appetite isn't that good either." Her voice started to quiver as tears welled up in her eyes. Struggling to maintain composure, she turned her head away and looked out the kitchen window.

I hesitated to go and put my arms around her because I knew she was afraid she'd break down crying and didn't want to appear weak. Instead I stroked her back with my hand and said, "It's okay, Mom. I'm here. You don't have to be so strong. We'll get through this somehow."

She lingered by the sink awhile longer looking out the window. "I'm okay," she said as she turned away from the window. "Come on, I'll heat up the supper for you."

I didn't feel hungry anymore. "You know, Mom, I think I'll just have a cup of tea."

She went to the stove and turned on the gas heat under the teakettle. "I don't know if I have your kind of tea. I just have Lipton."

I smiled at her. "That's okay. I have some in my travel bag."

She sat down at the table as I took off my jacket and placed it around a chair. My eyes slowly glanced around the kitchen and took in its familiarity. My parents had lived in this house all my life and memories of my childhood seemed fixed in the walls. It was an old farmhouse, about seventy-five-years-old, and they had slowly remodeled it. There was both a stability and fragileness about it—just like the couple that lived in it.

The kitchen felt warm and cozy from the heat register and the room had a golden hue from the overhead fluorescent light. It reminded me of the feeling one has sitting in front of a fireplace. The teakettle started to whistle and I went to the cupboard and picked a cup with a black and white cow on it. As I poured the hot water over a chamomile tea bag, I heard Dad walking into the living room and thought to myself, "Are you ready for this?" I turned from the stove and saw him standing in the kitchen doorway. His appearance was shocking and I fought to control my emotions. The last thing I wanted was for him to see the horror on my face at how he looked. There was nothing left of his beautiful, thick, silver hair except a few thin strands sticking out all over. His face was drawn and his eyes had a glossiness to them. He was thin and his pants were baggy. He looked sick! I swallowed and breathed in quietly to steady myself and slowly felt a centering occur inside.

"Howdy, howdy, howdy," he said in a weak, raspy voice. There was a grin on his face. "What do you think of your good old Pops without any hair?"

I smiled back at him and said, "You remind me of the character Pig Pen in "Charlie Brown" with crazy, wild hair sticking out of your head." He laughed. I walked over and touched a couple of strands. "Well, Pops, at least you won't have to worry about getting it cut for a while." Mom chuckled behind me.

"Yeah, that's for sure," he quipped back.

We hugged and my hands detected a boniness to his back. There was a hesitancy on both our parts to embrace longer and he pulled back from me saying, "I bet you never expected to see me like this."

"Nope, Dad, can't say that I did."

There was a moment of awkwardness between us that was broken as he spoke. "You want to see my new hair?" He grinned at me with a mischievous smile.

"What did you do, Dad, go and cut the tail off a horse?" I was curious about what he meant. I thought he was going to pull some kind of joke on me—as he was notorious for doing. "Okay, I'll bite, Dad. Show me your new hair."

As he turned and walked out of the kitchen, I looked at Mom, who was smiling. "He bought a toupee. He was so self-conscious after losing his hair, we went shopping for one. He paid a couple hundred dollars for it."

I took my tea and sat across the table from Mom, giving me a clear view of the entrance into the living room. A few minutes later Dad came prancing back into the kitchen with his new hairdo. There was a twinkle in his eye as he did a little dance with his feet to show off his new look.

"What do you think?" he proudly asked.

My immediate reaction was to laugh because it looked so outrageous. But I didn't. I was afraid if I did, it would hurt his feelings. "Dad, you look like a different man. Do you like it?"

"It's not bad. At least it keeps my head warm and I can wear it till my hair starts growing back. The neighbors certainly turn their heads when they see me. Gotta always give them something to talk about, you know." He chuckled.

I smiled watching Dad. Thank God, he hadn't lost his sense of humor. I felt a twinge of pain in my heart seeing him like this. I knew how proud he was about his appearance. This had to be tough on him. It certainly was for me.

"I've got something else to show you," he said. Walking across the room to the corner of the kitchen cabinets, he took the calendar hanging above the cream-colored telephone off the wall. "What do you think of this?" he asked with a proud smile on his face as he tossed it on the table. It was a five-by-seven color photo of Dad in his hunting outfit kneeling next to an eleven-point buck he had shot during last fall's deer hunting season.

"Hey, Dad, it's the prize deer you bragged about. Are you afraid us kids will forget what a great shot you are, so you made the photo into a calendar? You've gotten smart over the years. Of course the only problem is later on you can't exaggerate the size because now there is proof of how big it actually was."

We all laughed. For once he didn't have a quick comeback. He slowly pulled out a chair and sat down across from me. He had aged dramatically and no longer looked a youthful seventy. The spark of spunky vitality was gone from his eyes and it was difficult for me to look at him and not feel the emotions bubbling inside.

There was silence as the reality of why I was there rippled through the room. I wondered if they were feeling awkward also. I wished I possessed my brother Vernon's outrageous sense of humor to ease the discomfort. Whenever he was around, there was usually considerable laughter and more of a sense of lightness. Even though he used it to hide his emotions, it had its benefits.

Deciding to address the unavoidable, I asked, "So, Pops, how are you doing?"

He looked over at me as his hands rested on the table. His voice squeaked and he spoke slowly. "Some days are good and some days are not so good. I was sicker than a dog after getting that chemo. I've lost most of my voice and can't seem to keep much in my stomach. The doc said I would probably be tired, but I never thought it would be this bad. Nothing they seem to give me helps with the pain. I can't figure out why. You'd think there would be something that could take it away." He sounded frustrated and angry.

His response didn't surprise me at all. "You look like you've seen better days, Pops. This must be rough on you."

"You can say that again. Really took the zip right out of me. Two months ago I was feeling great in spite of this rib pain. That I could handle. This is something else."

I turned to look at Mom and watched as she gave Dad a concerned, loving glance. The camaraderie between them seemed to have deepened their relationship.

"Can I get you anything Dad? Something to eat or drink?" I asked.

"Nope. I'm afraid to put much in my stomach. Afraid I'll throw up."

"Have you been taking the Essiac tea I sent Mom?"

"I was. Then I started heaving my guts out from those drugs and now I'm afraid it will make me sick, too."

After Dad had first been diagnosed, a friend had told me about this tea. It is a Native American remedy of natural herbs, found effective in treating some types of cancer by strengthening the immune system and purifying the blood. Through my research, I found documentation by medical doctors in Boston verifying its effectiveness. One of John Kennedy's physicians claimed he was cured of cancer by using it. I sent Mom a book about it and was able to purchase the tea in Los Angeles. I knew it wouldn't hurt Dad and, if anything, might strengthen his body. Mom liked what she read and decided to try it. They both had been drinking it for over a month. I was disappointed to hear he had quit taking it.

Mom turned to Dad and inquired, "Were you able to rest?"

"Not much. The pain in my ribs keeps bothering me and I couldn't get comfortable. I'll need to take a pain pill soon, so I can sleep through the night." As he talked, his hands rubbed his lower back and there was scorn on his face. It was apparent he was in pain. He turned back to me and said, "You're lucky you weren't here a couple weeks ago. I was really miserable then. Mary came home and helped change some of my pills. I've been feeling a little better since then. At least I'm able to keep more food down now."

I had talked with Mary before flying back and she had mentioned her visit was spent more being a nurse than a daughter. Dad had been really irritable and grouchy and she was exhausted when she left. I was hoping my experience wouldn't be the same.

"Pops, are you still able to get out in the woods?"

"Yeah, but not every day. When I feel okay, I'm out. Johnny's getting the better of me, though. Those piles of logs are getting higher and higher." He chuckled. In the winter my brother worked with Dad in the woods. They had done this for years and it seemed to be a nice balance for both of them.

"How's L.A.?" he asked. "Tired of all that traffic and ready to move back yet?"

"Well, Pops, it's still crazy, but winters are going to have to get a lot milder and the summers a lot longer before you see my face around here for any length of time."

"I'll take the cold weather any day rather than having to be around all those lunatics. I bet they don't have any of this fresh air." His voice cracked and he started to cough.

"Do you want something for your throat?" Mom asked.

"Yeah, give me one of those lozenges." He looked at me. "Thought my voice would have come back by now." I could tell he was getting tired and wanted something for his pain. He looked uncomfortable and kept shifting in his chair. "Is it time for my pain pill yet?" He glanced over at Mom.

"I'll check." She walked to the medicine cabinet and studied a sheet of paper taped to the door. Listed on it were all his drugs and the times he took them. Mom brought him a glass of water and put a pill in his hand. I didn't ask what he was taking. "Tomorrow you can put on a new pain patch and that should help more," she told Dad.

He swallowed the pill and said, "Well, kid, I gotta go to bed. Glad to see you. How long are you home for?"

"A week, Dad."

"Good, good. I'll see you in the morning." He got up slowly from the chair and turned to Mom. "You coming?"

"In a few minutes."

"Good night, Dad. Hope you can sleep. It's good to be home. See you in the morning."

"Good night." He turned and walked into the bathroom and closed the door.

I turned to Mom. "Well, how do you think he looks," she asked in a way that hungered for reassurance that my response would be: "He looks great, Mom."

"He looks like he's been sick, Mom. This must be hard on you."

"I keep telling him he's going to beat this and I'm not giving up my hope." She sounded weary.

"I'm proud of you Mom. That's the best attitude you could have. I'm glad to be home. I bet you could use a break. Just let me know how to help out." My voice was quiet.

"I'm glad you're home, too. He is much better than he was. Mary being here helped a lot. At least she was able to straighten out some of his medication. Everything has happened so quickly we haven't known which way to turn. Ann and Dave have gotten the brunt of it. They've both taken off a lot of time from work driving with us to Marshfield. I feel like we've become a burden to you kids. Everyone is calling all the time and I know you're all worried." Good old Mom always thought about everyone else first.

"Well, Mom, if you can't depend on us, who can you? After all, you and Pops have certainly been there for us. How are you holding up?"

She fidgeted with her fingers as she replied, "I spend most of my time with him. Sometimes I just sit next to him when he's lying on the couch. You know, he is dealing with this better than I am. He doesn't say a lot, but there are times when he talks about it more. We're praying he'll be cured. He told me if he isn't then it's God's will. A couple of times we've cried together. The hardest part for him has been the weakness and throwing up. It's hard for him being sick because he has always been so active. It's helped having you kids around. I know he misses not having all of you closer. He has never said that over the years because he hasn't wanted to interfere in any of your lives. He always likes it when we're all together. I think it makes him proud how you've all turned out. I know I am, even though I don't say it much."

It was apparent how much Dad's illness had affected Mom. I sensed her words reflected equally how much she felt, even though she was referring to Dad.

I reached out and touched her hands. "Mom, just remember we are always here for you. Don't be hesitant to reach out at any time. Regardless of where we all are, I think each of us would drop everything to be there for you and Dad."

She squeezed my hand and then said, "I'm tired. I need to go to bed. If you want something to eat, there are leftovers in the refrigerator. Just leave the dishes; I'll clean up the kitchen in the morning. Could you put a log in the fire before you go to bed?"

"Sure."

She got up and gave me a little hug.

"I love you, Mom."

"I love you too, Susie. Good night."

Good night, Mom."

She walked slowly out of the kitchen. It was ten o'clock. Staring into my cold cup of tea, I felt numb. My parents' voices in the bedroom were a dull drone through the kitchen wall. Soon there was silence in the house, except for the ticking of the kitchen clock on the wall above the stove. Occasionally the wind outside whispered to the solitude of the barren sleeping farmland. Every now and then its force gently blew against the house, creating a whistle-like sound as if to say, "I am the winds of change." The thought made me shiver.

I glanced toward the window sill overlooking the back yard and a plot of land that lovingly became my mother's garden every summer. Normally at this time of year, she would have replaced her special knickknacks on the ledge with cut-off milk cartons containing tomato seeds she had planted with tender, loving care. She nurtured them into small plants until late spring, when she transplanted their sturdy little roots into the fertile garden soil. As a kid, I would watch her look through the seed and flower catalogs during the winter months, the way most women would browse through clothing catalogs choosing their spring wardrobes. She would spend hours immersed in them, deciding on her selection for that year's planting. Her flower and vegetable garden had always been a source of great pride and joy. Relatives and neighbors had complimented her many times on her bountiful garden and she was sought out for her delicious tomatoes.

But this year there were no milk cartons lining the window sill. Instead two ceramic oriental vases and a ceramic little girl (all of which belonged to her mother), an African violet and various other special jewels given by her grandchildren adorned the window ledge. Either she did not have time to plant her tomato seeds or the thought of planning a garden without Dad around was too much for her to bear. My reflections created a feeling of sadness, and I found myself missing the moments of joyous, childhood carefreeness and the sense of being secure and protected by Mom and Dad.

There was a slight chill in the kitchen as the wood burning furnace in the basement became low on logs. Putting my cup in the sink, I went to stoke the fire with enough wood to last until morning. I tiptoed into the bathroom so as not to disturb my parents, whose bedroom connected with it. The house was poorly insulated and sounds could be heard easily through the walls. Then I turned out all the lights in the kitchen, except for the night light over the sink, and carried my suitcases upstairs. I was careful to avoid creaks in the steps that were still familiar after all the years of sneaking in late from a date.

It was freezing in the room I shared with my sisters growing up, since little heat was coming up through the register. Even the storm windows did not prevent the draft and winter briskness from entering. I lit a candle on the vanity and undressed quickly, putting on long underwear beneath my pajamas. Crawling underneath the patchwork quilt, the bite of cold sheets made me shiver and eager to pull the quilt up around my chin. It took a long time to get warm. The candle light flickered with a soft glow on the ceiling as my thoughts contemplated Mom and Dad, hopefully asleep, directly beneath my room.

They had both been born in the Midwest—Dad in Chicago and Mom in Antigo. She was raised on a dairy farm a few miles from her present home and had four brothers and four sisters. She had a strong Catholic upbringing that had remained a dominant influence in her life. Mom's family was closely knit and everyone except one brother still lived in the area. Raised in a rural area, her companions and best friends were her siblings. Mom met Dad through her brother Vern, who was a close buddy.

When Mom graduated from high school, she worked as a secretary at a local bank for a year and a half and loved it. When she married Dad, she quit her job because no wife of his was going to work. She had always wanted to return to part-time employment after all of us kids were grown. It never happened. Dad put up too much resistance and Mom became tired of the battle and gave in to his control. Her desire to work outside the home had always been a bone of contention between them.

Mom was less outgoing than Dad. She had a tendency toward shyness and never thought she was pretty. She had always lived a sheltered life, surrounded by family. Her only sense of independence came when she lived with her sister after high school. Mom was refined and graceful, although she didn't see herself that way. From pictures taken when she was younger, one could see she had been tall, slender, attractive and looked like a model. She had a beautiful smile. She loved to dance and was aesthetically pleasing to watch when she did. She was an intelligent woman who didn't believe she was. She had always lacked self-esteem. She kept her feelings tucked deep inside and rarely shared what was really bothering her. When we were kids, she didn't like to "rock the boat" when it came to confrontations with Dad. Through the years she had become more assertive.

Dad was the oldest of seven children—three boys and four girls. He had never had a close relationship with his parents and rarely spoke about them. His upbringing was Lutheran, although he was not a frequent follower of his faith. He turned Catholic when he and Mom got married. When he was in the sixth or seventh grade, his parents moved from Chicago to a small town about twenty miles from Mom's roots to try their hand at farming. His parents purchased a farm from a realtor during the middle of winter without ever seeing the property. They were told the land was tillable and ended up being taken in the deal. While they struggled to make the farm work, Dad was sent back to Chicago to live with his grandmother and finish high school. He never did. After eighth grade, he became lonely for his family and his love of the Wisconsin wilderness, so he left Chicago. A short time later, his parents had to sell the farm because it was not profitable. They returned to Chicago but my father refused to go. Instead he worked odd jobs and supported not only himself but sent money to his parents. He spent a couple of years with the Civilian Concentration Corps (CCC) and loved it. He was disappointed when it closed down.

They were married when Mom was nineteen and Dad twenty-six.

Within the first five years of married life, they bore five children— two boys and three girls. I was the youngest at that point, and my Dad's favorite daughter. At least that was what I was teased about for many years. Eventually two younger brothers were born, each four years apart.

When my parents were first married, Dad had a milk route, hauling ten-gallon metal cans of milk from various dairy farmers that he delivered to the local milk factory. They lived in the upper floor of a friend's house for about a year and then purchased the dairy farm where I grew up. At the time, no banks would give my father a loan because he did not have any credit. Someone loaned them the money, and over time my father was able to expand the acreage of the farm to one hundred and fifty-nine acres, milking twenty-four head of cattle. It was considered a medium-size dairy farm during those times. He became a self-made man through hard work and determination. Mom once told me Dad didn't really care for being a dairy farmer, but he didn't know what else to do that would provide him independence.

Dad had a free spirit about him and was outrageously outgoing. He always seemed to be the life of a party, with his teasing and charisma. He was opinionated, dominant, controlling and not afraid to say what he thought. He had a temper and loved to be the center of attention. While he was rough around the edges, he was very sensitive inside.

By present day standards, we were considered poor. The house consisted of a kitchen, small living room and one bedroom downstairs, two bedrooms and a storage room upstairs. My two sisters and I slept together in a double bed. My two older brothers shared another room. When my two younger brothers were older, the storage room was cleaned out to accommodate all us kids upstairs. Later Dad put an addition onto the house that became the living room. We did not have an indoor bathroom until I was in the fifth grade and used an outhouse instead. We took a bath every Saturday night in a large tub Mom placed in the kitchen and filled with hot water from the gas-burning stove. She had a ringer washing machine and hung our clothes outside on a clothesline, regardless of the season. Later she got a regular washing machine and dryer that eased the job of keeping everyone in clean clothes. I never thought we were poor until I was in high school and saw how some of my friends lived. Whatever money Dad made went into keeping the farm running. We always had a used car and I never had a new bike. I don't remember if any of my older brothers and sisters ever did either.

I was raised in a very patriarchal family. Women were seen but not really heard. My father was the head of the household, and you knew it. My mother, as most women in that generation, was the caretaker for not only us kids but Dad as well. It was expected that she make all the meals, raise the kids, keep the house clean, wash all the clothes, as well as milk the cows and help with the farm work. My mother didn't know how to cook, sew, or raise a garden when they got married. She taught herself. She sewed most of our clothes when we were little and we always had a new outfit for Christmas and Easter. She easily went without new clothes for herself so we could have them. She became an excellent cook and no visitor ever left the farm hungry.

Dad would tell the story about when they were first married and he came home one day from his milk route and found Teddy, their dog, sniffing at hard pellets inside his dog dish. Apparently Mom had tried to make baked beans, but forgot to soak them first. Her attempt to hide the evidence wasn't even appealing to the family dog, who ate whatever you put in front of him. Although Mom was no longer a neophyte in the cooking category, they continued to chuckle over this story for years.

Mom became a great baker. Every Saturday she made a sweet dough that came out of the oven as yummy caramel rolls that melted in your mouth. She also made kalatches, a Czechoslovakian pastry filled with cooked fruits, poppy seeds or dates. She baked all her own bread and one summer she made eighteen loaves in one week. She also planted a huge garden that could feed an army. She did all her own canning and the fruit cellar was full every winter. We never went hungry. Our freezer was always full with a butchered dairy cow that no longer produced milk as well as venison, rabbit, partridge and fish from Dad's outdoor adventures.

My parent's relationship was an enigma to me as a child. I under-stood it more after having been married, realizing the ups and downs that occur with any relationship. Mom was not affectionate and I rarely saw her hugging Dad. He would put his arm around her and kiss her on the cheek and tease her. I never saw them hold hands. They didn't talk about their emotions, yet it was easy to tell when one of them was upset. Dad would lash out with his anger and Mom would become quiet. Whenever something was bothering Dad, he eventually blew up and then was fine. Mom carried around their arguments as hurt and resentment.

There were cycles of good times and cycles of trying times. I never knew whether this was normal in other families because I didn't share upsets at home with my friends. It was just how it was. I never knew how Mom and Dad's disagreements affected the rest of my siblings because we all coped in different ways. It was my tendency to numb my feelings without realizing until later the affect it had on my ability to be intimate. Any argument, large or small, healthy or not, made me cringe—and continued to do so into my adult life.

Mom and Dad's form of intimacy and closeness was more subtle. Dad always started the day by giving Mom a peck on the cheek be-fore he began his work outside. She would fix his favorite meals. On Mother's Day, he would bring her wildflowers he had picked. At times there was a harmony between them that was undeniable. They seemed to fall into a groove with each other's rhythms, a groove that had a sweetness about it. They were well aware of each other's quirks and flaws and, while their type of relationship wasn't one I would chose for myself, they hung in there with each other. When Dad was diag-nosed, they were two years short of having been married for fifty years.

Their relationship softened as they aged. Dad no longer walked all over Mom and she was less afraid to speak her truth. They both mel-lowed in their stubbornness and pride. They did a lot of traveling together that probably would not have occurred had it not been for us kids living in various states. My father always said he had lived a full life. I don't think my mother felt she had.

We worked hard. My parents rarely took a vacation when we were small. As we became older, they trusted our ability to manage the farm so they could take a few days' getaway. We loved the freedom when they did. We were a mischievous lot and, if something happened while they were gone, we hid the evidence. One fall when there was a break in harvesting the crops, they left to spend a couple of days up north. My two older brothers, Johnny and Vernon, had the habit of holding onto the cows' tails after milking as they chased them up the path to graze. On this particular day, as they were playing wild men, the cows panicked and broke through a barbed wire fence. That evening we noticed one of the cows had severed its tail, causing profuse bleeding and requiring a visit by the local veterinarian. It was my responsibility to hold the tail up in the air during milking and we sweated for a while over the condition of the cow until the vet came. I have no idea whether Mom and Dad ever found out the real reason behind that particular veterinary bill.

It always seemed there were a lot of people visiting. Most of the time they dropped in unexpectedly. My father called the farm "The Other Place." He said if people weren't at their own homes, they were at ours—hence the name. We loved the company because it meant a break in our chores. We took advantage of the opportunities and, when we played, we played hard. I think we were seen among the relatives as a boisterous and crazy bunch. We were always on our best behavior visiting someone else, but on our turf anything was fair game.

All my friends loved coming over. Mom was easy to talk with and Dad was so outrageous they were always laughing at his endless stories and teasing, and were susceptible to the pranks he would pull on them. They were always fed well, both in their stomachs and in their spirits.

As we got older and the family became larger due to in-laws and grandchildren, get-togethers became even more lively. We had developed enough courage to begin pulling pranks back on Dad and whomever else we found gullible. Our last family reunion had been three years ago, when my brother Ron got married. Before that, it had been ten years. Mom said something strange at the time: she said she felt it would be the last time we all would be together as a family. She would be right.

The night had grown late and I snuggled warmly in bed in spite of the brisk, cool air circulating throughout the room. Losing myself in the past had created a safe and secure feeling inside. As I leaned over to blow out the candle, emotions of love and compassion for Mom and Dad filled my heart. I had missed them.

A crisp, cold, sunny winter morning greeted me. The snow crunched underneath my feet, like the sound of cornflakes. Downstairs I could hear Mom and Dad in the kitchen and smelled the aroma of fresh coffee. The thought of subjecting my warm, delicate skin to the wave of cold air waiting to pounce the minute I pulled away the quilt kept me snuggled under the covers. My body was no longer acclimated to the brutal winter weather and Dad always teased me that, if I "put more meat on my bones," I wouldn't have any problem. For a moment it felt like old times being back at home. I was curious what the visit would bring. Knowing that getting out of bed was like jumping into a cold pool, I braved the initial impact and threw off the covers. Shivering in my pajamas, I sorted through my suitcase to find warm, suitable clothing and noticed all the videotapes packed inside. The harsh reality for coming home hit me and I knelt at the edge of the bed to pray.

After a few minutes in silence, I forced myself to get up the courage to go downstairs. There was a nervousness in the pit of my stomach. Taking a deep breath, I made my way down the creaking steps to the kitchen and was greeted by a warm heat wave. Mom and Dad were sitting at the kitchen table, drinking cups of coffee.

"Good morning," I said to both of them, as I closed the upstairs door and stood next to the warm air emanating from the furnace air vent.

"Good morning. Good morning," my father sang back.

"Good morning, Susie," my mother quietly responded. She started to smile. "I bet it was freezing in your room last night. Were you able to stay warm?"

I laughed. "Mom, you can take the girl out of the country, but you can't take the country out of the girl."

Dad grinned back. "Well if you would put more meat on your bones, you wouldn't have a problem with our wonderful Wisconsin winters." Now where had I heard that before?

"Want some breakfast or your usual cup of tea?" Mom asked.

Her memory for remembering one of her children's unique habits caused me to smile. "Just the tea."

"I figured that. The teakettle is hot." She poured water into a cup and put a tea bag in front of me. I noticed tiny rainbows all over the kitchen walls, moving back and forth like small dancing fairies. Glancing toward the kitchen window, I noticed an octagonal crystal I had given Mom years before hanging from a nylon string. Sun rays glistened in the window, striking the crystal and radiating brilliant colors that filled the room. I felt like a little kid at Christmas watching the magical sparkles.

"Mom, you still have that crystal."

She smiled. "It's one of my treasures. I love seeing the rainbows when I get up. They are the most vivid in the wintertime because of the direction of the sun." We all gazed at the floating colors as she spoke.

I sat at the table next to Dad. "Pops, I'm glad to be home, even if it's freezing out." I wanted to ask how he had slept but I didn't want to appear focused on his illness right away.

His response surprised me. "I'm glad you are, too. But I want you to promise me something. I don't want you talking about cancer while you're here. Not a word. I made up my mind to get chemo, and that's what I am doing. Right or wrong."

I was speechless! There went all my carefully researched information. Dad was staring at me with determination ingrained in his sickly brown eyes. I looked at Mom and she appeared just as surprised by his remarks. The anxiousness in my stomach resurfaced and I swallowed nervously.

"Okay, Pops, I promise," I said in a surrendering tone.

"Good. The only thing I will let you do is take my blood to send to that doctor Vern mentioned." My brother and his wife Margaret had been pushing Dad to see Harvey, an American medical doctor practicing in Mexico, who worked with experimental drugs to treat cancer. "Vern says this doctor can find out where my cancer is and I'm willing to send this off if he can do that. Then I could have it cut out. I don't know why they can't do that now. They can cut everything else out." There was frustration in his scratchy voice as he spoke, and I sensed his desperation about wanting his cancer "fixed."

Tears began to well up in the corners of my eyes and I struggled to contain my emotions. "Sure, Dad, I can take care of that for you."

"Good. Margaret sent all the stuff. You just have to prick my finger and then follow her instructions. Let me finish my coffee first."

He picked up his cup as I stared at the table counter. I had never thought I would have to deal with either of my parents getting sick at this point in my life. Perhaps it was denial that had kept me believing they would be healthy for a long, long time. They were still so young.

Just one phone call and everything had changed.

Chapter Four
Who Is My Father Beneath His Illness?

There was a quietness in my apartment that was soothing to the tiredness filtering through my body. Even the electric energy of Los Angeles seemed calm for once. A cool breeze gently blew through the window in my studio, fanning the candle flame on my altar. There was a bitter sweet feeling about being back in L.A..

The memories of my trip to see my parents were fervently imprinted in my heart. Memories I would cherish for a lifetime. I so strongly desired to capture the richness of that experience on paper to preserve all the precious moments. Yet I struggled to find words that could grasp the fullness that lay delicately in the intricate layers of my being. I never imagined I would be able to view the probability of Dad's dying as a beautiful, rewarding process. In my humanness, my heart hurt and wept with yearning to have him healthy and full of spunk as I had always known him to be. I didn't want him to be sick with cancer and miserable from the effects of his chemotherapy. I didn't want him to die, certainly not this way. Yet that was what was happening.

I had watched something subtly transform inside of me while I was with Dad.

There was no escaping the harsh reality of his imminent passing. It was before me every minute with his physical deterioration. I could choose to deny it or embrace it. I knew the former would leave me with regrets; the latter could provide freedom and fulfillment. In my soul, there was no struggle over what my choice had to be. I wasn't going to acquire another biological father in this lifetime. Pops was it. I believed we choose our parents before we enter this world. I didn't think it was just hit and miss with respect to whom we end up having as our mother and father. Something as important as that isn't just a number in the lottery system. God is too grand for that. So I could experience Dad to the fullest with what time he had left, or miss out on the profound gift that awaited me in this package wrapped in his dying. There wouldn't be another Pops coming into my life to give me another chance.

The moment Dad asked me to promise not to talk about cancer with him, I felt stretched. It left me to look beyond speaking about his illness and merge with him as my father, the man—to unite in our human frailties and perhaps one last time as father and daughter. For here was a man who was not just my father but a soul yearning for freedom as well. Freedom from this lifetime of unfulfilled dreams, unresolved sorrows and a body filled with disease. He was wise in making his request of me. He gave me gifts far greater than I could fully realize at the time.

I wondered what went through his mind as he watched his children come and visit, knowing we were making special trips now that he was ill. Did he also search for a communion with each of us as his time drew to a close? Did he savor the moments as much as we did? Dad had never been much of a philosopher. He was more practical than that. Yet I knew he was a thinker. His think tank was his nature as much as was his workshop. He spent endless hours in both. He was not a man who shared his innermost thoughts. He rarely had. I had never talked much about God with him, yet I knew he had a deep faith. It was refortified every time he walked through his forest land. I sensed that was where he was closest to God. We were very similar in this way.

I watched him lying on the couch in the living room. Several times throughout the day, I would see him there, void of energy, with his eyes closed. I assumed he was sleeping. Mom told me many times he was just thinking. She said when he wanted to escape from facing the pain, he would imagine walking in the woods planning next year's deer drives. She said he found peace this way. What else was going through his mind as he lay there? Did he think about dying and was he preparing for it? Did he know his days were ebbing away or did he feel he would beat this? Was he afraid? I never asked.

Honoring my commitment to Dad was challenging in light of what Solano had shared. If there were a perspective that could be helpful to him, I needed to trust that somehow, within the ground rules Dad had created, a window of opportunity would occur for that to be shared. Solano had told me not to bring much in the way of material to leave with Dad. "Bring him simply one thing. And in that one thing, know there will be a door that opens that allows you to speak of more and other things." Ignoring Solano's advice, the image of my suitcase loaded with videos caused me to laugh aloud. There was great wisdom in simplicity and I had learned a big lesson about thinking more was better. The illusion of thinking I might teach Dad something had turned out to be just the reverse.

When I was forced to let go of preconceived ideas and my mission in visiting Dad, it created a whole world of possibilities for sharing time together. He just wanted my being there to be normal and to experience his daughter coming home—not because he was sick, but rather to be with "good old Dad" because I missed and loved him. The week was one of the richest I ever shared with him. My only agenda left was finding a way to let him know how much he meant to me. Not wanting to create a forced conversation in which to do so, I waited and watched for the moment when it would naturally happen. It was quite magical how everything unfolded.

Dad was weaker than I had ever seen him so we were limited in what we did. One day we drove out to his land on Turtle Lake, a small fishing lake close to where his parents once lived briefly. Dad had recently purchased a new blue Chevrolet truck with four-wheel drive that was his pride and joy. For once he had splurged and was proud to show it off. I felt like a little girl wedged between my parents as we drove on windy, two-lane roads, listening to country music. The eight acres of lake property Dad owned was not plush resort land. It was wilderness. Getting back to it required driving on logging roads that were rutted and bumpy. No summer cabins silhouetted the landscape. Instead timber trees of oak, maple, white birch and poplar dominated the habitat. Deer, bear, porcupine and eagles were its residents. Dad owned an additional one hundred and sixty acres of woodland near the lake property and had created logging roads to give accessibility in maintaining upkeep of it. He thrived in this environment. There was a similarity between Dad and his land. Both had a rugged and untamed exterior, but on the inside there was profound wisdom, silence and simplicity.

When I was little, Dad would take us fishing in a green, wooden row boat and teach us how to catch the crappies, blue gill and northern that were abundant. He knew all their hiding places like the back of his hand and rarely left our fishing adventures without a catch. On days when the fish weren't biting or he wasn't catching, I learned how to row the boat. My attempts were clumsy and awkward as I tried to maneuver both the oars moving in the same direction at the same time. More times than not, they would clank against the sides of the boat, scaring away whatever fish were hiding in the mysterious depths beneath us. My awkward maneuvering usually led us in circles, much to the chuckles and frustration of whomever was in the boat.

Occasionally a couple of us were treated to sleeping overnight at the lake with Dad, in a thirty-foot black and white, used travel trailer, nestled among the trees. We would go after the evening chores were finished and return early the next morning. It was always exciting to break away from the daily routine, and staying at the lake always seemed like a wonderful adventure. As an adult I could still recapture the musty aroma of the trailer, lying in a squeaky bed, the kerosene lamp burning dimly through the globe and listening to whippoorwills awaken the eerie stillness with the sweetness of their song. At the crack of dawn we would be on the lake, bundled in warm clothes in the early morning dampness, privy to the masterful art of a self-taught fisherman. I felt special to be chosen to partake in these events because we rarely spent any time alone with Dad amid the constant business of the farm. These occasions made life feel magical and precious.

The air was cold and dry as my parents and I stood on the frozen tundra overlooking the lake still covered with ice. The trees, naked and exposed, falling prey to a lack of protection from the harshness of the winter elements, paralleled what Dad was going through with his cancer. I listened to him reminisce about deer hunting and his acquisition of land, and could feel the memories rekindle his intense love for nature. I sensed our drive that afternoon was for him to reconnect to life that brought stability, strength and security, something that was being robbed from him by his illness. Seeing his vulnerability caused me to feel helpless. Silently I prayed to God asking for his soul to be filled in a way I didn't know how. In the winter of Dad's illness, the only place to go was inside.

Our drive back home led us to a small local bar, the River Wild, that Dad visited occasionally, chatting with the owners and swapping deer stories. I was not particularly interested in sitting in a noisy, smoke-filled bar since I was chilled from the cold and didn't drink alcohol. Mom didn't seem to mind even though she rarely drank. The bartender John was the son of a couple who'd had a small farm next to my parents' during my childhood. His parents John and Norma became good friends with Mom and Dad, sharing many a laugh and fun times. Several years ago John Sr. had passed away from lung cancer.

This spontaneous stop gave me two amazing gifts. One was apparent almost immediately. The other didn't occur until over a year later. It was clear a friendship existed between Dad and John. As they bantered back and forth sharing stories about deer hunting, I saw Dad in a new light. There seemed to be more of a freedom about him when he didn't have to maintain an image of being the strong, responsible head of a household. Here was a carefree, mischievous, laughing boy who was endearing to watch. In that moment, I was no longer his little girl, but a curious woman intrigued by the person sitting next to me. Through her eyes I saw the richness of a man I never allowed myself to truly see because of limitations placed on him as "my father." There was an honest, open, humble way in which he told John about being sick that brought tears to my eyes. He had no pretense about him at all.

In spite of his sickness, we had many laughs together. Three nights in a row, we watched videotapes of Johnny Carson. My heart was warmed hearing the ring of his laughter fill the living room as we all let ourselves slip back into happier times. Each following day, I saw a sparkle return to Dad's eyes and more of a spring in his steps. It was extremely healing for all of us. Laughter has such a way of lifting spirits and taking away the edge found in darker moments. I didn't want these evenings to ever end.

As I learned how to be present and open with Dad in a new way, he responded. The most extraordinary moment was when he allowed me to give him a massage. His mere willingness was profound in itself, as he never had one before. My offer was very spontaneous. Dad had not been sleeping well because of continual pain in his ribcage. He was stiff from lack of his daily outside routine and seemed tense. From my own experience, I knew how helpful massage can be. The body is such a reservoir of stored emotions and thoughts that can build up to create illness if there is no way of externally releasing these feelings. It was clear Dad was dealing with a lot, not only emotionally but physically. The chemotherapy drugs and other pills combating side effects were foreign to his natural rhythm and were like sludge clogging an engine that was used to fresh air and exercise as its fuel. When a friend of mine who was a chiropractor mentioned he had a massage table, I jumped at the opportunity to borrow it. I had ulterior motives. Since I couldn't offer words for healing I could provide love through the touch of my hands. Either way, I was determined to offer my gifts.

There is such synchronicity in how God operates to support good works. The evening of Dad's massage was uninterrupted by phone calls or visitors. Unbeknownst to him, the living room had been silently blessed and a candle in the corner inconspicuously lit in preparation for what I considered to be a holy ceremony. Dad thought he was just having a simple massage.

He appeared shy as he climbed onto the table in his boxer shorts and I covered his body with a sheet. I asked Mom to sit nearby so he would feel more at ease and she could watch. I was hoping to give her a massage later. Joking with him helped ease his nervousness and helped him relax. I explained again that massaging his muscles would help him sleep better and take away some of his soreness. I closed my eyes before beginning and said a prayer: "Dear God, I offer myself as a pure vessel through which your love and healing can enter Dad's body and soul. Remove any physical and emotional pain that hampers his ability to become healthy. Please give him courage and strength and let him feel our combined love. I ask this in your name. Amen."

A gentle peacefulness moved through me as I glanced down at Dad. His head was turned toward Mom and his eyes were closed. He looked very innocent lying practically naked under the sheet. I was overcome with a feeling of love to see the weakened form of a man who once was my strong, healthy father. I quietly took a deep breath to control the tears welling up in my eyes.

Mom didn't have any massage oil, so I substituted the sunflower oil she used for cooking. Rubbing my hands together to warm them, I immediately began to feel intense heat in my body. It was an unusual sensation. With each stroke of my hands, I felt more emotionally connected to Dad. The closest physical contact I had ever had with him was kissing him on the cheek or giving him a hug. Now I was allowed a window of intimacy because his illness had removed our masks. Of all the gifts I ever gave him, this was the most meaningful. Despite his weight loss, I could feel his powerful muscles that had developed over years of hard, physical labor. His arms and back that once lifted hundred-pound sacks of potatoes and bales of hay were defined and solid. Legs that carried his sturdy, proud frame were toned and streamlined from many miles of constant walking.

Two years earlier Dad had had bypass surgery to replace six arteries to his heart. Noticing the scars on his chest, I couldn't help but correlate the operation with his cancer. Both left his heart vulnerable to events over which he felt little control; both required a great deal of faith. I enjoyed massaging his head the most since it allowed me to gaze upon his face and gently stroke his roughly, bearded cheeks. It was as though I could feel all the wisdom he had acquired throughout the years ingrained as indented lines on his forehead. Allowing my hands to linger, delicately caressing his baldness, my thoughts asked to release his brain of any worry, doubt or fear. What amazed me most was the softness and whiteness of his skin, just like a baby's. Underneath his exterior hardness, was revealed a tenderness he protectively shielded. Whether it was conscious or unconscious on his part, lying on that table he exposed an innocence no amount of words could ever relay. I felt humbled.

Something remarkable happened while working on Dad that surprised both of us. The longer I massaged him, the hotter my body and hands became. It wasn't just a mild heat, but intense. Even Dad remarked about it several times. He thought the heat was because of the oil, but I knew it was something else. Pondering whether to be truthful about my understanding, I teased him by saying it was all the fire in his belly coming out. Both he and Mom laughed. But my answer left me feeling uncomfortable. Resorting to humor diminished my own integrity and my belief in how the power of God works. My concern was that I not jeopardize Dad's feeling of safety with the massage. Torn by what to say, I remained quiet. When he commented again about the heat, I sensed discomfort and anxiety in his voice. I decided to be honest.

"Dad, it isn't the oil that is making my hands hot. It's only used as lubrication to prevent friction when rubbing your skin. What you're feeling is God's love and healing coming through my hands. Before the massage, I prayed and asked him to send his energy through my body. I'm not using any kind of magic potion. I believe God is here in the room with us, and my hands are just the vehicle for him to work on you."

He became very quiet. Then Mom asked to feel my hands. With a shocked expression she said, "Your father isn't kidding. Your hands are hot as an iron." I smiled and winked at her.

Shortly thereafter, Dad said he had enough. Even though he appeared more relaxed and slept peacefully, he was not open to any further massages. Later I wondered if my honesty had been such a good idea.

One afternoon while Mom and I were watching one of the angel videos, Dad came into the living room and joined us. While his interest took me by surprise, it was right up my alley. The topic was inspiring, uplifting and extremely Catholic. Here was common ground where we could safely relate because there was nothing threatening, confrontational or conflicting. Having watched the video several times, I was curious to learn what his reaction would be. I waited for some negative comment, but he had none. Instead he shared a couple of great stories.

One spring evening, he and two of my brothers, Vernon and Johnny, were burning dry grass in a field, something he had done many times before. All of a sudden the wind changed from a mild breeze into strong gusts and the fire started burning out of control. The rapidly spreading flames jeopardized not only our farm but those of several neighbors as well. As he and my brothers frantically dug furrows to stop the fire, he became alarmed, fearing the worst was about to happen. Too far from the house to run for help, they kept frantically fighting the flames. Just when he believed they had lost the battle, the wind switched directions and began to subside, allowing the fire to become manageable and finally to be put out. Dad said he knew the hands of God were working overtime that night and it was an experience he never forgot.

Miraculous things always seemed to happen during deer hunting. On numerous occasions he would instinctively know to raise his gun just as a deer walked into an opening. One season, a group of guys with whom he hunted had scared up a deer in thick underbrush and it lost its track. As whistles went back and forth among the hunters, designated trackers began scouring the woods for what they believed was a buck. Since their doe (female) tags had already been filled, they could only shoot if they saw horns or risk being severely fined. Standing quietly at his post, Dad spotted a deer move in a clearing of timber trees but couldn't see any horns. Out of the blue, he heard a voice as loud and clear as if someone were talking to him say, "Shoot." He hesitated, still unable to see horns. He heard the voice again: "Shoot." He pulled the trigger and down went the deer. Nervously he made his way through the trees to the opening and was surprised to learn it was a buck. The horns had been completely concealed by frozen snow. If he hadn't heard the voice, he would never have fired his gun. That was a new one for me—angels on deer hunting patrol?

His most unusual story was one I vaguely remembered. One fall afternoon while plowing a field, he glanced down at one of the wheels on the tractor. He was startled to see a small ball of fire burning there. Becoming alarmed, he stopped the tractor and jumped down from the seat to check on it. By the time he got to the wheel, the fire had disappeared and he found no evidence that one had ever existed. Accustomed to unusual circumstances happening on the farm, he kept plowing but also kept an eye on the tractor wheels. Nothing further happened the remainder of the afternoon. Later that evening he was shocked to learn his grandmother had died around the time he saw the ball of fire. He had been very close to her and she had come to say good-bye.

I was enthralled by our whole conversation. This was what gave life meaning. Not wanting the conversation to end, I told my parents about my bicycle experience. When I finished telling the story I had kept from them because of my mother's tendency to worry, Dad reminded me of another close encounter when I was sixteen.

Dad had a contract with a local pulp mill he supplied with peeled timber. Around June each year, he would cut poplar trees and we would be responsible for removing the bark once they were felled. Since the sap on these trees was only moist during a certain time of the year, when school let out in late spring, our days were spent assisting him before haying season began. That particular summer he was harvesting trees from his property at Turtle Lake. Dad would select an area in the woods that needed to be thinned and cut them down with his chain saw. Since five of us kids were usually peeling, we had to maneuver ourselves between a lot of fallen trees and many branches in a pretty dense area. We would mark the fallen trees in eight-foot lengths or sticks, up to a certain diameter, chop off all the branches and then peel away the bark. Each tree averaged about five sticks. We were constantly bending over fallen trees in whatever way possible to loosen all the bark. We used a steel tool called a "spud" that was about sixteen inches long and sharpened at one end to run a bead up the tree. The spud was then placed under the moist bark to loosen it and we gradually worked our way up the tree, stripping away the rough exterior until the marked areas were completely free. It was hard work and could be dangerous. The sap from the trees made the bark extremely slippery and we had to be constantly careful not to step on any discarded wet pieces, or trip over chopped branches. At times Dad used the chain saw to cut the trees in sections to make it easier for us to peel. This also created a risk for the logs to slide or roll.

On this particular summer day, I was working on a difficult tree and was not a happy camper. I was fed up with all the mosquitoes, my elbows and knees were bruised and I was hot, sweaty and cranky. Peeling pulp was never one of my favorite jobs. To make the days go faster, we would compete with each other to see how many trees we could finish by the end of the afternoon. As usual, I was behind and Vernon and Johnny teased me about being a slow poke. The tree suffering from my frustration was on the top of a knob and had been cut into sections. I was on the downside of the hill trying to unwedge my metal peeler from one of the logs, when it started to roll toward me. Caught by surprise and without thinking clearly, I began running down the hill with the log in wild pursuit. The voices of my brothers from the distance sounded as though they were cheering to see who would make it to the bottom first. Dad was yelling as he watched in horror at the sight before him, afraid of the outcome. At the last moment, I felt myself jerked to the side just as the log came crashing past me. Dad said I was one lucky kid and hadn't escape harm on my own accord. It had been a long time since I remembered that incident.

Although he only recalled those specific memories, both he and Mom said there were many times when they knew to check up on us kids just at the moment we could have gotten hurt by some piece of equipment. They always felt blessed because none of us had ever been seriously injured while we were growing up. They couldn't afford any health insurance and believed God had to have been looking out for them.

For a long time afterward I sat on the couch, enriched by what Dad had shared. It was amazing to think how an illness or crisis provides pathways to opportunities or conversations one normally believes are not in the realm of possibility. Once again I realized that, although I had come home to enlighten him, the opposite had happened. What was revealed was the simplicity in how he lived with God, not from an intellectual understanding but from personal, everyday experiences as a simple Midwestern farmer. His connection to God was more vast than I had ever realized. From where did it come? I had never seen him read the Bible, nor any books about spirituality. He didn't always go to church on Sunday and wasn't particularly fond of the local priest where we attended services a mile and a half from the farm.

Confronted with the challenges of raising a family on a limited education, he had come to trust in his own unique form of faith. To trust that when he planted his fields every spring they would yield a harvest that would feed his cattle throughout the winter. To trust that when he went hunting and fishing he would be supplied with food to feed his family. To trust that his dairy farm would provide him an ample income upon which to live. Even though he was raised on one faith as a child and practiced another as an adult, I sensed his belief in God was beyond any religion. God was just God to whom he prayed every night on his knees, and whom he experienced plowing his field on the tractor, hunting deer in the wilderness or lying on the couch alone with his illness. It seemed he had come to know God personally and drew deep strength from this relationship. I felt comfort knowing that somehow he would draw from this relationship to help deal with his cancer. His sharing of angel experiences revealed to me more about that relationship than I could have ever ascertained from an intellectual discussion. What a wonderful insight into Dad.

Even though Dad was unwilling to discuss his cancer, Mom and I talked openly throughout the week. I shared with her all the items I had brought, and we talked at length about simple ways she could start offering options to Dad. She was very open to exploring new ideas and seemed receptive to learning. I was hopeful she would be the door for him to consider alternatives to his chemotherapy. She had heard of Bernie Siegel and Norman Cousins and was inspired by their approach to healing the body. But, as I found out later, her liking a concept and believing in it were two different things.

Perhaps my reason for bringing everything was more for her than Dad. The foundation upon which she had built her life was faltering and she was afraid. While Dad had been seen outwardly as the stable rock, Mom was really the glue that had kept everything together. Surprisingly she was stronger than I had ever realized since she had been overshadowed by Dad all these years. It was interesting to see how one could doubt one's capabilities until given an opportunity to step into uncharted waters and have them validated. I hoped she finally saw the strength of who she really was. Dad would certainly be lost without her.

The opportunity to express my feelings to Dad occurred the last night of my visit. While I was washing dishes with Mom and sharing how much I missed her wonderful, home-cooked meals, Dad came into the kitchen. Standing by the microwave he said teasingly, "Yeah, you never tell your good old Pops how great he is."

Immediately I knew this was my moment. In one split second the stage had been naturally set and no amount of preplanning could have made it happen so effortlessly. Again God's timing was perfect. In spite of a tightness forming in my throat my mind was sharp. Taking a deep breath, I turned from the sink and smiled at Dad. "You know, Pops, you're right. I haven't told you in a long time how much you mean to me. I am extremely proud of you. I'm proud of how you and Mom raised all of us kids. Even though you had a stern hand, you both taught us good values, morals and a sense of responsibility. None of us have had any alcohol or drug problems and—aside from a few of us who are a little crazy—we all turned out great. Of course, I'm not going to say which one of you is responsible for some of us being a little crazy..."

We all laughed. He hadn't moved from the microwave. Although he seemed a little awkward, he made no attempt to stop me from talking.

"All kidding aside, Dad, I have learned a lot from you. I admire how you and Mom started out with nothing and built the farm into a self-sustaining operation. Although we have never talked about the fact, you only have an eighth grade education, yet you are smarter than most men who have a college degree. I have never seen you as lesser because you didn't finish high school. People yearn for the kind of wisdom and common sense you have.

"I admire your honesty. You're not afraid to speak your mind and tell it like it is. People know they can trust your word. That is a rare quality. You're dependable and have a generous heart. If someone needs something, you are right there. I believe there isn't one thing you wouldn't do for us kids if we were in need. I've never forgotten when you took time to help me move back here the summer I graduated from college or when my car broke down up north and you came after chores and got me. I'm always amazed to hear stories about how you pulled someone out of the ditch in the middle of the night during a snowstorm. Most people aren't like that."

If Dad somehow set me up for this conversation, the look of surprise on his face demonstrated he was getting far more than he bargained for.

"I love how you respect the land. You put as much tender, loving care into it as Mom does her garden. When other loggers are stripping forests naked to make a fortune, you don't. Instead there is a sense of dignity when you harvest trees. It's as though you are giving honor back to the earth when you remove old ones to make room for young saplings to grow. You know you could be a rich man if you clear cut just the forties you own, but money never seemed that important to you and Mom."

He finally responded. "I don't feel I own the land. I'm just watching over it. No sense in having something if you don't take care of it right. It's not just for me to enjoy, it's for you guys, too. Once the land is gone, it's gone. Those woods supplied me with a lot of deer meat to put on the table over the years. Your old Pops never let you starve. Wouldn't trade all the money in the world for being out there. It taught me a lot."

The room became silent as we both took in our exchange. "You know, Pops, I believe my love of nature and adventure comes from you. You taught me how to take risks, to be independent, feisty and stand up for what I believe. And you taught me how to problem-solve. There wasn't anything you didn't eventually figure out how to do. You and Mom are both hard workers. I know many times you two sacrificed for us and you rarely took a vacation. Maybe the real reason you didn't get away was not so much the responsibility, but more fear about what kind of trouble we would get into while you were gone."

Mom was chuckling next to me while Dad started laughing.

"I don't know how you handled so much with seven mouths to feed, watching over us, running the farm all at the same time and staying sane. You always kept a sense of humor. I also want to thank you for everything you have done for me. I'm very grateful even if I haven't told you much. Of course, I know I was the perfect child who never gave you any gray hair and about whom you never had to worry."

Both he and Mom responded in unison, "Yeah, right."

"Actually, Dad, I think the reason you have lost your hair is from all the years of stress having to put up with me as your daughter. It just finally caught up with you."

Mom sounded as though she was trying hard not to laugh as Dad piped up, "Isn't that the truth. You certainly gave your Pops more than one gray hair, I can tell you that. Keeping up with you kids always kept us on our toes. Never knew what you guys were up to next. It was easy to keep track of you because of Smokey. Wherever he was, you'd be right behind." Smokey was our black and white collie Dad had gotten from a neighbor when I was one-year-old. There must have been some karmic relationship between us because we were inseparable until I left home at age eighteen. He was my best friend.

"Yeah, Pops, I guess we were hellions on wheels. You know what they say though, 'the apple doesn't fall far from the tree.' If Uncle George were here right now, I bet he could tell a few stories about you as a kid that would make us look like saints." George was really Dad's uncle but they had been like brothers growing up and had remained close throughout the years. We had always called him "Uncle George."

Mom was trying to contain a grin that finally spread across her face. Dad was laughing. I was sure he knew my statement was more truthful than he'd ever let on. His silence spoke volumes. Feeling I was on a roll with my teasing, I continued, "You are a great Dad even if you have a temper, of which I've been on the receiving end on numerous occasions. I admit, it was probably justifiable the summer I burned up the brakes on the tractor. I thought every neighbor for miles around could hear your yelling."

In April of that year, Dad had gotten his long bed truck stuck in one of the muddy logging roads during the spring thaw. In an attempt to free the truck, a jack was used to lift the tires so boards could be placed under them. Vernon was underneath the truck when the jack slipped off the axle and he was pinned to the ground. By the grace of God, he was not killed and fortunately only broke his back. He was out of commission that summer and couldn't help during the busy haying season, so I took his place. One day as I was driving the tractor out to the field to rake the cut hay, I forgot to release a brake I never knew existed. Part way to the field, the tractor tires started smoking. Concerned something was wrong with the tractor, I turned it around to take it back to the yard. But before I could get there, it stopped moving because the brakes had frozen solid. Dad was livid and I felt awful. It was an expensive mistake, both in terms of time and money. Every single person who drove in the yard the next few weeks heard about what I had done. Dad never let me forget the incident and it had become a way to tease me throughout the years.

He rallied to my kidding. "Yeah, you and those brakes. Darn kid, thought you knew how to drive that tractor. Had to look after you like a hawk after that. And you wonder why I don't get behind the wheel with you. We'd probably end up in the ditch somewhere." He was grinning and his eyes were sparkling from the challenge of trying to get one up on me. Our sparring back and forth had always been an even playing field for us. It allowed a sense of playfulness and expression of love that he appreciated as much as I did. It was especially meaningful this trip.

"Well, Pops, at least you'll never be able to say I didn't bring a little bit of excitement into your life, ruffled feathers and all." I smiled back at him.

"That's for sure. You kids were never boring."

"Like I said, Dad, the apple never falls far from the tree." We all laughed. I felt as if my moment were drawing to a close and saying much more would take away the sweetness that had been exchanged. I reminded myself, less is better. "Pops, I'm honored you are my father, quirks and all. You are a remarkable man, perhaps in more ways than you'll ever know. I hope one day I will be able to give as much to you as you have to me. I love you a lot."

There was an awkward, potent silence in the kitchen and I could feel my heart pounding. Some families can so easily express their feelings for one another, but ours was never that way. I didn't expect to hear Dad return any accolades and he didn't. Neither of us attempted to hug each other. Emotionally it was all I could do to hold myself together.

He looked at me and quietly said, "Thank you. That's mighty nice to hear about your Pops," as he walked out of the room. As I turned back to the kitchen sink, tears dropped into the soapy water. Mom didn't say a word.

The day of my departure the mood in the house was somber. I dreaded my leaving as much as they did. On one level I was ready to go. My visit had been emotionally taxing and yet it was very freeing and fulfilling. My reluctance to leave came from missing out on being geographically closer. I wanted to be there for them and didn't want to experience another shock in seeing the drastic change in Dad's physical condition. Selfishly, the distance allowed a safety net for my emotions. I wondered how those who were closer were able to cope with the constant ups and downs. Perhaps it was easier for them because they experienced the changes gradually and weren't confronted with the challenge of being so far away. The truth was, it was hard on all of us. My job and home were in Los Angeles and that was the way it was. Fortunately Mom and Dad were surrounded by friends, relatives and the security of their own home. They had their roots and were fed by them. They were facing Dad's illness together—unlike Mary and I, who were facing it all by ourselves.

Shortly before leaving, I broke my promise to Dad. As much as he needed to be true to his own inner needs, so did I. I didn't want to leave with regrets because I had not said all I wanted. Once again the timing seemed perfect when I found him sitting alone on the couch an hour before I left. As I sat nervously a few feet from him, he turned and asked, "You getting ready to go?"

I cleared my throat, aware of a returning churning in my stomach, and my voice started to quiver. "In a little while, Pops." Looking down at my hands, I searched for courage to continue. Dad was quiet. Automatically one of my hands started scratching the side of my head, mirroring one of his habits.

"Dad ... you know I've respected your request the whole week by not talking about your cancer. But I need to say something now that I want you to think about. There is a reason you have two daughters who are nurses—one who is more traditional and one who isn't. Maybe we both have insights that can be helpful to you. I believe there are many ways of treating cancer and many people have been cured of it. If you want to discuss some of them, I'm always open to exploring these ways with you. I don't believe you have to die from your cancer, and I don't want you to. It's hard to see you sick because I feel helpless in what to do for you."

Pausing he responded, "I don't like being sick, either." His eyes ached with sadness and it was difficult to look at him and not start crying.

I forced myself to continue. "Dad, what is most important is that you have faith and trust in your doctors and the kind of treatments you choose. That's half the battle. You can either spend your days sick and miserable, or you can find joy in the moments like those we've spent laughing together. Maybe, as a result, you won't end up feeling sick and miserable. I won't push my philosophy on you. Just as you've let me make my own decisions, I know you have to make yours. But anytime you want to talk about options for your cancer, I'm willing and happy to do that with you. But I won't bring it up unless you do. As hard as it is for me, I trust you know what's best for you. Even if my picture looks different, I just want you to be healthy again, temper and all. I'm sorry if I broke my promise but I couldn't leave without offering something from my perspective... That's all I wanted to say."

There was an awkward silence between us and I prayed my sharing hadn't offended him. Reaching out, I touched his hand and then got up from the couch and went to the window. Tears began rolling down my face. I heard him walk into the kitchen. Just at that moment my sister Ann and her husband Dave drove into the yard and waved at me from the car.

Mom came into the living room and I hugged her good-bye. We embraced for a long time and her arms around me were soothing. My heart was filled with tenderness and love for her and the little girl in me didn't want to let go. She told me to be careful on my drive back to Minneapolis and to be strong. "Remember, Dad is going to beat this." She started crying. She always cried whenever any of us kids left after a visit. For some reason she was afraid she wouldn't see us again. I knew this time her crying went much deeper.

I told her I loved her and that I'd be back soon. "Remember, Mom, you are not alone. God is with you all the time and so am I."

She gave me another hug as I heard Ann and Dave in the kitchen with Dad. They came into the living room, leaving him alone.

Dave teased me and said, "We took your keys so you can't leave."

Joking back, I responded, "Thank God for an extra set. Of course, if you are really serious, you can go back to work for me."

"Not in that rat race," he retorted.

Ann chided as she usually did, with a smile on her face, "You can always get a job here. The hospital is always looking for nurses. And we know some men we can fix you up with, too." As much as they were kidding, I was well aware of how rough it was for them looking after Mom and Dad.

As I hugged Dave good-bye, his bear grip felt so strong I thought my ribs would crack. With my arms around Ann, I told her to call if she needed anything.

I walked into the kitchen to say good-bye to Dad. He was standing by the sink watching me walk toward him. The sparkle that had been displayed throughout my visit had been replaced by a deep hollowness. My knees were shaking as I stood for a moment to look at this fragile man who once was filled with a bountiful zest for life. Wanting to savor what I believed would be the last time seeing him alive, I was at a loss for words. A smile formed on my quivering lips as I grasped to impart a final tease. There was none.

"Pops, it has been really precious spending time together. I'm sorry I have to leave."

His raspy voice whispered, "Thanks for coming home. It was great having you here, too."

As I hugged him, for once he didn't pull back quickly. My hand stroked his bony back and the natural scent of his body filled my nostrils. My head rested gently against his and I no longer felt like his strong daughter. A tear rolled down my cheek as Dad released his embrace. Gently stepping back to look at his face, I slowly stroked his whiskered cheek as my other hand softly touched his arm. His eyes were filled with tears. He whispered, "Take care of yourself."

My hand tenderly stroked the side of his face again, imprinting the feel of his bristled cheek in my memory. As I looked into his eyes, my voice choked on the words, "I love you, Pops. Take care of yourself and I'll see you soon." Tears began to stream down my face.

As my hand let go of his arm, he said, "I love you, too."

With one last glance, I saw him raise his hand to wave good-bye. Then I turned and walked out the door.

As I got into the car, my hand was shaking and it was difficult to put the key into the ignition. For a moment, I put my head on the steering wheel and could feel a surge of emotion rise up through my body. A voice inside said, "Just drive out of the yard." Ann, Dave and Mom waved from the living room window, as the gravel underneath the tires echoed the familiar sound I'd come to love. I waved back, struggling to maintain enough composure to drive the car. Three-quarters of a mile down the road, I pulled into the driveway of the old, two-room grade school that graced my presence until fourth grade. A tremendous feeling of aloneness came over me as the impact of the trip finally hit me. I stared out the window longing for things to be different. Years of pent up feelings flooded through my body and I wept uncontrollably.

By the time my plane had arrived in Los Angeles, I felt a greater sense of completion with Dad. I had dared to be bold in many ways that had led me into uncharted waters, resulting in treasures beyond what seemed possible. The wise counsel of Solano had hit its mark. There was nothing more I wanted to tell Dad.

81

Many moments during my visit, I had felt awkward, vulnerable and uncomfortable. It was difficult to escape into my usual "mental" way of being because of the constant physical reminder that Dad was different. I constantly reminded myself of my desire to walk through the eventuality of Dad dying in a new way. I wanted to experience its gift, to find beauty and embrace its sacredness, and not to be left with deep scars of grief, regret or guilt. Spiritually strong in my belief in God, I knew the soul is eternal and death just a changing of form. When he died, Dad would return to a beautiful, glorious place of incredible freedom and unconditional love. I would always have a relationship with him; that fact would never change. It could only grow richer because the human barriers we had both erected would be broken. These thoughts would be a constant source of strength in the days ahead.

Chapter Five
Lightning Strikes Again

I was on my way to work when the phone rang. "Susie, it's Mom." The tone in her voice indicated she was not calling to check up on me. Perhaps Dad had gotten worse.

"Hi, Mom. You're calling early. Is everything okay?" My voice was calm.

"I found a spot in my panties this morning. Ann says it's nothing and I shouldn't worry about it. She told me to just go to the doctor and have it checked out, but I don't want to. Look what happened to your father when he went." Her voice quivered and she tried not to cry.

"Mom, it's probably nothing. Are you having any kind of cramping or are passing clots?"

"Nope, there was just this tiny spot."

"Mom, I agree with Annie. It's better to go see someone than to sit and worry about it. You know you will if you don't. And what will that serve you? It will just make you miserable and not able to sleep at night. Did you tell Dad?"

"He said the same thing both you and Ann said. I'm just afraid they are going to tell me that I have cancer, too." There it was again, her greatest fear. I tried to understand how she must be feeling. First her husband had been diagnosed with cancer that began with just a pain in his side, and now what might be in store for her? I sensed panic rising up in her.

"Mom, what are your choices? Not have it checked out and worry yourself sick, or go see your doctor and, perhaps, have your mind relieved that it is nothing. You don't need to make yourself crazy about this. It won't do you or Dad any good right now. For once in your life, make your health a priority."

Mom had always disliked going to the doctor and rarely did, unless there was some sort of crisis. A couple of years before, a prolonged cold had turned into pneumonia and she had been on antibiotics that left her tired and weak for months. How different she was from Dad.

"Okay, I'll make an appointment. But you girls better be right. I don't want to be sorry I went. I'd rather not know if something is wrong." She sounded frustrated and scared.

"Mom, maybe it's just stress. You know that's very possible. You probably are wearing yourself out taking care of Dad. Wouldn't you rather feel silly over worrying if they find nothing, than put yourself through agony fearing the worst?"

Her voice sounded resigned. "I know. You and Ann are probably right. You can't tell me you wouldn't be worried, too, if it were you."

"Mom, I really don't know how I'd feel. I would have it checked out, though. You at least owe yourself that. You deserve to be healthy, too. You can't continually give and give to Dad and not reserve something for yourself." It was always so much easier to give advice when the shoe was on the other foot. Now I sounded like I was the mother.

She replied softly, "I know."

"How's Dad doing?" I was curious if the chemo had started working, and yearned to hear he was getting stronger. Since I had last seen him, his right lung had continued to retain fluid, causing him difficulty breathing. Finally the doctor had sealed it off to stop the build up. He had had another round of chemo, less in potency, that had created minimal side effects.

"He's the same. Some days he can be outside longer, but he is still weak and his voice is still raspy. He feels good when he first wakes up in the morning, like he's brand new, and then it hits him. He seems more cranky and irritable. You know he doesn't like being sick. He never did. I keep telling him he is going to beat this. And he is." Her voice sounded stronger. It had always been easier for her to rally to the needs of someone else than to her own.

"Tell him I love him and not to give up, otherwise his spunky daughter is going to come home and give him something to really be grumpy about."

She laughed. "You're the only one he would take that kind of stuff from. I'm sure he'll get a chuckle when I tell him." Her voice softened and I sensed for the moment she was feeling a little more uplifted.

"Promise me, Mom, that you aren't going to hang up the phone and start worrying. Go outside and smell that fresh spring air and pray to God. This is going to be nothing."

"Okay, I promise. I'm glad I called you. I needed your words. They always help. You better get to work now. I love you."

"I love you too, Mom." We both hung up the phone and I sat for a moment on my sofa. Convinced Mom's spotting was probably stress, I hurried out the door to Sabrina's.

Mom had seen her doctor. He found a small lesion in her vagina and said ninety-eight percent of the time it was nothing, and not to worry. Mary had arranged for Mom to get a second opinion from a specialist in Marshfield. She had an appointment the following day. I was still convinced it was nothing, and refused to allow my thoughts go in the direction of worry. Instead, my focus was on seeing Mom healthy.

It was another beautiful, sunny, warm morning in Los Angeles, and I was sitting at my desk working on a book project. As the phone rang, I was jolted from my thoughts by hearing Mom's words on the other end of the line: "Susie, I have cancer."

She was crying. I stared out the window and, for a moment, I was lost in nowhere. As I was unable to concentrate, Mom's voice sounded like a rumble and nothing she said registered in my mind. Her sobbing jarred me back into my body and I was keenly aware she needed comfort. I was quiet while she continued to sob and I struggled with what to say. Gone was my inspiring and confident self. Taking a quiet, deep breath, I closed my eyes. What could I say? I had been wrong, I realized, as my words to her fifteen days earlier popped into my head. Her tests hadn't given her a clean bill of health.

"Mom, what exactly did the doctor tell you?" My voice was calm in spite of the turmoil going on inside my body. Her sobbing had stopped and her voice sounded like that of a lost little girl.

"He told me they found cancer, but they aren't sure what kind it is. They said it's rare, just like your father's. I shouldn't have listened to you girls and gone to the doctor. I should have just ignored it. Then I wouldn't have to face any of this. I knew they were going to find cancer. I just knew it."

She was angry and I felt responsible. I had encouraged her to go to the doctor, truly believing it was the best choice and would turn out to be a mild form of stress from coping with Dad's cancer. Had my advice, Ann's or even Dad's not been the healthiest choice for her? Had she once again been pushed into doing something she didn't want to do? Had what I thought was best for her turned out to be just the opposite?

"Mom, I'm really sorry if I pushed you into doing something you didn't want to do. I felt all along that it would be nothing and that, if you didn't see the doctor, you would let the worry fester inside, and you know how unhealthy that is for you. I truly apologize if my advice was wrong for you."

She didn't respond. All I could hear on the other end was crying. I was not sure what to say at this point. She was still silent.

"Mom, at least in knowing you can do something about it. You do have choices, and I still believe cancer doesn't mean death. There are a lot of people who have been healed from cancer. We talked a lot about that when I came home to see Dad. Remember all the videos we watched and how optimistic you felt for Dad afterward? Don't throw all that away now. Tell yourself what you keep saying to Dad: 'I'm going to beat this.' If other people can, so can you. God isn't selective about who can be healed. I know we have different beliefs about God, Mom, but we both believe in miracles. And I believe that neither you nor Dad need to die from your cancers. You have to believe that, too. You may not have any control over what Dad thinks, but you do have control over what you think. And that's where you need to start focusing. Don't let your emotions run wild. You know what happens when you do. You spin into a cycle of depression that does you no good. It never has."

I felt like a cheerleader at a pep rally, speaking as much for myself as for her. I prayed I didn't sound like I was preaching, that some of my words would resonate in a place where she could find some footing. If I could only be there at that moment. The best I could offer was to be strong for her. She was already carrying so much of the weight of Dad's illness and struggling to maintain some sense of stability.

Mom was no longer crying, but was quiet. I tried to sense what she was feeling or the space she was in. "Mom, has anything I said helped?"

There was silence for a moment longer. Then her tired voice said, "Yes, a little. I am just so scared. I should have never said when your father got cancer that I wished I had it instead. I didn't really mean it, I just didn't want him to be sick. Is that why I got this?"

Chills reverberated through my body at what she said. I had been taught well that our thoughts create our reality and the spoken word, strongly stated, is like a prayer sent out to the Universe. The phrase "Be careful what you pray for" came into my mind. Mom could never face that perhaps what she had thought or said had influenced what she was currently going through. In my heart, I didn't believe Mom or Dad consciously wished to have cancer. For her to be diagnosed with cancer within three months after Dad seemed pretty remarkable.

"Mom, when did you make that remark?"

"It was after your father got his first round of chemotherapy and he was really sick. I was upset and angry at the time. You know how you say things you don't really mean. I didn't expect for it to actually happen to me. You're not going to tell me I caused this, are you?" Her voice strained at the other end of the line.

"Mom, I don't know what caused your cancer. It doesn't matter how you got it. I just know it's important what you think and say.

You can begin by believing it can be cured, because that's where your healing starts. It's in your belief, your belief in God and your belief in your own body."

"So you're telling me I caused this. Right? I don't want to hear that. I can't talk to you anymore right now. I have to go." She was crying again.

I heard the phone clank down on the kitchen counter and the sound of muffled voices in the background. I felt awful. Instead of giving her comfort, I had exacerbated the situation.

My brother Vernon came to the phone. He had flown home to visit Mom and Dad a few days earlier and had been with them when the doctor gave them her results.

"What did you just say to Mom? She's even more upset."

I repeated our conversation and started crying.

There had always been a close bond between Vernon and myself, existing since we were kids. Much of it was unspoken. There had been long periods while I was married when we didn't see each other or talk often—yet the closeness remained. We were like kindred souls who connected in a place that had no definition. It was just there. I had grown to understand him better since he had gotten married and we had spent time together while I was living in Seattle. Since Dad had been diagnosed with cancer, we had become closer spiritually and shared similar viewpoints about healing and God.

"Don't worry about it. She's just overly sensitive right now and scared. I'll calm her down."

I was glad he was there. He had a way about him that could ease the tension in a situation or make it worse, depending on which family member he was around. He often interjected humor that some family members found offensive. I found it refreshing.

"I'm so glad you are there instead of me. I couldn't have handled this with them, it would have been too much." The mere thought sent shudders through my body. "How are you doing with all of this?" I asked.

"I'm fine actually. I mean, it isn't easy to hear that Mom has cancer, but somehow I knew I was supposed to come home when I did. You know, this was the first break in my work schedule that allowed me to get away. Every time I scheduled the trip, something came up so I'm trusting this is the time for me to be here."

We chatted for a little while longer before we hung up. It provided some comfort to my aching heart. I didn't know which hurt more: knowing Mom had cancer or my upsetting her. I stared out the window like a zombie, immune to the surroundings. Sabrina's voice startled me from behind.

"Suzane, what happened? I've been calling out to you the last five minutes." As I turned from my desk to look at her, she exclaimed. "You're white as a sheet, you look like you've just seen a ghost."

Tears started flowing down my cheeks. "My mother has cancer. I can deal with having Dad die … but I don't know if I can handle Mom, too."

Sabrina wrapped her arms around me and I wept. In her comforting way, she encouraged me to spend the night. Telling her I needed to be alone, I asked to leave.

I found myself getting lost driving back to my apartment. Familiar windy streets became confusing, leading me in circles. Finally I reached my apartment, relieved to be able to shut out the external world. The blinking red light on the recorder caught my eye, and I sensed both my sisters had called. My intuition was correct.

The cocoon of my apartment was soothing and I was glad to be alone. Fixing a cup of tea, I stared out the window. Just as I was challenged to see Dad's illness with a new set of eyes, before me was a similar opportunity. Yet the news that Mom also had cancer had stirred up a whole different set of emotions.

Our relationship had more intricate layers than the one I had with Dad. It had been tumultuous during my youth, especially on my part. Through maturity, I had accepted that Mom had been the best mother she could be. Any faults I once projected upon her were a result of my inability to see beyond my own judgments. And I had plenty of them, more than with Dad. I had not been an easy child to raise. My independence, stubbornness and pride were sources of frustration for her on many occasions, and led to a few fights between my parents. So whenever I teased them about being the 'perfect' child, it was more my own acknowledgment that I hadn't been.

Perhaps denial was my coping mechanism, but somehow I didn't believe Mom's cancer would be fatal. She had never had to cope without Dad and, maybe, this was a gift that would re-establish her own strength separate from him. She would have to shift her perspective so she didn't focus as heavily on him. Perhaps, too, this was the catalyst for him to let go. How would he be able to cope with her cancer, let alone his? She had always taken care of him. Once again I was forced not to see cancer as negative. There was a much bigger picture at play here.

I realized that what was really waiting to be faced emotionally was that Mom, too, had cancer. In just four short months the stability my parents provided—or its illusion—had suddenly become dismantled. Even though I had been on my own since eighteen, the farm was still what I called 'home.' No matter how many directions my life had taken, the dependability of those roots had always stayed constant. Suddenly they were being uprooted. The changes happening so quickly left little breathing room to adjust. I had faced challenges before, but nothing that penetrated to such a deep core. The pillars of my childhood were tumbling down. Wanting to cry out, there was nowhere for my voice to be heard.

A call to Mary informed me Mom had lyomyosarcoma of the uterus, a rare form of cancer that occurs in about three percent of women. There are two ways to medically treat it: chemotherapy and a hysterectomy. The doctor was initially recommending chemotherapy. Mom was unsure what to do. Mary and I compared notes emotionally and shared our disbelief. We didn't, however, share similar thoughts about treating Mom's cancer. She knew I was against chemotherapy because I didn't want Mom to end up in a debilitated condition like Dad. I respected my sister's tremendous medical knowledge and knew she was an excellent nurse. She was well-versed in the area of oncology and administered chemotherapy drugs on a regular basis to her patients. She accepted that some individuals improve as a result and others don't, yet felt the risk was worth it. Sensing Mom and Dad would now be leaning even more heavily on her expertise, I wondered if she were beginning to feel more like a nurse than a daughter.

Mary and I had always had a close relationship. Even though we were at opposite ends of the country, we talked frequently on the phone. The fact that both of us were divorced and childless had created a unique bond between us. Although she and Ann had spent more time together growing up because they were only two years apart, I'd always felt a special closeness with her.

As the days passed, the impact of what was happening to my parents began to hit. I felt numb and devastated. My emotions were out of control and all over the place—in and out of disbelief … to anger … to sadness … to overwhelm. My limited perspective shouted out the unfairness of it all. I prayed to find knowingness and strength inside and to feel that connection strongly within me … to taste … to touch … to hear God … never to question but always to go within first for solace and understanding.

One night after returning from work, I was compelled to meditate and pray in front of my altar. Sitting on a pillow, I lit a pink candle, closed my eyes and thought of Mom and Dad. Almost immediately I saw before me an image of Jesus. While his face had appeared before during meditations, it always startled me when it happened. His eyes had a loving, penetrating feel to them that drew me deep inside. Then his vision disappeared. Sadness began to engulf my body with overwhelming grief that became frightening and I struggled not to be overcome by it. All of a sudden an image of my parents' bedroom appeared and with it a sense of being pulled there. It was dark in the room and they appeared to be sleeping. The grief inside continued to grow and I began to weep uncontrollably. Somewhere in a distant place in my mind, I was calmly watching myself, aware that the feelings going through me weren't just mine.

There is a collective consciousness we tap into on a frequent basis where not all thoughts and feelings are our own. They can come from a larger whole that accumulates as an energy field. If a person thinks a certain thought or has a certain feeling, it circles above that individual like an invisible cloud. As other people experience similar feelings or think similar thoughts, this frequency is drawn into the invisible cloud like a moth is attracted to light. Then one is not just feeling a personal emotion, but an accumulation of collective feelings with intense power.

Because I was able to understand what was occurring in my body, it was less fearful to feel the depth of grief. Thinking that perhaps I was a conduit for releasing some of Mom's and Dad's emotions gave me comfort. Several of my close friends had often shared with me that when they felt the pain of a child it felt as if they were experiencing the universal pain of all children. Conceptually I understood what they were saying, but I had never experienced an intensity of that level. However, that night I felt I did. Within an hour, the incredible grief subsided and was replaced by a peaceful, cleansing sensation.

I had been thinking a lot about death. I didn't know when Dad would die from his cancer, but it felt likely it would happen sometime that year. I had mixed feelings about it. Sorrow arose from imagining him gone, along with the opposite reaction of freedom. It was an odd sensation I had never experienced before. But then I had never faced one of my parents dying. Society does not teach us to view death as something positive. It certainly wasn't seen that way in my family.

The only time death was ever mentioned was when we were faced with it. And then it was never really discussed, not in any kind of intimate way. Dad's parents had been killed when they were fifty in a car-train accident. I was a year old so I couldn't remember them. They had driven from Chicago to visit and were struck by a train in an unmarked railroad crossing a few miles from our farm. Dad arrived at the scene of the accident a few minutes after it happened. He almost never talked about their tragic deaths. Once when I was in college, I asked him how he dealt with it. He said, "When I saw them I was sick to my stomach. I was the oldest in the family and just did what had to be done. Handling the funeral arrangements with the responsibility of all you kids and running the farm, was all I could handle. You never talked about your feelings and just went on with life. And that's what I did. They were gone and there was nothing I could do to bring them back." He never talked about their deaths again to me. And that was how he dealt with death. He just went on.

Mom had greater difficulty with death. When I was in my early teens, one of her sisters died at the age of twenty-eight as a result of rheumatic fever she developed as a child. Mom mourned her death for a long time. Her father died in his seventies of a heart attack a few years after her sister. It was hardest for Mom when her mother died. They lived only a few miles from each other and talked every day on the phone. Mom never got over her death and had a lot of regrets. I was shown that death was black hearses, black clothes, traumatic, deep wounds and a lot of sadness.

I wanted to believe that no matter how death presented itself, it was still a gift and a blessing. A soul was moving on to the foreverness and beauty of the place from where we all originate. And yet I had no real experience of that perspective.

Shortly after Dad's diagnosis, I sought counsel from Solano and shared my history with death and my ideal of what I felt it could be. He said, "Hold strong to your belief that death can be a time for great love, intimacy and celebration. Much insight and gifts about the mystery of death will be revealed and it will be one of the most potent experiences in your life. It is even more potent in many ways than birth. For birth is simply a welcoming of new life. Death points the direction your life will go and with that comes great curiosity and yearning to know."

I asked him how to do this. His response was simple: "Remind yourself how you want to experience your father dying whenever that may happen and the rest will unfold. If you look for the intimacy and beauty in it, that is what you will find. Allow yourself to feel your emotions, but don't allow yourself to be pulled into the depth of despair by others. You're on a great journey. For one day you will walk in the steps of your own dying and be able to find it quite remarkable. You can walk away from this and feel inspired and uplifted. And remember you are not alone in this process. You have God with you—always."

I didn't want to go into fear about death—neither my parents' nor my own. Did we fear because of the unknown to where our soul returns at the completion of its journey on earth? Was it because we had not lived life to the fullest and there was regret? Was it because we associated death with pain and suffering? Who feared it the most: the person preparing to pass on or those left behind? And what about individuals who died tragically or at a young age? Was the impact greater on their loved ones and was their process of grieving different from that of persons saying good-bye to an elderly person? If we were taught differently to accept the profundity of death, would it not matter how or when someone passed on?

I believed our soul chooses when it is time to leave an earthly body, regardless of age or society's expectation about how that is supposed to look. If we can sense it is time to change jobs or move to another location, then the soul must sense when its work is complete here. Perhaps someone lives a short time to teach about love or forgiveness and that soul's intent is to depart as soon as that has been accomplished. And maybe a death that is tragic to the loved ones left behind isn't necessarily tragic to the person who has died. Maybe manifesting an illness is the souls' message it is time to move on. If our soul knows the way, we have to be able to tap into its wisdom and trust in that flow. There has to be a healthier and more honoring way in walking the path of death.

In the months that followed, my continual surrender to God was what sustained me on this journey.

Chapter Six
Two Faces of Cancer

Mom was scheduled for a hysterectomy and I was flying home for the operation. She was terrified to have surgery and getting her to confess she wanted someone to be with her had been very difficult. She never wanted to burden any of us kids by asking for help. Both my sisters graciously volunteered, but they had already sacrificed time away from their jobs since Dad's diagnosis. It felt like my turn. My choice wasn't from a place of obligation, but rather desire. I truly wanted to be with her, to offer my love and spiritual strength in return for all she had done for me. After all, it was her womb that gave me life. When I told her of my desire to be with her and to care for Dad while she was hospitalized, she finally responded by saying, "I would really like that." She would stop whatever she was doing in a minute to be there for any of us kids, or even for her brothers and sisters if they were in need. Yet for her to reach out and be at the receiving end was another story.

While packing for what was to be a week-long stay, I felt a strong urge to bring my blue silk suit. It was an odd thought because, aside from being with Mom in the hospital for her surgery, most of my time would be at the farm with Dad. His cancer had progressed slightly in spite of the chemotherapy and the doctor had recommended no further treatments for the time being. Even though he continued to have weakness and persistent pain in his ribcage, he was still able to go out in the woods a little each day. I had no logical reason to bring the suit, but I packed it in my suitcase anyway. The thought that Dad might die during this visit never crossed my mind.

It was evening when Ann and Dave picked me up at the airport. As we drove back to the farm, they updated me on the latest change of events. My sister and her husband seemed to be holding up well, but then they always did. Their philosophy of "what else can we do, except just accept what is, pray for the best and keep moving on," reflected the predominant thought of the whole family.

Hearing Mom was having a rough time didn't adequately describe her state of mind when we arrived at the house. Her depression and fear were beyond anything I had imagined. She broke into tears the minute I hugged her and hardly spoke a word. Gone was her fighting spirit; it had been replaced by the defeatist attitude that doom was around the corner.

Seeing Dad again wasn't as much of a shock this time, yet it still affected me and brought even closer the reality he was dying. Although he had lost more weight, his physical condition didn't appear grossly different. Emotionally the strain showed in his eyes and he looked haggard. The energy in the house felt like a morgue. Was this what it had been like for them the past three weeks? How had they been coping? I shuddered to think of the unbearable pain they must be experiencing.

It was difficult to squeeze out of Mom what she was feeling. As we sat alone together at the kitchen table, all she did was look down at her hands. Ann and Dave had left and Dad had retreated to the living room. My only inkling about his emotional state of mind had been in a conversation we'd had a few weeks ago. When he called me on the phone, I thought he was reaching out to talk about his cancer. Instead he asked if there was some kind of pill Mom could take to help with being depressed because he was at his wits' end in knowing what to do for her. She had been on an antidepressant for several years because of a tendency to become melancholy during the long winter months, which deprived her of her love for gardening. With the devastating shock of the diagnosis, even those pills were ineffective in maintaining a balance.

Listening to the solitary ticking of the clock, the agony of the situation was indescribable. There was no life in this house at the moment, stripped away by the destruction of three terrifying words: "You have cancer." Touching Mom's hands, I felt how cold they were. I squeezed them hoping to bring some warmth to her shattered heart. After coaxing her to speak, she finally confided she was petrified of the surgery. My attempts to get at the roots of what scared her about the operation were futile. Her continual response was, "I don't know." Nothing I said seemed to ease her emotional pain or broke through the terror. I had no concept of what she was going through and, as we parted for the night, the only comfort I could offer was my loving embrace.

Lying upstairs in bed, my own pain surfaced. Tears rolled down my cheeks and with them a burning desire to be held. My heart ached for all of us, and our lives that had been so dramatically turned upside down. I didn't want Mom and Dad to hurt or suffer, nor the little child in me, nor the adult woman either.

It would be easy to run from the emotional chaos before me, or fall prey to the potent sorrow in the unfolding circumstances. And I could rage at God for the awful tragedy that had befallen my family. But what would that serve me? I knew all too well where stuffing my emotions had taken me. I wanted the gifts, the pearls in the oyster, the blessing from God that came in this mysterious package. I would not let myself or my family be torn apart over this.

Tired after the long flight from L.A., I yearned for a good night's sleep. Mom and I had to be on the road by five o'clock for the two-hour drive to the hospital and the day would be emotionally taxing. Sleep never came. Instead, my mind started racing with intense worry and doubt, as a crescendo of fear, terror and panic gripped my entire body. Tossing and turning in bed, I was unable to calm the inner turmoil with meditation. A downward swirl of energy sucked me inside, and with it a feeling of being trapped by its powerful grip.

I had no idea what was happening to me, never having encountered such a compelling, fearsome force before. My thoughts kept repeating, "I am losing my mind, I am losing my mind." The intensity of emotions continued throughout the night like a crushing vise and I felt as though I were fighting for my life. I wondered if I were going insane. My mind

thrashed back and forth inside, frantically trying to escape the excruciating black hole of despair. Just as my brain felt it was going to explode,
the emotions stopped, and with that came total exhaustion. Slowly my
mind returned to a sense of normalcy. Gone were the thoughts about
being crazy. I felt more like myself. Glancing at the alarm clock, it was
four in the morning and time to get ready. So much for getting a good
night's rest. Lying in bed, I pondered my sleepless night and where the
feelings had come from. Suddenly it dawned on me that this was what
Mom had been going through all night! Whether it was conscious or
unconscious, somehow I telepathically had tuned into her terror about
surgery. What powerful emotions. How did she have the strength and
control to keep it together? As I crawled out of bed there was a greater
compassion and understanding about how both fragile and strong she
was.

If Mom had a horrendous night, it never showed on her face. She
was alone in the kitchen looking out the window and turned to say
"good morning" as I closed the upstairs door. Although she was calm,
she looked worried. She commented about the blue silk outfit I had
decided to wear for good luck. "Susie, you look really nice, but why
are you wearing your good suit and not something more comfortable? Your feet will get sore all day in those heels."

Thank God she didn't ask how I slept. Smiling at her, I responded,
"Mom, I want everyone to know you're not just any woman having
surgery today; you're special because you're my mother. I may not
have a powerful job, but at least let them believe I'm someone important. They'll think twice before messing with you."

My remarks put a smile on her face and she replied, "Susie, you're
something else."

Walking over to her, I fastened a ceramic angel pin on her sweater
and told her it was a reminder she was being closely watched over and
loved today. She looked at me and said, "Thank you. I need that
today."

Mom walked out of the kitchen and I could vaguely hear her talking with Dad in the bedroom. I wondered what they said to each

other that she didn't share. It was a private moment that was none of my business.

When we got into the car, I gave her a special stone from my altar and asked her to hold it in her hands to let her know my strength and love were with her. She placed it in the corner of her palm and wrapped her fingers through her rosary beads. She was quiet for most of the drive to the hospital and appeared to be a million miles away as she stared out the window. Every now and then she stroked the little brown stone, while her fingers rotated the crystal rosary beads. The country roads passed through acres of rolling farm land, waking to the sun as golden rays greeted the clear morning sky. It was a beautiful drive that would soon become familiar territory for frequent future visits by several of us in the family. My exhaustion was removed by the sheer amount of focus the day entailed. There was no time for feeling tired.

The closer we got to the hospital, the more tense Mom became. As we drove into the parking lot by the main entrance, she panicked. "Susie, I can't go through with this. Just turn the car around and drive home. I can't do it. Please, just take me home." Her eyes had the look of a wild animal fighting for its life.

I was perplexed why she was so terrified. Was it because she was afraid she was going to die during surgery? Turning toward her, I held her hands as she tightly grasped my fingers. There was a soothing quality to my voice and I felt like a mother comforting a frightened child. "Mom, why are you so afraid? Women have hysterectomies every day. Do you think for some reason you're going to die?"

She was quiet and then responded, "I'm afraid to have them put me to sleep. I'm afraid I won't wake up. Please, just take me home. What's so wrong if I just do nothing about treating my cancer?" She clutched my hands harder.

"Mom, I promise you'll come through the surgery with flying colors. This kind of operation is done all the time. If God were sitting here right now, he would tell you the same thing. It's going to be okay. You will feel relieved once it's done. I'll be with you the whole time until you go into the operating room and will be waiting in your room after you come out of recovery. You won't be alone, God and your guardian angels will be there with you. Watch, later we'll laugh about why you were ever so afraid. We will."

No response.

"Mom, trust me. You will come out of the anesthesia. You're a healthy woman. If there were a risk, the doctor would have told you or he wouldn't be supportive of you having it."

She was not budging. "Susie, I just can't do it." Her voice quivered and she started to cry. Her whole body was trembling. I'd had patients afraid before, but none to this extreme. Her hands gripped mine tighter. I was torn about what to do and certainly didn't want to force her into the surgery. If she were in a more rational place and had changed her mind, it would be a different story, but fear had become rampant, immobilizing her ability to think clearly. Some kind of intervention needed to take place. What were the options here?

If I took her back home she couldn't continue to function in such a depressed state; it was not healthy for her, nor for anyone else. Dad wouldn't be able to handle her in his condition. She didn't trust any kind of alternative measures at this point, so that was out. The only plausible solution was to assist her in facing the fear of surgery. In my gut, I knew she'd come through the operation fine. Okay, God, help me walk her through this next step.

With great compassion, I tried another angle. "Mom, I know you're really scared. It's okay to let yourself feel these emotions, but it's not okay to let fear control you. And that's what is happening. Look how awful it's been for you the past three weeks. You can't just run away and hide. One way or another you will have to deal with this. I believe surgery is the best option for you right now. And as much as I'd love to drive out of this parking lot and take you back home, I won't do it. So you and I are going to walk into the hospital, with me right by your side and we're going to face this together. We'll ask the nurses to give you some medication to help you relax and it'll help diminish some of the fear. Can you at least trust that God sent me as your guardian angel today?" It was easy to see where part of my stubbornness came from.

Silence.

"Mom, would you feel better if we prayed together first before we went in?"

She whispered, "Yes."

Still clenching my hands, I closed my eyes and said, "Dear God, bless Mom today and all the people who will be taking care of her. Watch over the operation with all your love and guide the surgeon and anesthesiologist in providing her the best care possible. Let her come through the surgery healthy and strong and remove all the cancer. Please take away some of her darn stubbornness and thank you for the opportunity to be with her. Amen."

Taking a deep breath I squeezed her hand and said, "Okay, Mom, let's go."

Slowly she got out of the car. Placing my arm through hers, we walked into the hospital together. The minute I stepped in the door, old emotions stirred inside me, intensified because the patient was my mother. I felt a fierce protection of her, like a mother lion caring for a cub. My nursing experience became a true blessing as we walked through the maze of admission, pre-op (before surgery) procedures and the hectic flurry of unfamiliar people coming in and out of her cubicle. My heart went out to families who could easily become overwhelmed by all the dynamics in the hospital with no one to explain things to make them feel safe or comfortable.

I didn't know which was more of a challenge to the staff working that morning: Mom's depression or my constant request for them to explain everything they were doing for her. Somehow I knew my prayers were being answered or else my blue suit was magical, because everyone was wonderful. As busy as the staff were, they gave extra attention to Mom after learning she was terrified. Later some of the nurses thanked me for being able to verbalize Mom's needs to make their job easier.

Her surgeon was a different story.

Thinking it was standard procedure for surgeons to meet with their patients before surgery, I asked when the doctor was coming to see Mom and was informed that it would not be until she was in the operating room. Knowing Mom's state of mind, I requested to meet him so he could reassure her about the surgery. When he appeared at the cubicle, he was not pleased and I sensed he thought I was a demanding family member and a disruption in his hectic surgical schedule. He explained to me that at her last visit they had talked about the procedure and she understood what to expect. But hearing about something that will occur in the future is different from having it happen that day.

In spite of his seeming frustration with me, he rallied to my request and consoled Mom about her concerns. My intent was certainly not to ruffle his feathers, yet it appeared that I had. Not wanting him to carry any kind of frustration toward me into surgery with Mom, I touched his arm and acknowledged my appreciation for his extra time seeing her. My gesture didn't seem to warm him any and he walked out the door. In the past I would have taken his response to heart and felt bad for infringing on his time, but this time I didn't care. This was my mother and she deserved the best possible care. Besides it wasn't an unreasonable request.

Even after the surgeon's visit, Mom was still in a lot of emotional distress. They had given her a mild sedative but even that didn't penetrate her depressed state of mind. Neither did my attempt to uplift her spirits through our praying together nor the doctor's reinforcing words. I was beginning to sound like a worn out record.

Finally I asked for a chaplain. A little while passed and Dennis, a wonderful Lutheran minister appeared. Although Mom preferred a priest, none was available. After meeting Dennis, I knew he was one of her angels because he was able to reach a place inside her that was remarkable. While his words didn't sound different from what I had been telling Mom, it made a tremendous difference in her attitude. I quickly realized it was because he was a man of the cloth.

When I had made the choice to leave the Catholic Church many years ago, Mom had been concerned that somehow I had lost touch with God. Yet in many of our conversations, we had talked about God. She once acknowledged that she spoke about God more with me than with any of my other siblings. Yet, somehow I still lacked credibility on that level with her. She saw God and the Church as synonymous, whereas I saw God in everything and not just within the confines of the Catholic faith. Eventually what she perceived as a major difference in our beliefs became a need she sought from me.

Dennis became the catalyst who emotionally carried Mom through her surgery, and who was a great support during her stay in the hospital. She finally reached some sort of peace before they took her into the operating room. I was eternally grateful to this unique man who walked into our lives that Monday morning. It left me smiling as I thought how God opened doors to help us stretch and grow in the most unusual ways.

As they wheeled Mom away on the stretcher, I asked a nurse for the number of her operating room. She checked and told me it was the number seven, one of my lucky numbers. Locating a secluded waiting room, I began a prayerful vigil. I visualized the operating room filled with beautiful healing, white light. My hands clasped Mom's rosary and my little stone. I projected my love into the room, and felt its power strengthened by having had Mom hold the stone and also having touched the surgeon's arm, silently blessing him. As I felt a swirl of loving energy, an image of golden angels appeared. They were surrounding the table with sparkly glittering lights that twinkled like stars. I felt peaceful inside. The operation was scheduled to take four hours and I remained in prayer for the majority of it. I felt no lack of confidence about the success of Mom's surgery.

As Mom's surgery time drew to a close, Dennis found me in the waiting room. He was a comforting sight. Thanking him for his assistance earlier, I told him he had a great calling to touch others, which was especially needed in the hospital.

His sharing in return warmed my heart. In a soft, gentle voice he said, "Suzane, I don't know what kind of path you have been on, but your understanding about God is remarkable. There is something unique and different about you that is compelling. What a gift you are to your mother. She told me my words were very similar to what you had told her. I would love to hear about your life sometime and how you got to this place inside. You have a very strong spiritual foundation and it is refreshing, especially here in the hospital." The kindness in his voice and feeling of kinship with my soul brought tears to my eyes. We would become friends and later share our respective spiritual paths during subsequent visits bringing Mom to see her doctor.

When our conversation was finished, I went off in search of the floor and the room where Mom would be for the next several days. Much to my delight, she had a room to herself. I blessed it and placed a ceramic angel statue playing a harp at her bedside, along with her rosary and my stone. Then I went back to the waiting room.

Mom's surgery had taken longer than anticipated. Finally her surgeon appeared and took me into a tiny room off the surgical ward. He assured me the hysterectomy had been successful in removing the majority of cancer and gave her a good prognosis for treatment and recovery. He explained the operation had taken longer because of a clotting problem. Although that was unusual, he felt it was associated with the tumor cytology of her cancer and she would be fine. The only catch about the surgery was that he had left a tiny spot of cancer he categorized as a 'gauge' to be used in treating Mom with chemotherapy. His comment struck me as peculiar but my attempts to ascertain why he even left any fragments were futile. Either you cut out all the cancer if it was localized, or you didn't. With my attempts to understand his rationale for not doing that, through what I believed were reasonable questions, he became irritated and brisk with me. Suddenly he got up out of the chair and said he had no more time to talk and abruptly left the room.

I sat in disbelief, offended by his manner of departure. All I had been looking for was assurance and comfort that Mom would be okay and accurate information to pass on to my family. I hoped in the days ahead I would see little of him. His medical decision would linger with me and would plague Mom's thoughts in the months ahead.

Seeing Mom after surgery was a night-and-day difference. Gone was the severe depression and terror had been substituted with relief, hope and cheerfulness. Her first words to me as she grinned from ear to ear were, "Susie, you were right, I came out of the anesthesia fine."

Mom had asked me to call Dad when her surgery was over because he had promised to come and be with her. True to his word, a couple of hours later he appeared in a wheelchair escorted by my nephew Davey, Ann's son, who was home from college for the summer. Standing by the window, I'll never forget the exchange that occurred between Mom and Dad. He was wearing a French-looking tweed beret to cover his bald head and looked like some kind of dignitary. When he saw Mom, he got out of the wheelchair, walked over to her, kissed her on the cheek and laid his head on her chest. She stroked his forehead and said, "It's okay now. I'm here."

There was a precious tenderness between them that was profound. An overwhelming emotion came over me and I turned to look out the window. I was crying. No matter how much pain and suffering they were going through, this one moment of love was a gift beyond gifts. Hearts were being healed right before my eyes. Cancer had deepened their relationship, stripping away defenses. I felt extremely blessed to see such an innocent display of affection. No one would ever be able to tell me any illness was a tragedy. What my eyes revealed and what I was feeling reflected something completely different.

They were both back in some kind of flow, with Mom fussing over Dad and he was lapping up the attention. Sensing their need to be alone, Davey and I left the room to give them privacy. When we returned an hour later, Dad was tired and ready to go back home. I was spending the night with Mom in the hospital and Davey was staying with Dad. Davey was his oldest grandson and they had a unique bond and close relationship.

Just before they left, Dad was sitting in the wheelchair near the door, with Davey behind him waiting to push him out. I teased Dad, promising him I'd be back at the farm the next day to fatten him up with my cooking. Laughter filled the room. Dad had always been a basic meat-and-potatoes man and had been spoiled by Mom's culinary talents. He had never been shy to express when he didn't like the way certain foods were prepared. As my sisters and I learned how to cook, he had to succumb to our attempts to duplicate Mom's style or starve. I hadn't fixed him meals in many years. Wanting to give Dad one more ribbing before departing, I said, "I bet you can hardly wait to taste my food again, huh Pops?"

His response was priceless and left me speechless. A wide, defined grin formed on his face and he slowly put his finger up to his lips and went, "Sssshhh."

Both Davey and Mom started chuckling. The image of Dad in this pose warmed my heart as Davey backed the wheelchair out of the room. As they went out of view, I could hear my nephew's voice: "Grandpa, you really got her on that one." Looking over at Mom, we started to laugh. It was true: he had.

My choice to stay with Mom that night had selfish undertones. As much as she needed physical nurturing, I wanted to comfort my heart by being in her presence as mother and daughter. With the pressure of worry and fear gone, she was in great spirits. Although she was hooked up to a morphine pump to self-regulate any pain, she rarely pushed the button for medication. Interacting with her felt more carefree, just like old times, and our moments of silence were as rejuvenating as when we talked. At times our giggling had the ambiance of intimacy between two close girlfriends that was endearing. It was a relief to see her so relaxed and peaceful and more like the Mom I'd come to know. Knowing the scenario would change dramatically with Dad the next day, I relished the sweetness of our hideaway cocoon that allowed both of us to fortify ourselves for the days ahead.

Later in the evening, Ann came to visit Mom. They chatted like sisters and talked about all the local gossip. There was such an easy flow in their dialogue and it reminded me of how Mom had communicated with her own mother. Sitting on the empty bed across the room, for a moment I felt envious of how they related. They seemed to have so much in common. Living in the same town, they knew many of the same people, they saw each other regularly and had the motherly thread of raising children. Their exchange took me back to my childhood when I perceived that Ann was always her favorite daughter. Resentments had formed because of that. I smiled inside at the wonderment of ever forming such a belief and at the way innocent family dynamics could flush out the ghosts of experiences long-forgotten. The envy was fleeting because I was well aware that what existed between Ann and Mom was just as precious as the relationship she had with me or any of her other children. None of them were better—they each had their own distinct flavor. Mom was so lucky all of her children had such unique personalities that brought great richness to her life. No wonder she missed us not being closer.

The next morning I found myself stalling at leaving the hospital and returning to the farm to care for Dad. Mom continued to be in great spirits and there was such joyfulness in the room. It was a rare treat to have her all to myself and feel her happiness again. She was making a remarkable recovery from the surgery. She had slept comfortably all night and was beginning to take short walks down the hall. She had no problem with my leaving and was content to be alone and catch up on her rest. Normally there would be no issue about someone staying with her, but these were no longer normal times. I knew she was concerned about Dad and was eager for me to get on the road. I was not eager to face Dad in the shadow of death after the sharp contrast of Mom's life being restored to health. Oh how I wished things were different.

It was clear Mom was in good hands when the day nurse, Sharon, informed us her mother had been diagnosed with cancer and was cured. She was friendly with a positive attitude and Mom would be in her care for the next three days. I was relieved. God had sent another messenger to watch over her.

Dad was sitting with Davey at the kitchen table attempting to eat when I arrived mid-afternoon. He looked tired and, from the appearance of the food on his plate, his appetite was poor. The house had such a different feel with Mom gone and I was not overly excited at the prospect of holding down the fort until she returned. Dad was always ornery when he didn't feel well and became easily agitated. I reassured him Mom was doing well and gave him a hug from her. He asked when she'd be home. "Hopefully by Saturday, Pops." He seemed relieved.

Davey had some errands to run and planned to return in the evening to spend the night. Dad walked slowly into the living room to lie down on the couch. I was left alone in the kitchen. I wondered what would transpire between us.

Our next few days together were miserable for Dad. He really missed Mom. It was clear I wasn't a suitable substitute for her and he seemed more at ease around my nephew. He complained his pain medication wasn't working and would eat very little for me. Davey had more luck with him and told me I was not patient enough with Dad. It was awkward and frustrating for both of us. In my whole life, I had never spent more than a day alone with him since Mom had always been there maintaining a balance. Now his source of support and strength was gone at a time when he was most vulnerable. It was a comfort having Davey spend the nights because he slept downstairs and watched over Dad. I was beginning to question my own usefulness.

A few days later we had an appointment with Dad's doctor where Mom was hospitalized. It had been three days since they'd seen each other. Her doctor was recommending she begin chemotherapy to combat what little cancer might be left in her body so she would remain for another week. Dad's current medication didn't appear to be controlling the discomfort in his ribs, so the family consensus was to have him assessed for pain relief. We did not want him suffering and needing to consult a doctor on call over the weekend. He had a good rapport with his physician and we wanted to maintain that consistency of care for him. He had tolerated his pain more easily since learning about the appointment and I believed the majority of his restlessness was because he was lonesome for Mom.

The day before had been a pivotal turning point for him. We were sitting together alone in the living room after lunch. Aside from caring for his physical needs, we had not engaged in any lengthy dialogues. Most of the time he had been quiet. Out of the blue he turned to me and said, "I don't know what's wrong with me. Nothing is working right. I wake up in the morning and feel like my old self, thinking I'm back to normal. But a little while later everything seems to fall apart. I get so tired and I can't seem to do anything. I can't think straight and my body just doesn't function right."

Listening to him talk, I could feel his frustration as he struggled to make sense of what was happening inside. He seemed to be searching for some kind of truth that would set him free. I didn't realize it would come from me. Seeing the pain in his eyes was gut-wrenching and I wasn't sure how to respond. Looking at Dad, I shared my understanding of what I thought he had learned at the last doctor's visit. "Dad, your cancer is spreading. There are more spots in your lungs. That's why your body doesn't feel like it's working right. Remember the doctor telling you that the last time you saw him? He isn't giving you more chemotherapy because it isn't working. Plus you are taking all those pills and they are affecting your ability to think straight. It doesn't surprise me you're having a hard time."

Dad gazed back at me with a clarity in his eyes and said, "So that's what's going on. Now I understand." He paused for a moment and added distinctly, "If I had known chemotherapy would make me feel so miserable, I would never have taken it." Then he looked down at the floor and was silent.

All of a sudden it hit me that I had told Dad he was dying. My mind began questioning what I had done. What if his doctor hadn't really said the cancer had spread? What if I misunderstood Mom when she told me the results of his last visit? Maybe the additional spots in his lungs weren't that significant from his previous x-rays?

What if I had told Dad something that wasn't true? If he had heard this before, why did it seem he was hearing it for the first time? Oh my God, what had I just done?

Not knowing what else to do or say, I left Dad alone, walked outside to sit on the swing and felt sick to my stomach. Had I just taken away any hope he had left? Deep sobs racked my body. Mom wanted to believe that Dad would beat this cancer so had she interpreted what the doctor said differently from what she had shared with me? Or was the real truth that, in Dad's aloneness from her, he was finally accepting the reality of his condition? There were no thoughts to give me comfort because I had just told my father he was dying.

Finally able to compose myself, I walked back into the house and found Dad still sitting in the living room. There was a peacefulness about him. He looked up at me and all he said was, "What time do I have to see the doctor tomorrow?" When I told him the time, he said, "Good."

When my nephew arrived later to spend the night, I was glad to escape to my bedroom. My heart had been heavy the remainder of the day and I yearned to be alone to find comfort from what had occurred earlier. It came from my prayers. "Trust in what you were led to tell your father. You were not wrong. He wanted freedom and he sought out the truth from someone who would give it to him. Trust in the unfoldment of what is to come."

On our drive to Dad's appointment, his eyes were closed most of the time. I thought he was sleeping but every now and then he would open them and tell me which road to take, as if I had never made the trip before. I was still feeling numb from the impact of our conversation the previous day and was in my own space. There was such a contrast in making the journey with him this time compared with the trip a few days earlier with Mom. He didn't show any degree of worry or fear on his face and no words were necessary to comfort him.

Our wait to see the doctor was short. Upon examining Dad, he recommended admitting him in an attempt to regulate the pain with a morphine pump. As the physician listened to Dad's lungs with the stethoscope, I became emotional and looked out the window to hide the tears streaming down my face. I was not sure what had triggered the depth of sorrow that had caught me off guard. Dad was calm and clear when he asked questions and had no issue with being hospitalized. He actually seemed relieved. The doctor said he would probably only require a few days' hospitalization until the morphine dosage had been properly regulated. Then he should be able to return home.

It never occurred to me sitting in the room with Dad that he would be embarking on his final days. Later I learned from my brother-in-law Dave that Dad told him he knew he wouldn't be coming home from the hospital. What must have been going through his mind as he drove away from the farm one last time and as he sat so stoic and strong while the doctor examined him? Somewhere in his process he had made peace with his imminent passing.

Chapter Seven
The Pearl In the Oyster

Dad passed away Sunday, June 3rd at 12:45 in the morning. He had been hospitalized for nine days. It felt as though a lifetime had been lived during this short span of time. While my heart felt sadness, my soul was at peace. Dad was finally free, released from the shackles of his illness.

His dying mirrored the way in which he had lived his life. It was not without surprises, intrigue and humor. He did not talk about dying nor about being afraid. He just accepted it was going to happen and went about living his death. In the end, his willful journey became a rich tapestry as it wove its illusive threads throughout the intricate layers of our hearts. It was potent with unfolding levels of human emotions and spiritual awareness.

It felt as though the worst of times and the best of times were all wrapped together. While Mom grew stronger each day, Dad subtly grew weaker. When he was admitted to the hospital, they were initially in the same room. It was bizarre seeing them in adjoining beds wondering which way the flow of life would take them and then observing it leading in opposite directions. I felt as though I were watching a movie of someone else's life. There was no way of knowing what would unfold each day or what to do with all the diverse emotions going on inside. It seemed we were all on a fast-moving train and most of the time none of us knew how or what we were feeling.

Dad rallied the first few days. He was more at ease and peaceful being back together with Mom. Once the doctors were able to regulate his morphine dosage, he rested comfortably and rarely complained of pain. Mom's need to take care of Dad gave her renewed strength and purpose, diminishing the focus on her own illness. She was making great progress from her surgery and had started chemotherapy. Aside from feeling a little weak and tired, she had no side effects. This was a real contrast from Dad who had become quite sick from chemo.

Being in a hospital setting, especially the cancer ward, was challenging for me. It felt more sterile and impersonal than what I remembered from working as a nurse. The pace of the floor was busy and mechanical. I hungered for the medical staff to be the same faces so we could share intimately in our journey. They weren't. Nurses were assigned to different patients every couple of days to prevent emotional attachment and more objectivity with their care. All they knew about Mom and Dad was what they read in their charts or what was passed on from nursing reports at the change of shifts. This was unlike my experience with cancer patients in Seattle. We had worked in teams and were assigned to individuals until they were discharged or passed away. Each patient could depend on the same group of nurses caring for them and our interactions were much more personal. We came to know our patients and their families intimately, carrying home a little piece of them in our hearts every day. Our relationships with family members became as important as those with the patients. Each situation had its own diverse richness that lent honor to participating with them in their journey. We knew our interactions played a large part in what became imprinted in their memories.

I expected a lot from all the people caring for Mom and Dad. I wanted the best for them because we all deserve that. I yearned for them to be seen as special because they were my parents. Instead it was a reality wake-up call to the dynamics that go on in a hospital and that can create a sense of isolation and formality. It was also a lesson in tempering my frustrations and using discernment in speaking out. While the overall care of my parents was good, one particular incident provoked an intense reaction inside me.

The nursing staff became concerned that Mom was becoming tired focusing too much attention on Dad because they were in the same room. I was torn over having them separated but did not want to jeopardize Mom's recovery. After consulting with Mary and Ann, we decided to have Dad put in an adjoining room.

The first night turned out to be disastrous for him. Since both Mom and Dad were stable, I had been driving two hours back to the farm each evening to take a break from the hospital. Every morning I would arrive early and spend the day with them. On this particular morning, I learned Dad had had a very restless night and had been strapped to the bed. The nurses reported he kept trying to get out and was disoriented. They said his medication was making him confused. Yet when I had left him the night before and when I saw him that morning, he wasn't disoriented at all. Upon learning they had tied him down, I became outraged. All the time Dad had been ill at home or in the same room as Mom, this had never happened. Something seemed really off to me so I questioned the nurses. Had Dad been told Mom was in the room next to him? Had they inquired of her whether he had been disoriented or brought her into his room to see if it made a difference? Had anyone tried to call me? The day shift didn't know. They said the night nurses weren't staffed to give one-on-one care to Dad and did what they felt was the best course of action so he wouldn't hurt himself. I asked to talk with his doctor and inquired if this were normal hospital policy with cancer patients. He said "no," and told me he was unaware of the nurses' actions. He apologized for what had happened.

It was apparent why Dad had been restless. He had never slept alone from Mom, except when she was in the hospital. When he'd had chemotherapy months earlier, she had always stayed in the room with him. He was afraid, his mind was fuzzy from the medication and in that state of mind he didn't remember where he was. A few minutes of sitting next to him, holding his hand and assuring him he wasn't alone because Mom was in the room next door could have been all that he needed.

The following evening I slept on a reclining chair in Dad's room. We brought him into Mom's room and explained where she was and that I would be with him all night. Several times when he awoke and appeared restless or afraid, I comforted him and he fell back asleep. The next day an order was written to have Dad see Mom nightly before he went to bed. His restlessness subsided and there was never another incident of restraining him. He and Mom remained in adjoining rooms, but I still wondered whether separating them had been the wisest choice.

One of the most revealing and valuable aspects of Dad's dying was watching his internal process. I was aware of the stages a dying person goes through from pioneers such as Elisabeth Kübler Ross, who described stages of denial, anger and bargaining that eventually led to acceptance of death. Maybe it was because I hadn't been around Dad much at first, but I didn't witness him going through these stages. If he did, they were snippets, because early on in his illness he spoke about the "will of God." Later he became grumpy and agitated, but that was his normal response when he wasn't feeling well. Through it all, he displayed a grace that was vastly different from what happened for Mom.

A few days after he was put on the morphine pump, he went into spells during which he was confused and he talked about things that didn't seem to make sense. When the nurses told us Dad's medication was causing him to hallucinate, it became clear what was really going on.

One evening Ann and Dave stopped by the hospital after work and Dad and Dave started talking. I was sitting on a chair between both beds and listening to them while Ann visited with Mom. Anyone walking by would have thought they were having a normal conversation. Dad was reliving the memory some thirty years earlier of having cows when our milk was stored in ten-gallon metal cans. Only he wasn't talking in the past tense, he spoke as if it were occurring at that moment. Dave wasn't even married to Ann then. Here they were chatting back and forth and I wondered how Dave understood what Dad was talking about. At one point Dad turned to me and said,

"Now make sure you clean those cans out good. Don't get the numbers mixed up with the old ones." (Each farmer had numbers on their cans so the milk factory could identify the owner.)

I wasn't quite sure what he meant and decided to just agree. "Okay, Dad, I'll do it later."

In an agitated voice he replied, "No, go get at it. Now get going."

I looked at Dave bewildered but Dad was already off on something else. Later when I asked Dave about how to respond to Dad, he laughed. "I didn't have any clue what he was talking about. I just pretended I did and said 'okay' to whatever he asked. He saw me as whomever he wanted me to be at the time."

Everything started making sense. Dad was reviewing his life. I remembered something that was taught in my spirituality classes. There is a natural process that occurs in preparation for the soul leaving the body. It is unique with each person. A person who is ill and feels his time is drawing to a close begins to detach from the physical form and earthly connections. The person usually reviews her life and makes peace with how she has lived it. The process of assessing starts with the dying person's current life and regresses back in time. That's why someone who is dying may not make sense when they refer to a loved one as a brother or sister when that person is not. Or the dying person may believe he is some place different. The person flows in and out of this exchange until his internal review is finished. Some individuals may verbally share this process, others do it in the privacy of their own thoughts. Dad did both.

Many times it appeared he was sleeping when he wasn't. His eyes were closed and he was thinking. On various occasions when someone spoke to him, he wouldn't respond. Yet the doctor would appear and say "hello" and Dad would open his eyes and say, "How we doing Doc?" When he did engage in dialogue, he was tying up loose ends. It reminded me of completing last minute details before leaving on a trip. Dad was doing the same thing. I liked to think he was sitting on top of the jammer of his red pulp truck, picking up scattered logs and neatly stacking the cords of wood of his life.

One remarkable incident during this process led to a huge surprise. When I arrived at the hospital one morning, Mom shared that Dad had been acting peculiar. He had come to her bed several times during the evening and once again early that morning to tell her where to find the money. She thought he was confused. Something told me to press her about their conversation. She couldn't understand most of it except he was really adamant she understand where he had put the money. He kept saying, "Do you know where I'm talking about?"

Mom told me that when we were younger Dad had taken money out of their account and she hadn't known what happened to it. Years later she found out he hid it behind a beam over the furnace because he didn't completely trust the banks. The Depression had left an indelible imprint about looking out for himself.

Believing Dad's persistence wasn't merely confusion, my curiosity kicked in. I began asking Mom all about Dad's old hiding place and whatever else I could ascertain from her recall of Dad's earlier interlude. She had kept the books since they were married and knew how much money was deposited in the bank. She couldn't imagine at this point in their lives not knowing about a secret stash.

Our conversation stayed in my mind throughout the day. That night to appease my inquisitive nature, I scrimmaged around the basement after getting home from the hospital. It was midnight. For anyone observing me from the outside, it would have been amusing. One room in the basement had a large, old wood-burning furnace with several pipes that connected to vents and a brick chimney. Unfinished wooden boards formed the ceiling and the floor was cement. To the left of the furnace was the hot water heater and next to it, in the corner, boards covered a large hole where the well once was. The basement was typical of cellars in old farmhouses. It was dusty with cobwebs and a little eerie, especially at night all alone. If any money could possibly be there, I was determined to find it. I felt like a female version of Sherlock Holmes looking everywhere, trying to figure how Dad's mind might have thought. I had to use a step ladder to reach the ceiling beams. My hands searched for openings that might contain a treasure. There was nothing but slivers in my fingers. The chimney seemed like the logical place and I found a loose brick near the floor. I was ecstatic. In the old movies this was where they always stashed something.

My adrenaline was pumping as I knelt on the cement, pulling away the brick. Shining the flashlight into the opening, all I could see was black soot. I stuck my hand deep into the hole to feel for anything. Again, nothing. Sitting on the cold cement floor leaning against the fireplace, I started to laugh. "Dad is in the hospital dying of cancer and Lord knows what is going to happen to Mom. Here it is two o'clock in the morning and I'm searching for money Dad may have hidden. I must have gone crazy."

By this time, I was cold, filthy and exhausted and ready to give up my quest. Just before leaving to go upstairs, for some reason I turned to look at the boards covering the old well and heard in my mind, "Don't go over there. Just leave it alone." Tiredness overshadowed my will to explore further and I climbed the cement steps to go to bed.

The next afternoon, the mystery of a possible secret stash was revealed. Since information travels quickly in our family, my midnight escapade was not lost on my nephew Davey. He returned to the scene of my search and went right over to the old well. Lifting up the boards he found a garbage bag lying to one side. Inside was a silver box filled with hundreds of dollar bills fastened together with paper clips. A note was addressed to my brother Johnny in Dad's handwriting: "Distribute this among all the kids and grandkids." Farther down the paper was an addition that had been written more recently. In a more shaky style were the words, "Make sure Mom is taken care of, too."

Wanting to give Dad peace of mind, I went to his bedside after hearing about Davey's discovery. He appeared to be sleeping but I knew he wasn't. I whispered in his ear, "Dad, Davey found the money. Thank you for your generosity and caring for us all these years."

His eyes were closed and although he moved his arm slightly, he never said a word. Tears filled my eyes and my heart was overwhelmed thinking about Dad's sense of responsibility to make sure his family was taken care of. He must have been setting aside money for a long time from the milk checks and timber sales, adding to it bit by bit.

The days were up and down with Dad's health fluctuating. In many ways it seemed he was dying not from an illness but from a natural progression of his life slowly ebbing away. There were times when he was more talkative and others when he was just quiet. I took him for rides outside in the wheelchair so he could have fresh air. Close to the hospital was a little park and we would sit for brief periods. We didn't talk much and I wondered what he was thinking. He never shared. He didn't like being away from Mom for long so our excursions were limited. It was clear she provided him stability and security. The first couple of days, when Mom and Dad were in the same room, they watched television together. One evening when a few of us were visiting, it was time for the Lawrence Welk Show. While their style of music was playing, they would look at each other and smile, lost in another time of their lives. In a bizarre kind of way it was like old times. As strange and difficult as it was to see them both hospitalized, it was comforting to know they had the companionship of each other. We all drew strength from that.

Our visits alternated between their two rooms. It was typical in our family to watch how the men would congregate in Dad's room and the women in Mom's. Some things never seemed to change even with illness. When Mom wasn't getting her chemotherapy, she would be in Dad's room, holding his hand. She remained in good spirits the entire time and never anguished outwardly over Dad's changing condition. She probably thought he would get better and that sustained her hope. The silent contentment between them was quite extraordinary. Their exteriors showed the wear and tear of all the years and the pain of their illnesses marked their faces. Yet within their hearts I sensed a pureness of love and true appreciation for each other.

At times it felt like a party, with visitors coming and going, laughter filling the room and good-byes being said without knowing they were final. Shortly after Mom's surgery, her sister Rosemary came to visit. Rosemary was unaware Dad was also hospitalized and had a surprised look on her face when she walked into the room. Bending down to say hello and kiss Mom on the cheek, she whispered in a concerned, serious voice, "Edna, do you know there is a strange man in the room with you?"

Chuckles erupted. Turning to my aunt, I gently touched her arm and said lightly, "Rosie, we know and he really is odd. That's Dad in the other bed."

Later I wondered who was more challenging for the hospital staff: my parents or the rest of us. Our sheer presence in numbers alone could be intimidating. Add to that all our diverse personalities and we were a handful. Anyone who ever considered marrying into our family could attest to that. Being quiet and without opinions was not a weak point and teasing was a natural form of communication. When all these components were wrapped in a package, a surprise always appeared. The hospital staff were not only faced with caring for Mom and Dad, but also subjected to our many questions, frequent visits and creative interactions. It was probably safe to say we were seen as somewhat demanding or a little insane.

One night, Dad's doctor made an unexpected visit while most of us were gathered in the room. Dad started introducing each one. "This is my daughter Misery. I mean Mary. This is my son John. And this is my daughter, Suzane, Susan, Alex, or whatever name she goes by now." (For several years while working in the television industry, I had used Alex Ramsey as a pseudonym. While my birth name was Susan, I preferred Suzane.)

When Dad had finally finished with his round of introductions, the doctor looked at him and said, "John, you certainly have a crazy family."

Dad responded with a laugh. "Yeah, and if they weren't, we made them that way."

These humorous moments were the brush strokes covering the canvas of important work occurring underneath for all of us. Five months earlier, our parents had been a vital life force and now everything was so different. The lightness of laughter was soothing to our tender hearts, helping ease our pain while maintaining some sense of stability when it felt as though there was none.

Around the fifth day of his hospitalization, Dad required oxygen due to low levels of saturation in his body. In layman's terms, his body wasn't able to absorb the proper amount so he was put on an oxygen mask. What followed was a valuable insight in trusting the knowing of someone dying as opposed to following standard medical policy.

Dad didn't like the mask and kept trying to pull it off. He went back and forth with the nurses. They would put it on, he would become agitated and soon he would be pulling it away from his face. Once it was removed he was fine. When the nurses said they would need to consider strapping his hands down because they felt he was confused, I stepped in. The solution seemed pretty simple to me. Dad didn't want the mask on and his choice needed to be respected. I asked to talk with his doctor and shortly, after my request, he appeared at Dad's room.

I liked this doctor. He was kind and compassionate to both Mom and Dad and never became frustrated with our questions or concerns. He had a good bedside manner and could handle Dad's nature. He had a way about him that was always gentle and comforting.

Stepping out into the hall with the doctor, I explained Dad's reaction to the mask and inquired about the possibility of using nasal prongs. He explained there was a greater chance Dad would die quicker without the mask. I turned to him and said, "But shouldn't that be his choice? Our family knows his days are limited. We'd rather he have some dignity than wrestle over something he doesn't want. We just want to support what's best for him."

The doctor was quiet for a moment and then replied, "You're absolutely right. It should be his decision. I'm willing to switch the order to nasal prongs but you need to know it may cut short his time."

As we talked, we had a view of Dad lying in bed and Mom sitting next to him holding his hand. A few moments passed between us in silence and then I said, "If this were your father, I'm curious what you would do."

"Probably exactly what you are requesting."

The orders were changed and much to the surprise of the doctor, Dad's oxygen saturation remained the same without the oxygen mask. We had scored a victory for Dad.

It was after this incident that I felt Dad beginning to let go. Having to rely on oxygen seemed to be his cue that his body was starting to shut down. Although up until the last day he could sit up in a chair or walk around, he was much weaker and needed a steady arm to lean on.

We were notified that Dad's condition had changed dramatically. Our family came together at the hospital and began to wait. While we all had come to accept it was Dad's time, our feelings of sadness were intertwined with happiness because Mom was becoming healthier. It was confusing. Here we were engaged with the face of life and the face of death, going back and forth between the two adjoining rooms. Up until a few days before Dad passed and it was clear he wouldn't leave the hospital, I kept believing he would be going home with Mom. There was little room to emotionally prepare for what was occurring. And the fact that we were all so blessed Mom would live seemed to take the sting out of Dad leaving us.

During this critical time for Dad, Mary came home and we were given a unique gift. We were driving back to the farm on a two-lane stretch of road that was heavily wooded. It was late one afternoon and we were both tired from splitting time with other family members at the hospital. I was driving and saw what looked like a large black dog in the middle of the highway. As we slowed down and got closer, we realized it was a large black bear. It was just standing in the middle of the road and seemed like it had been waiting for us. It never moved as we got closer and we had to come to a complete stop. The bear looked directly at both of us for what seemed like minutes and then slowly started to cross to one side of the road. It turned one more time, glanced at Mary and then ambled into the trees. We looked at each other in amazement and shock. I said, "This is a sign. We have just been blessed with bear medicine. And Mary you have been given a double dose. That bear looked at you twice."

In the Native American culture, bear represents courage and intro-spection. In the winter, bear enter a womb-like cave to hibernate and digest the year's experience. Within this deep place of Mother Earth, nourishment is given and, in this void of silence, all becomes known. Many tribes have called this void the "place of inner knowing." It is where death of the illusion of physical reality overlays the expansive-ness of eternity. Our family was certainly needing both courage to face what was ahead and the wisdom to understand a greater mean-ing behind what was happening. I believed our prayers of strength were being answered and a bear had been one of the messengers.

Dad rallied and everyone returned to their respective homes. He was to die three days later.

During this period, there was a natural flow, like pieces of a puzzle fitting together. Mom was on her last day of chemotherapy and get-ting ready to be discharged. We were concerned about what to do with Dad. He was more suitable for hospice care than the cancer unit and our family was faced with the decision of where to put him. Mom wasn't strong enough to drive back and forth from the farm every day and yet she didn't want to leave him.

One afternoon we walked over to the hospice unit to check it out. It was very nice and had more of an intimate atmosphere. Yet some-thing didn't feel right about moving him there. Mom had concerns as well. Turning to her, I said, "Mom, I don't know how it's going to happen, but everything is going to fall into place. You aren't going to have to leave Dad and he isn't going to have to adjust to a different floor and new nurses. I just know God is looking out for us."

She looked at me and said, "Susie, I think you're right."

On Saturday, the day of his passing, I decided to take a break from constantly being at the hospital and from the two-hour drive back and forth. Since it was the weekend, other family members were off from work and could spend time with Mom and Dad. Mom was doing great and Dad's condition hadn't really changed. Although weak and using oxygen, he was still conscious and able to talk. It was a beautiful, warm, sunny day and I decided to surprise Mom and plant her garden. Around mid-morning while hoeing the soil in my bare feet, a voice clearly said, "You need to go to the hospital. Dad is going to die today."

Unbeknownst to me, my brother Mark, his wife Kate and their kids were driving up from Madison. During the trip, Mark had the thought run through his mind, "Today's a good day to die."

That same morning, my brother Johnny presented Dad with a lasting memory and a fitting send-off. The previous fall, Dad had killed a large buck during their annual deer ritual, one of the nicest ones he had ever shot. It was the same one in the photo he'd had taken and made into the calendar hanging by the phone. Since buck fever had always run high in my father and three of my brothers, horns were usually saved and mounted as a memento of a particular year's bounty. Although one of the walls in Dad's garage was filled with all his trophies, he'd never had a deer head mounted. If the head and neck of a dead deer could be considered beautiful, this particular one was professed to be so by the proud hunters. Thus, Dad had been encouraged to have a taxidermist mount his trophy. Although normally it takes a year to complete such a task, it was miraculously completed the night before Johnny was coming to visit Dad. It had taken seven months.

In his own way of showing love, that morning, Johnny snuck the mounted deer head underneath a sheet through the hospital corridors and into Dad's room. I unfortunately missed my brother's thoughtful gesture—but not its repeated accounting. Here was my brother, carrying a large, white, outrageous-looking form with spearlike objects protruding from it, and not one person stopped and asked what he was carrying. The hospital was not a small, country hospital, but was known throughout the Midwest for its cancer treatments and was quite a busy place. He walked through the main lobby, up the elevators and past the nursing station as though the object he was carrying were invisible.

Dad was alone in his room and appeared to be sleeping when Johnny arrived. He removed the sheet and was standing at the bedside when Dad opened his eyes to the vision of a buck standing before him. He reached his hand out as if he were reaching for his gun and then he grinned. Johnny asked him if he knew what it was and he smiled and said, "Yes."

Johnny placed the deer head in a chair and it sat there as if it were a natural part of the family. More than one startled nurse walked into Dad's room wondering what was before her eyes. A human heart had been reconnected one last time to a passion that fed it. A loving gesture between a father and son had been created that would forever be cherished. Those were the last words Dad would speak.

By the time I arrived, it was clear Dad was making his final transition. Everyone was there except Mary and Vernon. The day was spent stroking his head, holding his hand and telling stories. It was not without laughter and silent tears. I brought Mom's walkman from home and hooked earphones into Dad's ears and played angelic music. I was teased about it and Mom said he probably would have preferred the honky-tonk of Patsy Cline. Knowing him, that was probably what he was hearing anyway. His body was hot and almost felt as if it were burning up.

By late afternoon, his feet were starting to feel cool and the pace of his breathing had changed. By ten o'clock that night every one, except Mark, decided to leave. Mom sat with us for a while and then became tired and went back to her room to rest. Although she was calm, she looked weary. It had been a long five months for her.

Mark and I were on both sides of the bed holding Dad's hands when he passed two and a half hours later. Neither of us spoke much, alone in our own thoughts and process. Dad's transition was gradual. His breathing started to lesson and became more like short intakes. You could almost see his spirit slowly move up his body as his feet started turning blue. Then his breathing became shallow and quick and he gracefully took one last breath.

We had not woken Mom before then, I'm not sure why. As soon as he passed, we went and got her. She cried, held his hand and stroked his face. I asked for a chaplain to come and bless his body. A woman arrived and gave him the last rites. Mark took Mom back into her room and I stayed with Dad for awhile. I did my own blessing and prepared his body to be removed from the room. I asked that his soul know joy and freedom and that his transition to the other side be swift and peaceful. I was surprised I didn't cry. Instead I felt relief. His days of suffering were over. We had all given our love as best we knew how and said our good-byes.

Some people say they can feel the spirit of a loved one leave the room. I was hoping to, but didn't. Mark said he did.

The next morning Mom was discharged.

The following days were a blur. Mom held up well and seemed relieved that the pressure of looking after Dad was over. Two days after he died, she woke and said to me, "I feel so great. It feels like cement weights have been lifted off my shoulders. I hope I continue to feel this way."

I told her she should be proud of herself. She had done an incredible job taking care of Dad and she could find peace in that he died with dignity and ease.

Our family drew strength from one another, each contributing a unique flavor. We had the last laugh on Dad when we went to pick out a casket. It was such an odd sensation going into the funeral home storage room looking for the one that reflected his spirit. It almost reminded me of buying a car. There were the "Cadillac" models for someone going out in real style, your middle-of-the-road moderate comfort and the practical, reliable, plain ones. We found nothing that suited the originality of Dad. Inquiring whether "was this it," we learned the Amish make a casket from poplar trees. We all started to laugh. That was the one. For all the years of suffering through mosquitoes and bruises from peeling poplar trees, we would have the final chuckle. Sight unseen we bought one. It was beautiful. All natural wood and simple. It fit Dad to a tee.

When we went to pick out flowers, Johnny asked if he could go along with Mom and us girls. I thought his desire was great because this wasn't normally a man's thing to do, certainly not in our family. As we were looking through floral arrangement books, Johnny decided Dad should have a little tree. Off he went to find a small pine. His touch of intuition was perfect and the tree was later planted in the yard. Years later it was still thriving and had doubled in size.

There were things I needed to do to feel closure for myself. The day before Dad's viewing, I went alone to the funeral home. I wanted to make sure he looked good before Mom saw him. Kneeling by his casket, I started to cry. What a unique man he had been, so outrageous and full of mischief, and now he was silent. He had taught me a great deal and I would miss him. As I knelt there, tremendous emotion overcame me and I prayed for strength in the days ahead. All of a sudden, I felt a wonderful sense of peace go through me and I felt Dad's presence. Afterward, I asked the funeral director to smudge the room where the viewing would be held. In the Native American culture, smudging is a form of cleansing the air in the same way a Catholic priest uses an incense pot. The funeral director looked at me a little strangely and I explained its purpose. He said "okay" and led me to an empty room. It felt cold and lifeless. I lit some sage and walked through the room asking that only the essence of Dad be felt and that those who came to say their last respects would feel his zest for life.

The evening of the viewing was extremely long since I had been going nonstop for two and a half weeks. It felt more like a party than a funeral wake. At one point I went downstairs to the bathroom to have some breathing space. Coming back up the steps, I could hear loud laughter filling the hallway. Dad would have loved all the attention.

I offered to do Dad's eulogy and didn't realize what an undertaking it would be. Having never written or given one, especially for someone so close to me, I had no idea where to begin. All I knew was that I wanted it to be inspiring, uplifting and to capture Dad's essence. There never seemed to be any time to collect my thoughts and write. And when I would sit down nothing came. No matter how hard I tried to think of something, my mind was blank.

The morning of the funeral, I woke about six and went and sat by Dad's woodshed. Since he had spent a lot of time there, I hoped it would provide me with some insight. After a few minutes, a warm feeling came over me and it felt as if Dad were sitting right next to me. I heard the words, "Dad was like a multi-faced crystal, each facet unique in its beauty." For a short time, the thoughts flew onto my piece of paper. Then they stopped. Looking at my watch, I saw it was time to get dressed for the service. Still not finished, I began to panic. The rest didn't come until I was sitting at the funeral home before going to the church. The words appeared like magic. At one point Ann came up to me and said, "You look like you are writing pages and pages. Don't make this wordy. Just keep it short and sweet so we can keep it together." It sounded like something she would say and I smiled.

Dad's service had a simple beauty, just like him. It was a beautiful day and the little pine tree stood proudly at the base of the altar. Mom was magnificent, full of grace and composure. I don't know how I got up to speak. My knees were shaking and there had been no time to rehearse what I had written. But when I stood in the front of the church, Mom smiled at me and everything seemed to flow. When people laughed at certain places, I knew I had captured the humor of Dad and created a feeling of upliftment. He would have been proud.

It was a good death for Dad. He died with dignity and peace. He was able to make choices for himself that suited his style. He was surrounded with the love of his family and had a touch of home brought to his hospital room. Although his physical body deteriorated, he gained in spiritual and emotional healing. Solano was right. Being engaged fully with the transition into death could bring freedom. Dad didn't have to be any other way than how he was. His process was his alone and that was what worked best for him. I felt sadness, but there were no deep scars of regret or turmoil of things unsaid. Love had reigned supreme in helping heal this weary old man and tender his soul onward. The pearl in the oyster had been revealed to me.

Chapter Eight
Uprooting and Planting New Seeds

I had just returned from spending ten days on a spiritual trip to Peru and my studio apartment was messy from partially unpacked suitcases. Although it was another gorgeous morning in sunny California, I was feeling out of sorts adjusting to the frenetic energy of Los Angeles. It had been two months since Dad passed away and the reality of his being gone filtered through my body.

My thoughts drifted back to the moments of quiet solitude meditating on the top of Machu Pichu and the magnificent peacefulness that had permeated every cell inside me. The energy of the Inca ruins nestled in silence among the majestic mountains, like soothing arms that cradled me deep within its womb. Early one morning, I had trekked alone to the sacred grounds to do a sunrise prayer ceremony for Mom and for Dad's spirit. Amidst the pristine air and awesome vastness of nothing and everything, images of Dad began flashing through my mind. And with them tiers of sadness peeled away like layers of an onion. It was a potent experience and rejuvenating for my soul.

The trip had been an unexpected blessing and in retrospect, divinely guided. About a month after Dad had been diagnosed with cancer, I had learned that a dear friend, Jacque, was organizing a group of individuals to travel to Peru in June. My intuition told me to go, yet my logical mind doubted its feasibility because of Dad's condition. When Mom was diagnosed with cancer in May, taking such a trip seemed even more impossible. If I went and Dad passed away, the logistics of getting back, as well as regrets over not being with him, would weigh heavily on my mind. While my gut kept telling me to trust the flow of things, that knowing was clouded by external family dynamics. It was challenging to keep a clear perspective of what was my voice and what belonged to others. My plans for the trip moved forward, yet remained silent from my family, especially Mom and Dad. They deserved to know my priority was with their lives and not selfishly my own. I could always go to Peru. Although it was apparent I had no control over when Dad would die, something was guiding me to take this trip. From a distance, it didn't seem that these two events were related. In the end not only were they connected, the trip was an accelerated healing in preparation for a far greater challenge than Dad's death. Not knowing why my intuition led me there was a great lesson in trust and surrender.

Three weeks after Dad passed, I found myself in a completely different culture. The simplicity of the people and the country, combined with being unable to speak their language, afforded me great solace. Free to be alone in my thoughts with no demands on my time was therapeutic. I had the space to just "be," without having to "do" anything. The timing for a new perspective was perfect. It was good medicine for me. There were two experiences that validated my reason for going on this trip.

Shortly after arriving in Cusco at the beginning of the trip, members of our group had an opportunity to see a well-known woman healer in the city. One evening several of us sat in silent prayer in the living room of her home waiting for individual sessions. At the same time, a small group of musicians outside began strumming their guitars and singing in joyous harmony as they marched down the street. Among the noisy laughter, I quietly prayed to be cleansed of any remnants of sorrow from Dad's passing. When it was my turn, I was led into a small, plain room with one chair, a desk and a massage table. The only source of light was candles and the room had a warm, peaceful quality that felt intimate. I was directed to sit on the table. The healer spoke no English and used a male interpreter to communicate. He explained she used eggs to conduct the healings. Hearing this, I began to question what I had gotten myself into.

The woman had no knowledge of my history and asked no questions. In a Peruvian dialect, she began explaining what was about to occur. In her culture, she believed every person has an energy field around them that strongly influences their physical health. If this field is surrounded consistently with negativity, such as anger or unhappiness, the individual is at a high risk of developing an illness—similar to coal miners who continually breathe in polluted air. Whether the pollution is visible or invisible, it still has adverse effects on the body.

While the Peruvian healer believed there were many ways to clean an auric field, her preference was to use raw eggs. The liquid inside the egg acted as a receptor drawing in unhealthy energy and capturing it within the shell. While raw eggs was a stretch as an alternative form of healing, this woman's philosophy about energy fields was not unfamiliar to me. I felt comfortable allowing her to proceed. Taking a raw egg from a bowl on the desk, she held it in her hands and blessed it. Then she moved the egg in a circular fashion around my body as she spoke in her native tongue. When she finished, she cracked the egg into a jar of water. The interpreter explained that whatever unhealthy energy had been pulled from the body would be neutralized by the water. The healer then walked over to a vase of fresh flowers, withdrew one and returned to the table. Gently she glided the flower over my body, focusing on my throat and heart. I started to cry and felt a deep sadness being released. Through the interpreter, she explained I was carrying a great deal of my parent's vibration as my own and that it appeared as a mask around my heart. It was suppressing my individuality and need to express freely who I was. The interpreter went on to relay that because of my natural psychic nature I had a tendency to feel others' emotions as a way of easing their pain, and it was no longer necessary to do that. The flower represented the beauty and strength of my inner core and it was safe now to let my own light shine and not to be in anyone else's shadow. I was told Dad was much freer now but that his energy was still lingering around me wanting to connect. She said the sorrow in my heart would soon turn into joy. Considering that the healer did not know my father had died, the information she shared was surprisingly accurate.

Leaving the room, I felt more peaceful inside but somewhat skeptical. Not knowing the Peruvian culture, my rational mind questioned whether everyone had been told the same things during their healings. Jacque, the organizer of our trip, had stayed in the room with each of us and later shared that each healing was different. I was the only one who had her body blessed by a flower. In the days ahead, I noticed a difference in my body and more of a lightness to my heart.

The other incident tested my commitment to God. We had taken the train to Machu Pichu to spend a few days at the sacred ruins. We were staying at the base of the mountains in a tiny, isolated village. On the second day, the dilapidated buses stopped running up the windy, rutted, one-lane dirt road to the ruins. Since it was too far and treacherous to walk the road, we remained confined in the little town. It did not appeal to my hunger for being alone and praying, so I journeyed off to find a spot in nature. In actuality, all we were surrounded by was nature—forests full of it. Our rustic accommodations were next to a river that flowed parallel to the railroad tracks that had brought us from Cusco. Walking along the trestles, the mountains were thick with lush green trees. I could have sat anywhere to pray, but I wanted a place that felt right.

After about ten minutes, I spotted a sandy beach across the river. Getting to it was more of a challenge. Attempting to cross the river, the water was cold, the current strong and it was difficult to judge the depth. Twice I was halfway across but turned back because the current had too much force. I became frustrated and decided maybe it didn't really matter where I prayed. Finding an alternative grassy knoll to sit down, I heard inside my head. "Are you willing to give up that easily on where you are guided to go? You could be missing out on many blessings that await you. Have you come all the way to Peru to settle for less?" No sooner had the words registered in my mind, than I was up on my feet more determined than ever to cross the river.

Walking farther down the tracks, I passed grazing cows and soon came upon a small path trodden by hoof prints. Making my way to the river bed, I saw a young, dark-haired boy who looked about twelve helping his mother wash clothes. He was wearing a tattered shirt and tattered pants and had black rubber boots up to his knees. Smiling at them, I stepped into the water to once again attempt to cross the river. The young boy came over to me and started speaking. Unable to understand him, I pointed to the other side. He grinned, took my hand and we forged our way through the waist-deep river. He held my cloth bag with the sacred items for my prayer ceremony above his head. Upon reaching the other side, he inquired which way I wanted to go. I pointed to the right, and he began walking with me along the river bed. We continually crawled over large boulders to reach the spot I had seen earlier. Two hours had passed since I had first started out on my mission.

Wanting privacy, I smiled at the young boy, conveyed my thanks and pointed back to where we had just come, letting him know he could leave. Much to my frustration, he sat down on the sand watching me. Smiling once more at him, bowing to say thank you, I again pointed back in the direction we had just come. He smiled back at me and didn't move. Kneeling down, I placed my special objects—a few shells, some stones and a beaded cross—on a red flannel cloth upon the sand. Closing my eyes, I quietly began to pray, hoping my comrade would journey back to his washing duties once he realized this strange woman wasn't going to sacrifice any animals. After waiting a few minutes, it was clear he wasn't budging. Instead he began to pick up my sacred things and examine them. I felt imposed upon but decided to make the best of the situation. Turning my focus inward, my silent prayers thanked God for my life and the opportunity to be in Peru, and asked for Mom to become healthy and to continue providing my family and me with strength, courage and understanding in the days ahead. I asked to ease our sorrow over the loss of Dad, to bless his spirit, and guide him in his spiritual journey so his soul would flourish. Then I asked for a sign that he was happy and doing well.

A sense of deep peace came over me. After sitting in silence for a long time, my eyes were suddenly forced open. I looked across the river and upward at the mountain directly in front of me. Toward the very top was a white cross that appeared to be etched in stone. The sun which had been hidden behind some clouds began to shine directly on the white image as if illuminating a bright light. I was stunned. The cross had not been there when I first sat down to pray. In my amazement, all I could do was stare at the mountain top in awe at the vision before me. For a moment I began to doubt my own eyesight until the young boy leaned next to me, pointed toward the cross and grinned. We both sat in silence for a long time.

The wind started to pick up and, realizing it was getting late, I placed the sacred objects back in the cloth bag. My little guide stood patiently, committed to returning me safely back to the other side of the river. Our return trip took us on a short cut through the forest, along a worn path. The young boy knew his way well and we climbed over old decayed trees and through muddy pools of water. At one point he took my hand and helped me over a large boulder, putting his arm around me and smiling. Before I had time to react, his hand began to move up toward my breast. Quickly I pulled it away, turning to look at him. He grinned as if nothing had happened and then nonchalantly walked in front, leading the way until we reached the river bed. Once across, I gave him Peruvian money and found my way alone to the train trestle.

Walking down the tracks, I realized my commitment had paid off. I had been given my sign and knew Dad was happy. I didn't know which amazed me more: the image of the cross or the boldness of the young boy. I would see neither of them again.

The distant echo of the telephone transported my memories of the trip back to the apartment. I heard Ann's strained and controlled voice at the other end of the line. "Mom's cancer has spread and she wants you to come home and be with her." The deep peacefulness inside gave way to a sigh as my mind was flooded with questions and anxiety.

I had spoken to Mom twice on the trip and once just before getting on the airplane. Fifteen minutes before my departure from the Los Angeles airport, I'd had a strong sense to call Mom at the hospital. She was getting her second round of chemotherapy and would be hospitalized for five days. She sounded strange. Her voice was very weak and she said she wasn't feeling well. I asked if she had told the nurses and she replied, "I've been buzzing and buzzing them, but no one answers my light." Telling her not to worry, that I would get in touch with the nurses for her, I hung up the phone and called the hospital. I reached the nursing station on her floor and told them something was drastically wrong with my mother and to please get someone to go into her room right away. Then I boarded the airplane not knowing what was happening to Mom. It was fifteen hours before I could contact her again. After Mom's first round of chemotherapy, she had developed blood clots. The doctors were unsure why. They had put her on a blood thinner and she was having a reaction to it the day I called her. To prevent the clots from going to her lungs, they inserted a filter. Had I not called her that morning, who knows what would have happened to her.

The memory of this incident was strong in my mind and I wondered if there was more going on with Mom.

"Stay centered and breathe," I told myself. "Remember everything happens for a reason and everything has a gift in it." I heard my own inner dialogue at the same time as my sister Ann was speaking.

"Mom's chemotherapy isn't working and she doesn't want to be alone."

"Has Mom said she wants me to come home?" I searched to find out who was really reaching out. Mom had rarely been one to ask for any kind of help and was not one to impose on her children's lives unless she was desperate. Since Dad's passing, Mom had relied on

Ann and Dave much more. Dave was like another son to both my parents and they had baby-sat their kids as they were growing up. Somehow I sensed Ann's call for help was as much for her as for Mom.

"Well, I mentioned it to her and she thought it was a good idea," Ann responded.

I asked for all the details of what had been occurring with Mom since I had left for Peru and she updated me with all the medical jargon. I was more concerned about Mom's mental and emotional states since I was aware of their impact on the physical body. We talked a little while longer and hung up.

I walked to the window and looked at the courtyard below filled with pink and fuchsia flowers, surrounded by the greenery of shrubs. I saw and felt the delicateness of life and thought of Mom's love for her own flower garden. Tears rolled down my cheeks as I struggled with the thought of perhaps losing my mother, too. My voice screamed inside my head, "No, no. God, not again. Once was enough with Dad. She's too young. She deserves more. I can't lose her. Not yet. She's my Mom." I could feel my thoughts leading toward emotional pandemonium.

Struggling to maintain some sense of composure, the question arose: "Why is this happening to my family?"

No matter how many times I asked that, the only answer that came was: "There is a higher purpose at play here. Trust in a bigger picture and know everything is in order in its rightful place. Remember there is no such thing as death, only a changing of forms."

I sat quietly on the couch before picking up the phone to call Mom. Sensing something dramatic was about to happen, I felt uneasy. Within three weeks after returning from Peru, my life would undergo a radical change.

Mom's voice sounded flat and tired. "Susie, when did you get back from your trip. Did you have a good time? Are you all right?"

Good old Mom. Always inquiring about someone else first. It was good to hear her voice and reconnect. She had been on my mind a great deal during the trip. "My plane came in late last night, the trip was good and I'm fine. I'll tell you all about it later. How are you doing?"

Her voice was shaky, but she didn't cry. "The chemotherapy isn't working. The doctor sent me home. He didn't give me another treatment."

"How are you feeling Mom?"

"I feel weak, but the doctor said it is partially from the chemo and recovering from the surgery. I don't feel sick, but I miss your father."

My heart was re-engaged with all she had been through and memories of the trip now seemed to be in the distant past. Couldn't I have eased into the present situation a little more slowly? "Mom, I spoke to Annie this morning. She said you want me to come and stay with you. Is that true? Would you really like that?"

"Well, Ann brought it up initially. It would be nice if you could, even if it were only for a couple of weeks. I don't want to impose on you or your job, though." There was a shyness in her voice. She had never wanted to be a burden on anyone and I didn't want her to feel as if her asking implied such a thing.

"If I were to come, Mom, what would you want from me?" I was curious what her needs and desires were.

"Susie, I need your spirituality. I want what you have. I saw how strong you were with your father dying. I need that in my life." Her response surprised me. She was not asking me to come because of my nursing background, she was asking me to come because of my spirituality! What happened to my being lost from the flock?

"Mom, if I come, when would you want me there?" Somehow a two-week visit didn't seem like it would do the thing for her.

"I would love it if you could be here tomorrow, but I know that's impossible. Just whenever you can make it. Remember I don't want this to be a burden for you. If you can't do it, I'll understand." Beyond her words, I felt in my heart her unspoken plea for support and comfort.

"Mom, I need to meditate about this before giving my answer. This is all pretty sudden. Can I call you in the morning?"

"Susie, I don't expect your response right away. I know you need to meditate about this." She sounded relieved that I hadn't said, "No."

"You know I'll be there in whatever way I can for you. Remember you're not alone and you never will be. I promise to call you tomorrow. I love you, Mom."

"I love you, too, Susie. Take care." Her voice was soft and tender.

For the first time in her life, my mother had reached out and asked me for something. What a privilege. From a deep place inside, I already knew what my answer would be.

Before going to bed, I prayed for guidance about Mom's request and had a dream:

Dad came to pick me up in his old flatbed truck that he drove when I was a child. It was maroon with 'John E. Piela Farm Produce' printed on the side. He didn't speak a word but just waited in the cab while I climbed on the back. We began flying through the air with the wind blowing on my face, soaring just above the treetops. It was freeing and uplifting. Then we landed in Mom's and Dad's bedroom. I watched from a corner of the room as they looked at each other. They were both healthy and I wondered why I was there. I didn't know what they said to each other. Suddenly Dad was gone and I was left alone with Mom.

It was early when I awoke with the dream still very vivid in my mind. It felt as if it had actually happened. I could still feel the wind upon my face. I had asked for guidance and it had come—very clearly, with no room to debate its meaning. I was amazed by the quick response to my prayer. Mom must really need someone to be with her. It was apparent what I needed to do. Not knowing how long I would be gone, I decided to quit my job and give up my apartment. My guess was three to six months. By that time Mom would be strong and on the road to recovery as well as more adjusted to the loss of Dad. I believed she would heal from her cancer.

I called Mom and told her of my intentions. She asked how I arrived at my decision and I told her about my dream. She was surprised and became quiet on the other end of the line. Then she said,

"Susie, I'm really glad you are coming." She asked how long I could stay.

"Mom, for as long as you need me."

We talked about expectations. She didn't really have any of me. I, however, had some stipulations for her. In the end, we both agreed that neither of us wanted to feel a sense of obligation in case my being there didn't work out. We each had the freedom to say when we'd had enough. If she wanted to learn how I acquired my spirituality and become more so in herself, she had to be willing to do the internal work. She agreed and expressed a desire to learn how to meditate to find peace inside. She couldn't mope around the house feeling sorry for herself and had to look for the positive things in her life. At intervals we would assess how things were going and make changes to maintain a healthy balance. If either of us got frustrated or upset we had to be open and honest about our feelings. I would be able to fly back to L.A. periodically just for a break.

She had no problems with my requests. She was just happy that I was coming. Our arrangement sounded more like a business deal than a daughter going home to care for her mother. However, I wanted to feel some sort of control and was beginning to feel nervous over the sudden upheaval in my life.

She asked how soon I'd be home. I told her in three weeks.

The days passed quickly as I prepared to leave Los Angeles. It felt like a whirlwind with little time to absorb the sudden changes. However, there was a flow around the chaos and everything fell into place. My landlord had a waiting list for people to get in and had no problem renting my apartment. Sabrina was at a slow pace with her business and was supportive of my leaving. I had no real qualms about leaving Los Angeles itself, although I was more reluctant about leaving my circle of friends and spiritual support system. They had become a great source of strength since Mom's and Dad's illnesses. Not knowing when I'd return or even if I would, it was difficult saying good-bye to them.

A few days before my departure, the reality of what was happening hit. I was going into an unknown with no idea of the outcome. I was not moving because of a job that had hired me for specific skills or experience that created some kind of definition for what I would be doing. I was going home to care for my mother. There was no definition. I didn't know what I would be doing. It was about just being. That was scary to me.

A visit with my dear friend Jan helped put my situation into perspective. While our interaction didn't completely eliminate my anxiety, it helped and pointed to a direction for my life. Sitting in her apartment, it was a comfort to be able to share my uneasiness. While Jan had never faced losing her parents, she was not a stranger to dramatic change in her life, nor to losing people she loved. Our spiritual beliefs paralleled one another and we shared similar uncommon experiences in our mutual path of spirituality. I told her I really wished I could gain some insight into what this time with my mother would entail. She went to her desk, opened a drawer and brought back a bag filled with twenty-four ceramic stones with markings on them and a book called *The Book of Runes*. The runes are an ancient form of predicting the future through the use of symbols. I went into a prayerful state and asked three questions: What is the situation in my life as it is right now? What is the course of action to take? What will be the new situation that evolves? The first stone was "disruption," symbolizing events that seem to be totally out of one's control. The second stone was "unknowable," which stands for "having total trust." The third stone was "breakthrough," which means that the course of one's life is transformed forever.

On August 17 I returned once again to my childhood roots. My plane arrived in the afternoon—and with it nervous anticipation of what lay ahead.

It had been over twenty years since I had lived in this house under the same roof as Mom. I was no longer the naive teenager who thought she knew everything, and she was no longer the protected wife and mother secure about her life. Now she was a fragile, grieving woman alone for the first time facing her own mortality. We had very different lifestyles. While I was used to my freedom and independence, she'd had relatively little. I'd come to depend on myself whereas she had always depended on Dad. Nothing had certainty except that she was still my mother and I was still her daughter. That would never change. I wondered why God had sent me on this mission. Of all her children, Lord knew I had given Mom more grief than anyone. She had never been my best friend as some of my women friends had been with their Moms, but she had been the most I would allow her to be as my mother. While she hadn't understood many choices I'd made, she had respected them. All she had ever wanted for me was to be happy—no different from what I wanted for her. We were so similar yet so opposite. And now Dad's death and Mom's illness had brought these two unique women together. What gifts did we hold for each other? What possibilities existed for us? I didn't know if I would have considered such an undertaking had Ann not planted the seed in Mom's mind to ask and then trusted in the guidance of my dream.

Aside from having lost her hair, Mom looked the same. She did not have a sick look about her as had Dad. From her physical appearance you would not have known she had cancer. She looked healthy. I didn't have riveting feelings going through me about her illness as I'd had with Dad. Even though her chemotherapy wasn't working, I wanted to believe she would pull through this. Hopefully tender loving care was the best possible medicine. She certainly needed a lot after giving so much to Dad.

I moved into my old bedroom, bringing things to make it feel more like my space—some favorite pictures, a special handmade quilt Mom gave me for Christmas last year, my altar items, my computer and a few other things that provided familiarity and comfort. It was difficult to assess how I was feeling. Everything felt so strange and yet so familiar. What would this journey bring and what was I to learn? It would become the most profound year of my life.

A month had passed since I'd left Los Angeles. It was a beautiful fall day, warm in the afternoon and cool at night, the kind I'd always loved as a child. It was so wonderful to breathe fresh air again and to be away from the hectic pace that engulfed my life. In some ways it felt as though I was on an extended vacation. My support for Mom was more of a companion since her physical condition overall was good. Every morning she drove to the cemetery to visit Dad's grave. On days when his absence was rougher for her, she returned to the cemetery in the afternoon. She didn't talk about her frequent trips and I respected her privacy by not asking.

We spent a lot of time talking about anything and everything. Most of it was about Dad since she was trying to adjust to the emptiness of his being gone. It was apparent she felt the void of their routine and consistent togetherness.

At many moments it was very difficult for her. My heart yearned for her to find some joy. It was strange not hearing Dad's red pulp truck drive into the yard or hearing his familiar, "Howdy, Howdy." I missed him but didn't ache with the nagging sorrow some people talked about. Either I had successfully walked through his death to find closure and satisfaction, or my focus on Mom's illness didn't allow anything else to sink in.

I started to teach Mom how to meditate. It was slow going. She had difficulty stilling her mind for even small amounts of time and started to doubt herself. She was afraid to go inside, afraid she would discover some awful sin she had committed. Trying to reassure her that she would find God and peacefulness didn't seem to help. I knew she had regrets about her life and was concerned she would face unresolved issues if she were successful in meditating. In my own experience, varied emotions had arisen that were at times uncomfortable, but if I stayed with them, they eventually moved through me. Maybe meditating wouldn't be helpful for her, or perhaps the problem was with me. I tended to be strident and somewhat impatient and had to remind myself how it had been when I first started. She said she wanted to learn so we continued with our sessions.

Aside from emotional support, most of my attention went into upkeep of the grounds. In addition to the usual housework, there were two acres of lawn to mow each week. Most was accessible with a riding mower. The rest required a push mower for trimming the ditches and around the various apple, plum, evergreen and maple trees scattered throughout the property. With winter fast approaching, the basement needed to be filled with firewood. Near the barn was a metal shed where chopped timber was stored throughout the year for that purpose. The wood was transported from one location to the next. For a seasoned farmer like Dad, that wasn't a problem. All it required was hooking a trailer to a tractor, backing it up to the wood pile in the shed, throwing logs approximately a foot and a half long and six inches wide by hand into the trailer, driving several hundred yards to the front of the house, backing the trailer up to the basement window, inserting a small metal chute through the window and then tossing each piece of wood onto the chute leading into the wood room. Each piece of wood was then neatly stacked into rows until the room was full. It usually required six to seven trailer loads of wood.

Growing up, this was a standard chore mostly for my brothers. As we all grew older, no one was immune from the job. While it had been years since I drove a tractor, that wasn't my challenge. Once you learn, you always remember and you don't forget where all the brake attachments are located. What I never got the hang of was how to back up the tractor when it was connected to any kind of equipment. The trick was turning the tractor wheels in an opposite direction from where you wanted the equipment to go. That was my difficulty. Nothing ever backed up straight and it ended up in a jack-knife position. My impatience was inherited from Dad, and in the past I lacked the confidence even to attempt it.

Dave was gracious in coming over to help me acquire this ability. His patience was remarkable since what would take him less than a few minutes to accomplish took me up to half an hour. Through sheer stubbornness and determination I was finally getting the hang of it. One load of wood had already successfully gone into the basement. It was humorous to watch this city woman prove she was still tough enough to handle farm work. Mom was usually smiling when I returned to the house afterward and, from the grin on Dave's face, I could tell he probably chuckled all the way home. The physical work was enjoyable because it was easy to feel some sense of accomplishment at the end of the day. Sometimes I imagined being a pioneer woman fending for herself. I had always loved being outside and during my childhood would do anything to get out of housework. The physical labor helped me stay balanced with the emotional aspect of Mom's illness and I was glad for the distraction. Being gone from the farm for so many years, I'd forgotten how hard we worked. Although my muscles hurt in places where I didn't think I had any, I had no difficulty sleeping at night.

I spent the weekend of my birthday alone at a quaint bed and breakfast in the north woods of Wisconsin. It had become a ritual on my birthday to reflect on the past year and meditate on the new. A cozy fire was burning in the fireplace and I was curled on the bed listening to the wind outside. I was grateful to have time for myself.

I had been with Mom for two months. I didn't know which had been more of an adjustment: the loss of my freedom or the weather. It had turned cold shortly after I arrived and my body hadn't adapted to the dramatic change. I was used to just two seasons in L.A.: warm and warmer—and that certainly wasn't occurring any time soon in Wisconsin. Instead we faced the prediction of a long, cold winter. In spite of the cold, I had always loved winter because of the snow. The first snowfall took me back to feeling like a child as I watched magical snow flakes floating like feathers, caressing the barren earth with a warm blanket. And when the sun shone on them, they glittered and shone like mystical twinkling stars. Life seemed to slow down and bathe itself in the silence of the season. There was a subtle change to my internal rhythm and I basked in the resting period of doing less and listening more. It was the same as the earth having a chance to sleep and re-nurture itself before the next season of unfolding newness. This metaphor seemed fitting for Mom's process of dealing with her cancer. In the barren winter of her life, she waited to face the unknown. It continued to be difficult for her since Dad had passed away and memories of their life together were everywhere. Added to that was the constant reminder that medical science hadn't been able to cure Dad's cancer. She was confronting the same reality.

We had been to see her gynecological surgeon three times since I'd been back. The tiny spot of cancer that was never removed had developed into a tumor that drained vaginally. It gave off a slight foul odor and Mom was self-conscious about it. The doctor claimed there was nothing he could do medically to alleviate the smell and Mom was supposed to just live with it. Mary was exploring possibilities that could help but had found nothing yet. We inquired about radiation to possibly shrink the tumor, but got little support from Mom's doctor. I still felt friction between the doctor and myself when I took Mom for her appointments and he was brisk in his answers to my questions. Personally, I didn't care for him, but she liked him and that was all that was important.

Mom was sensitive about not having any hair, so we bought her a wig. It looked very natural and helped her ease her self-consciousness. She was now trying a different chemotherapy that didn't require hospitalization. She had a wonderful nurse who was compassionate and had a good sense of humor. Our visits felt more like visiting with a friend and Mom was usually in good spirits after her treatments. The doctor wasn't confident chemotherapy would work but Mom wanted it anyway. She kept telling him, "I'm going to be cured of my cancer." I didn't know whether she truly believed this or was just trying to convince herself. Regardless, at least she felt she had some control over her disease.

She had been willing to explore alternative measures and was taking the Essiac tea she and Dad had been on when he was first diagnosed. She drank it faithfully twice a day, but only if I fixed it for her.

After Dad had been diagnosed with cancer, I was guided to a book by Hulda Clark, *The Cure for all Cancers*. Dr. Clark had a doctorate degree in physiology and had worked as a research scientist for twenty-eight years and as a private consultant for sixteen. Through her studies she came to believe all cancer is caused by a single parasite, the human intestinal fluke. Normally the eggs live in the intestine and are passed out of the body through bowel movements. Occasionally eggs enter the blood stream but are usually stopped by the liver, whose function is to destroy and eliminate toxins from the body. In healthy individuals, this is not a problem. However, people whose immune system is impaired have a decreased ability to fight off foreign bodies. As a result, toxins continue to circulate in the blood stream and slowly diminish the body's resistance, making it more accessible to illness. Dr. Clark believed that once the intestinal fluke has been destroyed, the cancer would stop. The treatment was all natural products: black walnut tincture, wormwood, cloves, ornithine and arginine.

After reading her book, in which she substantiated her theory with a hundred case histories, I felt there was substance to what she had written. In my nursing education, we had been taught that creating a strong immune system was instrumental in maintaining optimum health. If these herbs could help fortify Mom's immunity, they were worth a try. She had agreed to take them. To show my belief in both the Essiac tea and Dr. Clark's treatment, I was also drinking the tea and taking the herbs. I could notice a subtle difference in my body: I had more energy and better assimilation and elimination of foods. Mom said she wasn't aware of any changes. Although her doctor wasn't opposed to her being on the herbs, he didn't support them either. What a "catch twenty-two." She was open to trying more natural ways of healing her body and looking for support for her attempts, only to receive little encouragement. Instead she heard that, medically, her cancer couldn't be cured. Where was one supposed to turn for hope?

As Solano had said, "There are many ways of healing cancer. What is most important is to choose a method you are most comfortable with and believe in most." Where did that leave Mom? Perhaps she was just willing to experiment with holistic herbs to pacify my desire for her not to depend so totally on Western medicine. What was probably more accurate was that she was desperate. Regardless of where her physician stood medically, I wanted to believe our natural efforts were not in vain.

Yet no matter what she might put into her body, I believed her attitude was the key. That was where my greatest efforts were expended with her. I had been trying to get her to understand that what she thought affected how she felt. While it sounded simple, I knew the challenge for her because of what it had been like for me. She saw nothing positive about her and Dad getting cancer and his dying from it. She felt they had been punished and didn't see how there could possibly be anything to feel good or happy about. She questioned whether, if our roles were reversed, I would be able to maintain a positive attitude. I reminded her of our agreement. If she wanted what she perceived in me, she had to be willing to look at things from a different viewpoint. I pointed out that we faced different challenges because she didn't have to deal with her parents having a life-threatening illness. While her father had died of a heart attack in his seventies, her mother lived to be eighty-three. She asked me how I handled it and my explanation was I could choose to be angry and resentful about the fate of their illnesses or to look instead at the gifts. What kept me sane was the latter. And I saw plenty of gifts, gut-wrenching moments and all. She didn't respond. Either what I said was sinking in or she felt she wasn't being heard. I knew it is easy to see the bright side of things when one is healthy and a whole different ball game when one is not.

The newness of being home hadn't worn off yet. I was not used to the continual phone calls from my brothers and sisters checking on Mom, nor the frequent visitors dropping by. Sometimes it seemed like Grand Central station. A certain degree of suffocation had been creeping in and I felt I didn't have any room to breathe. Everything felt a little too close. A big part of me wanted to leave because it was emotionally uncomfortable and I felt vulnerable. These feelings were shocking to me. My emotional walls that been erected unconsciously were being slowly chipped away.

I was emotionally protecting myself around my family. At moments I felt the way I thought or what I said was being observed and I was concerned I'd be judged. These were my own created assumptions and barriers. No one was probably giving my being home a second thought. In fact, they were probably relieved I was home. It was just a different feeling having my life be so exposed, and not having my own home. My intention was not to be secretive, it was just my way of being safe, believing that what someone didn't know would keep me from being criticized or scrutinized. As much as Mom's illness was stripping away her security, it helped me overcome my limitations.

Since moving back, what I missed most were my friends, the independence of my lifestyle, and an environment that supported progressive ways of thinking. Sometimes I felt as though my wings had been clipped and I'd been put into a cage. My phone bills were high— and justifiable in my mind—to maintain a sense of normal balance while I was going through this adjustment phase. Hopefully once that occurred, I'd feel a greater sense of peace and ease.

At times I felt an overwhelming sense of responsibility, and I was aware it was my own agenda. Part of me believed the holistic daughter had been sent to bring Mom to the doorway of alternative measures. Intellectually it was a way of coping; emotionally it kept me safer. Mom depended on me to be strong. I could see it in her eyes. She said I reminded her a lot of Dad—confident, feisty and not afraid to speak my mind. Yet I had my vulnerabilities and weaknesses, too. Did she see that as well and feel the protective shell I wrapped around myself at times? How did she perceive her grown daughter who had come to live with her? I knew she was glad I was there because she told me. I teased her that she'd get tired of me and be happy to ship me back to L.A.. She said, "Never. You'll probably get fed up with me." Sometimes I thought she was concerned she'd become a burden and at some point I'd leave. I'd told her that would never happen. That I knew with certainty.

Being with Mom reminded me of dating, and it had its highs and lows. At times it felt like a marriage getting to know each others' ways and learning how to give each other space. I had not had so much consistent togetherness with one person since my ex-husband. In many moments, I cherished the intimacy of just being with her, learning anew who she really was from the perspective of her adult daughter. Since I'd left home, this was the largest block of time we had been together. It was so different from the times I had returned for short vacations. Then I loved the condensed time we shared but had been glad to be able to return to my own life.

In some ways I felt as though I had returned to the womb. The situation of Mom's illness fed me. The quiet, fresh country air gently re-fortified my soul. Although geographically isolated from my friends, the slower paced lifestyle afforded more inner time to reflect and assess what was important. It was almost as if I had become the lifeline for Mom and she for me. An illusory umbilical cord connected us to unknown possibilities. We both had an opportunity to grow through the daily interactions of our unique ways of dealing with her cancer. It was like a gestation period after a seed has been planted and all that is required is tender, loving care and trust that it will eventually bear fruit.

I had faced my own health challenge since leaving L.A.. For the past year, there had been a small nodule in my groin area, the size of a small pea and hard like a marble. My gynecologist said there was no reason for concern. However, it started getting bigger just after I arrived at Mom's. Because of her tendency to worry, I never mentioned it. Deciding to have it checked out, I flew back to L.A. at the beginning of October. Mom thought the purpose of the trip was for me to take a break.

After the doctor examined me, to my surprise he recommended surgery. It was not what I had expected. Because the cyst had enlarged so quickly, the gynecologist believed removing it was the healthiest route. He was concerned the growth could have partially lodged into the bone and to do nothing about it could be detrimental. I told him I needed to meditate about it before making a decision. Aware of my holistic beliefs, he was willing to work with me to arrive at a mutual decision. That night while staying in Sabrina's guest house, I prayed for guidance. A peaceful calm came over me, and it felt right to have surgery to remove it. Once my decision was made, it was remarkable how everything fell into place.

Two days after my exam, I was scheduled for out-patient surgery. The morning of the surgery I sat outside with my bare feet on the earth and asked for the cyst to shrink, so less cutting would be necessary. Not wanting my bone to be affected, I visualized in my mind the growth becoming smaller. There was no thought that cancer might be found.

While lying in the pre-surgery room, I felt the nodule and it seemed smaller, back to the size of a pea. In my excitement, I asked the doctor to check it. His assessment was that it felt the same as when he first examined me. Regardless of what he said, I knew it had shrunk. Before entering the operating room, I asked him to be silent with me in prayer. Having cared for his mother-in-law who died of cancer, he was supportive of my spirituality. The OR nurses, however, were a little less receptive. I asked that no music be played during the surgery because the body's energy field is susceptible to outside noises that can affect its healing ability. I also asked them to visualize my body being surrounded in white light and becoming healthier and healthier. They said my request was unusual but they would honor it. The last thing I did before going unconscious was to bless the operating room in my mind and ask God for everything to be normal.

It took a week before the biopsy tests came back. My stay in L.A. had to be extended by four days because the doctor didn't want me to fly. Since Mom was expecting me back sooner, I told her about the surgery. She was upset because I hadn't mentioned the cyst and responded just as I thought. She began to worry it would be cancer. When I flew back to Wisconsin she was amazed I wasn't pacing the floor waiting for the results. I told her that if I had been guided to care for her, my health would be intact. My surgery was just a minor inconvenience in the larger scope of things. What it did provide was an opportunity for her to see how I lived my beliefs and practiced my spirituality. I wasn't just telling her things for the sake of making her feel better or to falsely give her hope. I was walking my truth in the face of my own health challenge. If I could remain hopeful and positive, so could she.

The results came back negative. My doctor found the cyst was much smaller than indicated by his pre-surgery exam and the bone wasn't affected. He told me the nodule had a rare cytology (tissue variations) and that if it had occurred ten years earlier, the medical profession would have considered it to be cancerous and my body would have been "butchered." He told me I had been blessed and the results were a definite testimonial.

Chapter Nine
The Winds of Change

Mom had changed doctors. Her gynecological surgeon had said there was nothing further he could do and referred her to hospice care. The news was extremely depressing to Mom. The tumor had grown and so had the discharge and odor. She had resorted to wearing Depends, adult diapers, and was extremely self-conscious about it. My heart ached for her and I felt helpless about what to do. My positive approach seemed to be losing ground with her. At times I felt like a broken record she had heard once too often.

Through my brother Mark, we were led to another physician. He was an Associate Professor at the University of Wisconsin in Madison. Ever since Mom's original physician imparted the words, "I'm sorry there is nothing more we can do for you," we had been praying for a new door to open. My brother, who lived outside of Madison, was reading the Sunday paper when he came across an article about a doctor who was conducting a study using lavender oil extract to treat patients with cancer. We told Mom about it and she wanted to try it.

She was accepted as a candidate for the lavender study. Even though she knew it was experimental, she was drawn to the concept of utilizing the derivative of a natural herb that was less caustic than typical chemotherapy drugs. She was hopeful it could help her. She was willing to participate in the experiment not only for herself, but so others might benefit as well. The lavender oil was ingested in pill form every day and once a week her blood was drawn to determine the effect level. It was an eight-week study and she was on week two. Her cancer had neither improved nor progressed.

This new doctor turned out to be a blessing. Although he was a straight shooter, everything he said was couched in hope. In his position at the University, his expertise was equally divided between research and caring for patients. He spent a great deal of time with Mom during each visit and it was so refreshing not to have her appointments limited because of time. I liked him. His style and approach to Mom were far more supportive to her individuality than those of her previous physician. He was aware her condition was considered "terminal," yet he never spoke about days or months left to live, and he always talked about options. Even though he didn't promote holistic measures, he was open to discussing them. The greatest thing about him was his attitude. He was positive and encouraged Mom to live her life and not her disease. He was down-to-earth and actually came across as quite humble. Through my inquisitive nature, I learned during one visit that he had been born and raised on a farm in North Dakota. After hearing that, I knew he had been sent to us by God.

Our trips to Madison occurred once a week and the three-hour drive provided a wonderful change from the isolation of the farm. Having lived in Madison for ten years, I knew my way around the city easily and part of my nursing training had taken place at the hospital where Mom saw her doctor. Several of my college friends still lived there, which provided a pleasant diversion from the purpose of our trips. We stayed overnight with Mark and his wife Kate, which allowed Mom a chance to spend time with her grandchildren. On several occasions, my brother or Kate accompanied us on our visits to the doctor. The arrangement worked out well and I looked forward to our weekly excursions, although Mom didn't. She became tense and fearful the morning we drove down because she was always sure the doctor was going to give her "bad" news. Afterward she would be like a different person and became a "Chatty Cathy." Some of our best conversations took place in the car on the way back home, her fears having been relieved until the next trip.

It was impressive how our family had banded together through the whole ordeal with Dad and now with Mom. In the best of times tempers can flare and old wounds resurface within all families. A crisis certainly lets one see the best and worst in people. We'd had our moments during the past year, but they had been minimal and had not left us divided. There was no way to assess everyone's coping levels because we all handled things differently. I trusted my journey home had relieved some pressure for those closest in geographical proximity to Mom. I knew Ann and Dave had been able to return to greater normalcy in their lives. They still visited frequently but it was less out of necessity. Occasionally Ann stopped by before work or Dave stopped after work, and they always came on the weekend after church services with their daughter Julie. Sometimes I thought Dave stopped just to see if I'd done any damage in my pioneering efforts. Ann and I spoke regularly on the phone and the bond between us had grown deeper. She was becoming very dear to me and was a great source of support.

Ron and his wife Ann frequently made the trip from Minneapolis to see Mom. When Dad had first become ill, they had been home constantly because Ron was helping put Dad's financial affairs in order. I knew Ron the least of all my siblings because I had left home when he was about nine or ten. He was independent and ambitious. An avid sports enthusiast, he was a staunch supporter of the Green Bay Packers. He was rowdy in nature and knew how to have a good time. While tough on the exterior, he had a soft heart.

Mary had been back twice since Dad died and took Mom to her doctor's appointment when I was in L.A. for my surgery. I had not seen her since Dad's funeral.

Mark, Kate and their kids came less often now that Mom and I made regular visits to Madison. Kate's father had passed away a year earlier from a brain tumor and the current situation with Mom was especially challenging for them.

Margaret and their kids were planning to fly home for Christmas. My brother Vernon had not been back to see Mom since Dad's funeral. It was tough on him being so far away and his business didn't allow much freedom to visit. I sensed he had been having a difficult time since Dad passed.

Johnny and Gail usually stopped by on the weekends, as well. Because Johnny put in long hours for his job, he was not usually able to visit during the week.

When Davey, Pat and Shaun, the remainder of the grandkids, were home from college, they also spent time with Mom, so she was never void of companionship. Her spirits always seemed to lift after anyone's visit and she'd had a chance to fuss over everyone. Although she was less able to fix huge meals—which had been a major way of showing her love—she still managed to give special attention to whomever stopped by.

Sometimes the telephone never stopped ringing. I had become the thread that was continually interweaving between everyone regarding Mom's condition. It was interesting how an illness could change family dynamics. Growing up and being the youngest in the first group of five children, many times I had felt like a part of the woodwork, never seen nor heard. There had been a complete shift and now I couldn't escape being the focal point. What a way to finally be noticed and what a responsibility it carried.

I was learning a great deal about my brothers and sisters—this unique group of souls that comprised our family unit. It reminded me of looking through a camera lens. If I changed the focus or angle, I saw a different image. Through our constant interactions, more of each of my siblings was revealed. They all carried such diverse qualities that added richness to the whole. Because our family was scattered throughout the states, we rarely got together as a group. It was amazing how there was just a short, condensed period during the span of our entire lives when our relationships had developed. Consequently the memories and opinions we had of one another had been formulated when we were young and our hearts innocent. As adults we had grown through our individual experiences, yet we still saw each other from childhood perceptions, making it difficult at times to break the mold of old beliefs. I felt fortunate be able to look at them from a fresh viewpoint.

Mom's and Dad's illnesses had allowed our separate lives to reconnect, affording us an opportunity to reunite in a deeper way. We had a chance to contribute to each other that could either solidify the family or tear it apart. While we all—including me—had our quirky qualities, my choice was to look for the best in them.

Mary brought expertise in the medical profession, an intelligent and researching mind and all that came with being the oldest in the family. Johnny, second in line, brought a sense of fairness, teasing and a kind heart. Ann, the third oldest, added reliability, tenacity and dependability. Vernon, the fourth in command, was outrageous, bold and humorous. Mark, sixth in our generation, was gentle in nature, openly sensitive and had the heart of a child. Ron, the last heir to the throne, was aggressive and had business savvy and determination. Added to that were the significant others who brought their own flavor of richness to the composite. Gail, Johnny's wife, was loving and supportive. Dave, Ann's husband, was shrewd, mischievous and devoted. Margaret, Vernon's wife, was spiritual, graceful and curious. Kate, Mark's wife, had a tender and kind heart. Ann, Ron's wife and the last one to be adopted in our family, was thoughtful, spunky and willful. And we were all a little crazy. It had never been boring when we were all together and that hadn't changed with Mom's and Dad's illnesses.

My job was easier because of all of them. In their own ways they contributed to Mom's care as much as they could. I rarely made any decisions alone and no one demanded their way was the best. My tendency to be independent challenged me to keep them informed and included. We were all in this together and I couldn't do what I was doing without their support. The nature of the circumstances provided me with a greater understanding about the meaning of interdependence.

Mom and I had established a comfortable routine with one another. She knew when to give me space and I was learning her subtle quirks that made it easier to understand her needs. She was still able to care for herself and was determined to do as much of her normal activities as she could. She had not regained her stamina after the hysterectomy and was discouraged she ever would. I was in charge of all her medications, how many and when to take them. We had completed the parasitic cleanse and were still combining natural herbs with her pharmaceutical drugs. My efforts to help her meditate had been slow and we were less consistent with our sessions. She still had difficulty quieting her mind and was afraid to do so. I hadn't wanted to push her.

My outdoor responsibilities had diminished. Five loads of firewood had gone into the basement—two thanks to the help of Mark and his son Jimmy. I missed spending time outside where I had breathing room from the emotional intensity of being with Mom. I didn't, however, miss the weekly lawn mowing. The long winter days were beginning to feel endless and my stay looked as though it were going to be much longer than I had imagined.

Mom and I took a trip to Florida to visit Mary. We were there for ten days. Mom always dreaded winter and now that it was cold, we felt the warm weather would be good medicine, both for her spirits and her body. My original desire was to take her to Hawaii, especially the smaller islands, because of the healing qualities of their vibration. I also felt the dramatic change in environment might provide a fresh outlook on her life and a diversion to the focus on her illness. Having spent time on the island of Kauai during a low point in my life, I remembered how the gentle, balmy breezes felt like soothing arms that eased my pain. Mom didn't want to travel that far; just getting her to Florida was a miracle. I had to trust her time there would have the same effect. She had become entrenched in the familiarity of how her life used to be, constantly binding her to what had been lost. Nothing seemed to uplift her.

So far the trip had been magical. The cost of our airline tickets was incredibly low—a steal, according to my travel agent. There was a blizzard the day before we left that caused concern the airport might be closed. The next morning, however, it was clear and sunny and the runways were plowed. When we got to the airport, we were upgraded to first class without even asking. It was a real treat for Mom because she had never flown that way. A gentleman came by with a wheelchair and escorted Mom right to the gate. As we were making ourselves comfortable in our seats, one of the Smothers Brothers boarded and sat one row in front of us and across the aisle from Mom. She was so excited because she got to see a celebrity.

It was great to get away from the winter weather. The Midwest was supposed to be hit with a forty below wind-chill factor that would be brutal. Polar bear weather was not my idea of a good time since I didn't have much meat on my bones—well, you know the rest of the story.

Although Mary was working during most of our stay, her presence was good for Mom. My sister was upbeat, talkative and liked to do things. Mom had a tendency to isolate herself, and this had increased since Dad's death and her illness. If anyone could nudge her to get out and be more active, it was Mary. I was glad we had made the trip and so was my sister. The change seemed good for Mom, who had more lightness and peace about her.

I also needed a break from the constant focus on Mom. It was like having a newborn baby. You become aware of their every breath or moan and what it means. My ability to tune into Mom had become more astute and the fact that I was with her because she was ill never left my consciousness. During the past month I had been edgy and irritable. I was not quite sure why. Mary had even mentioned my mood. We had actually gotten into a huge argument over it. She thought I was being sharp with Mom. I didn't think I was. When I asked Mom whether she felt I was being that way with her, she said she noticed some crankiness but figured it was because I missed my friends and my old life. Then she responded, "I'm not taking it personally, so don't feel like you're doing something wrong."

I had no regrets or resentment about being with Mom. There were just moments when I needed to express my own humanness, to release or seek out a different perspective that afforded me a healthy balance to the dramatic changes in my life. I certainly hadn't achieved sainthood yet and carried my own set of unresolved baggage. I was questioning whether it had been a mistake to share some of my thoughts with Mary. Although we had always been close and helped each other through some rocky times, I sensed she wished she were the one home with Mom. Our argument cautioned me to be more discerning about how and what I shared with her. Perhaps my friends were a safer haven because they were neutral to the situation.

One day we took Mom out on the ocean. We laughed a lot and it was great for Mom. Mary made the arrangements and must have been guided in her selection of a charter company. There was no one else on the boat, and the captain was a woman. It was perfect. The day was sunny and warm and Mom loved drifting through the canals, looking at all the cottages peppered along the waterway, as we made our way to the open sea. Mary and I hoped we would encounter some dolphins, even if from afar, because Mom had never seen any. Not only did they appear, but three of them swam and dived along the boat, going back and forth from side to side as if they were guiding us. Mary and I told Mom she was being blessed by dolphin energy. Studies have shown dolphins emit a frequency similar to that of humans. They are extremely loving and sensitive and have been used in working with autistic children. It was remarkable to watch their playfulness and Mom's reaction to them. I knew God had gifted us with the miracle of their presence. It was a wonderful, rare afternoon to see such a childlike spark and innocence in Mom and to be able to share the experience with my sister.

It was also great to get Mom out of Mary's condominium. She had become weaker since we'd been in Florida and both Mary and I felt it was because of the lavender oil. She was really tired and was sleeping more. We called her doctor to share our concerns and he agreed with taking her off the pills. She had been on the study for seven weeks and it appeared she was not having any success with the extract that was supposed to combat her cancer. After his decision, Mom's spirits were low and it was easy to understand why. Another drug had failed. Where could she turn for hope?

One day I took Mom to a secluded beach to sit in the sun. Mary borrowed a wheelchair from her office because Mom wasn't strong enough to walk any great distance. There was a wooden pathway all the way from the small parking lot to the beach, and I was able to wheel Mom right to the sand. I watched as she sat on a beach chair, wearing a sun hat, just staring out at the water, a frown on her face. We stayed for a couple of hours and she was quiet for most of it. I wondered if she went only because Mary and I had said it would be good for her. She didn't want to go back.

I wished she would share more intimate feelings with me. I didn't think she did with Dad either. Maybe that was just her way. It was difficult to know what to do or even what to say anymore. Perhaps we had gotten into a routine with each other and the freshness of my outlook had become redundant. She continually reminded me to keep saying positive things because she needed them. Yet it was hard to gauge my effectiveness and I wondered if I were making any difference. My role was changing and, with it, the dynamics of our relationship.

Mary's outgoing nature was a breath of fresh air. Mom seemed to laugh more with her and had even gone out to dinner with some of Mary's friends. Spending time alone with Mom and then watching her interact in social settings made for a dramatic contrast. She was more alive and engaging. When she was like that, it reminded me of the old Mom. Sometimes I thought she was putting on a facade. How could she be one way with strangers and another way with me? Perhaps I had replaced Dad and she didn't have to hide her true feelings with me. Maybe that's how it is in all families. Oh how I wished things were different.

In a few days we'd be returning to Wisconsin. Mom was depressed about Christmas approaching and I was not looking forward to returning to the cold weather. It would be her first Christmas in forty-nine years without Dad. On the last night we watched "Highway to

Heaven," one of Mom's favorite shows. A father was dying and wanted to make peace with his son. I knew Mom was having a hard time with the show because she had taken off her glasses and was looking down at her hands. Later I asked if she were okay.

Mom's voice quivered and she said, "Yes."

She asked why I had asked. I said, "I thought the show might have been hard to watch and I wanted to know how you were doing."

She started to cry. She was sitting on a reclining chair so I went and knelt on the floor next to her, placing one hand on her leg and holding her hands with the other. She said, "I can't keep crying all the time."

I told her it was okay to cry and she should cry for as long as she needed because she was still grieving Dad.

She responded, "I'm through grieving him."

I looked up at her and said, "Mom it's only been seven months."

She kept crying and then pulled herself together and said she was going to bed. I watched her walk slowly upstairs and then heard her sobbing. Feeling her pain, I wondered whether to go to her. It didn't feel right. I sat alone, frustrated, not knowing what else to do. Fifteen minutes later her crying stopped.

I tried to put myself in her shoes to grasp what it must be like for her. It was challenging because even in some of my darkest moments, I'd tried to search for the positive. One evening about a month before, when Mom was really low, she had turned to me on the couch and said, "You keep telling me to look for the good in all of this. Well, I can't find one darn thing."

My heart had ached inside as I pondered what to say. Finally I had shared a little story—or perhaps it was a joke—someone once told me:

"A group of psychologists was conducting a study on children to assess how their upbringing influenced the way they responded to identical situations. Two small boys were put into similar rooms, each filled with horse manure, and left alone. An hour later the psychologists went to check on them. They found the first little boy sitting on top of the horse manure

sobbing and sobbing. 'I can't believe you left me all alone in this room with nothing but a huge pile of smelly horse crap. Why am I being punished? What did I do wrong?' With the second little boy, they encountered a completely different response. When they opened the door, there was horse manure all over the walls. He had a huge grin on his face and was flinging clumps right and left, while digging furiously. They inquired why he was so happy and excited. Turning to one of the psychologists, the little boy responded, 'Because I know there is a pony in here somewhere and I'm going to find it!'"

Mom had laughed and then become quiet. She might not have been digging to find her pony, but I was. If the shoe were on the other foot, I was quite sure I would have similar feelings. Yet at some point I'd start asking inside for answers and looking for another path. I didn't believe God intends for us to suffer. We make that choice by the way we look at a situation. That was why I loved the story about the two little boys and the horse manure. It was such a contrast in perception. All I could do was keep trusting in my reason for being with Mom and continue looking for the pearls.

Early on when I first came home to be with Mom, we had talked about how to change her thoughts. We were exploring ways of looking at her life now that Dad was gone. I saw that she had many choices. She could look to the days ahead as an opportunity for new possibilities or live in the past of regret and sorrow. It all depended on where she focused her thoughts. Years ago I had read a book called *There's a Hole in My Sidewalk*, about a woman who had a habit of marrying alcoholic men. When she realized it was a pattern, this woman had been able to turn her life around. Within the book was a section called "Autobiography in Five Short Chapters." This piece struck a chord inside of me and I had carried it around in my wallet for a long time. Thinking it might help Mom, I gave her a copy.

Chapter 1
I walk down the street.

There's a deep hole in the sidewalk.
I fall in.
I am lost ... I am hopeless.
It isn't my fault.
It takes forever to find a way out.

Chapter 2
I walk down the same street.
There's a deep hole in the sidewalk.
I pretend I don't see it.
I fall in again.
I can't believe I am in the same place.
But it isn't my fault.
It still takes a long time to get out.

Chapter 3
I walk down the same street.
There is a deep hole in the sidewalk.
I see it is there.
I still fall in ... It's a habit.
My eyes are open.
I know where I am.
It is my fault.
I get out immediately.

Chapter 4
I walk down the same street.
There is a deep hole in the sidewalk.
I walk around it.

Chapter 5
I walk down another street.

I always referred to this quote when I was feeling stuck because I loved the analogy of "walking down another street." It reminded me that I had choices and that ingrained habits, whether they are thoughts or actions, are just consistent patterns. They can be changed and don't need to control my life.

Mom liked this little saying and periodically when she was having an especially tough time I would say to her, "Did you fall in the hole in the sidewalk?" She'd smile back and it usually opened the door to a conversation about what she was feeling. Lately, however, it didn't seem to be working.

Christmas was a mixed bag of emotions. It seemed we were all trying to be strong for Mom to boost her spirits, putting up a good front to celebrate the holy season but not feeling that way ourselves. Because I hadn't been home for a couple of years, it didn't feel the same without Dad. His absence was deeply missed. Gone was the tradition of Pops going out on his land to find the perfect tree and puffing out his chest when he brought it home. Of course, his idea of a great tree and mine were never quite the same. One year I teased him that he must have forgotten to wear his glasses when he picked out the tree because it looked like a Charlie Brown version. He grinned at me and said, "Beauty is in the eye of the beholder."

I missed Dad joking about what he was going to get from Santa Claus and his ritual of serenading us with a few tunes on the harmonica while his feet danced a little jig. When we were little, it was a ritual to go to bed on Christmas Eve with the living room looking normal and to wake up in the morning to a decorated tree and Santa's presents stacked in piles with our names on them. As we got older and knew about Santa, we helped decorate the tree. Dad had two ornaments from when he was a child that only he could hang on the tree. One was a little red plastic horn and the other a plastic chicken in a sleigh. He reminded me of a little boy as he placed them delicately on the tree. I could tell they were special to him.

Dad loved the Christmas holidays and there was always laughter filling the house. There were days of non-stop relatives on their annual visit to see our tree and it felt like an on-going party. Because deer season was still fresh in Dad's mind, the most recent hunting adventures were shared over and over. He had a humorous postcard in his desk drawer and every time he brought it out it made him howl as if he were seeing it for the first time. A deer hunter was sitting in an outhouse in the woods. The door was slightly ajar and you could see his gun sitting in the corner. Behind the outhouse were two hunters standing next to some trees. One of the hunters turned to the other and said with a serious look on his face, "Joe, ssshhh, I think I just heard a buck snort." And that was how it was with Dad and Christmas.

In spite of his distinct absence, I could strongly feel Dad's spirit, encouraging us to be happy. While he wasn't there in physical form, the memory of him was. As I sat alone reflecting about how special he had made Christmas, I was sure the brightest twinkling light on the tree was him.

Mom had no spark about Christmas. In the past she would have spent several weeks baking cookies and making divinity candy. She always hung her Christmas cards with tape on the doorframe going into the living room and put out a manger nativity scene one of her brothers had given her. She would put fluffy angel hair underneath it and on the sides and then put small twinkling lights around it. She had no desire to do any of it this year and didn't even want a tree. Johnny brought one over and we asked Mom to do the honors and put up Dad's ornaments. She couldn't.

Ann and Dave and their kids and Johnny and Gail and their son spent the day with us. Even having the grandkids around didn't brighten Mom's grieving heart. Vernon, Margaret and their boys were soon to arrive from Seattle and would be staying for five days. It had been a couple of years since Mom last saw Vernon's children and I hoped hearing innocent laughter would ease the intensity of Mom's pain and lighten the burden of her heart. I was looking forward to their visit to help fill the emptiness of the house and provide me comfort.

It was painful watching Mom withdraw from everyone and go and sit by herself. I had rarely seen her that way. My heart ached for her. It ached for all of us. Not only was she dealing with the loss of her husband, as well as facing her own mortality, but her best friend Ann passed away two days before Christmas. She had lived just a few miles down the road and died from a rare blood disease. She had become sick a year or two before Dad. When we heard she had passed away, Mom said to me, "It's great to have kids, but sometimes you need a really good friend to talk to. I'm really going to miss her." I had thought we kids were enough to help her get through this. What an insight for me. Ann's funeral was going to be another tough day for Mom.

If I imagined looking through her eyes, it was apparent she saw the cards more and more stacked against her. Within two years her best friend had been diagnosed with a rare blood disease, then her sister's husband had been diagnosed with cancer. Next her daughter-in-law's father was diagnosed with brain cancer and died within six months. A year later Dad learned he had cancer, and then so had Mom. Dad passed away within five months, and two months later one of his brothers also died from cancer. Mom's own illness was progressing and now her best friend had also left her life. Mom's world had been completely shattered.

I gave up suggesting to Mom that she could see the cup of her life as half full or half empty. Just when she seemed to be gaining some ground inside, something like this happened and the flood gates of loss hit again with full force. I continued to struggle with what to do or even say. I had never experienced such frequency of death among the people I loved. She must have been overwhelmed with the depth of her emotional pain. I myself felt so helpless.

The day of Ann's funeral was tough on both of us. Although Mom held up better than I expected, it was apparent she was hurting deeply. Earlier that morning, I had heard her sobs from upstairs but when I went to offer comfort, she asked to be left alone. My heart felt as though it were breaking.

I had always liked Ann. She was warm and caring and had a softness about her. She and her husband had been good friends to Mom and Dad. They watched each other's kids grow up and gave neighborly support. Mom taught Ann how to plant a garden and started her growing geranium flowers. They were good companions for each other.

When my sister Ann and I took Mom to the funeral, something unexpected happened to me. While sitting in the church, I felt I was being transported to the future and the service was for Mom. Tears streamed down my face and I couldn't stop crying during the service. Later both Mom and Ann commented about it. I told them, "It's probably a delay in emotions from Dad."

I wished I could share the silent pain going on inside me. But how do you tell your fragile mother, clinging to hope for her own life, that you are crying for her? On the couple of occasions during the past few months when I had shed tears, her immediate comment had been, "You're not telling me something about my cancer, aren't you? That's why you are crying. The doctor told you something, didn't he?" No matter how much I reassured her I wasn't keeping something from her, she didn't believe me. Since then, I had only allowed myself to grieve in private.

Ann's funeral was a gift. It was an accepted place to cry, even if my tears were for another reason. It has been said that tears are a way of cleansing the soul and, for that brief moment, I felt that's what occurred for me.

I had been thinking a lot about grief. What is healthy and unhealthy grief? We all go through it differently and at our own internal pace. But at some point can it reach a place of unhealthy excessiveness so we become shackled to the grief because we are afraid to move forward? I watched Mom and wondered. She was certainly entitled to her grief with everything she had been dealing with. But she was a tough one because of her tendency to become depressed at times. I knew what that was like. You wallowed in its energy so long you didn't know how to get out. And once you were immersed in it, you questioned if there were another way of feeling. You became the depression and that was all you knew. But once you were out, you realized the depression had a force all its own that exacerbated what you were unhappy about to begin with. It got a grip on you and you thought the overwhelming sadness was all that existed.

There was such a fine line with Mom. The loss of Dad and now her best friend were compounded by facing the loss of her own life. Added to that was the powerful emotion of fear. It consumed her and it was hard to watch the effect it had on her. I had tremendous compassion, and wished there was more I could do. Yet I didn't want to diminish the importance of her internal process. While I didn't have any children of my own, it seemed similar to watching a child struggling. Sometimes all you can do is let them struggle and when they've had enough, they let it go. But what if they don't?

No matter how strong I was spiritually, dealing with dying was not easy. More and more I was beginning to feel as though Mom was my daughter and I was the mother.

Chapter Ten
Testing New Wings

Mom received radiation to her uterine area to curb the tumor growth. Just after we returned from Florida in the middle of December, we spent a week in Madison where she had daily appointments. Most of the drainage was gone and so was the repulsive odor. Mom was relieved. The treatments were not painful or uncomfortable, but afterward she was in excruciating pain. She had always had hemorrhoids and the radiation caused them to become raw. Every time she had a bowel movement, the pain was almost unbearable. My mother was not one to complain about pain, but this was almost more than she could handle. My frequent calls to the radiologist's office for effective medication were as frustrating to them as they were me. They felt I was exaggerating the intensity of her discomfort. Later when they gave Mom a follow-up exam and saw the tender tissue, they realized I hadn't been stretching the truth and apologized for what Mom had gone through.

For a week both she and I suffered through trying to ease her pain. Mom said it was ten times worse than bearing children. Several times all that seemed to help was rocking her in my arms. It was the greatest amount of physical pain I would watch her go through. As short a duration as it was, it made me grateful she did not have the type of cancer in which that kind of experience was the norm.

I thanked God when her ordeal was over. What an ugly disease cancer can be.

We had just seen Mom's cancer doctor. Since the lavender study had proven unsuccessful, he hadn't been sure what else to do for her. At least he hadn't said the dreaded words spoken by her first physician. Instead he said we would continue with our monthly visits, and they would keep exploring, so Mom could find some joy in her life.

He had encouraged her in the past to seek out a support group. We went several times to one that was held at the hospital. I didn't know who was more depressed afterward. To be fair, we didn't attend the full six-week cycle of classes and perhaps, if we had, the outcome would have been different. It just seemed all the people in the group, which averaged between eight and ten, talked about everything wrong with them. It was not what Mom wanted to hear. Usually she sat quietly in the group not wanting to share. Finally in one class she spoke out asking why no one was talking about hope. The nurse leading the group said they had discussed it the previous week, which we had missed. I wondered why it wasn't a topic of conversation in every class. We stopped going because Mom found no comfort or value in it.

After pressure from my sisters and me, Mom went three times to see a counselor—a nun at the local hospital. I attended the initial visit with Mom and did most of the talking. The nun/counselor seemed compassionate and qualified and had worked with many hospice patients in the community. She was a Catholic sister, which was in alignment with Mom's religious beliefs. Although she talked a few times about the will of God, I didn't feel it would be a hindrance for counseling Mom about her cancer. I was wrong. I let Mom see the nun by herself for the next two sessions, thinking she would share more openly if I weren't with her. After the third visit, Mom refused to go back and said "That woman is too depressing to listen to." She said I was more helpful than she was. That was the end of her willingness to seek counseling outside the family.

The doctor's news that they were at a standstill in treating Mom's condition wasn't a surprise. We'd heard the medical profession say before there was no effective treatment for her rare form of cancer. That mentality, however, was still difficult for me to grasp in this day and age, considering what is known about the body and its natural healing abilities. I didn't fault Western science for not being able to cure Mom and Dad. It wasn't intentional. They knew no other way and were not wrong in their approach.

The human race has evolved tremendously because medical science has paved extraordinary inroads toward discoveries and knowledge that has improved the quality of life for millions of people. Yet everything is not all right in the hallowed halls of the Land of Medicine. There is an imbalance. An imbalance in the consciousness of believing their way is the only and best way. That isn't true. There isn't just one right way for anything. Not for planting a field, constructing a building, designing an automobile or treating a disease. Each is unique to the specific situation and desired outcome. My issue with the medical profession isn't with their inability to cure an illness, it is with their unwillingness to encourage or support individuals to explore other options by holding a "lesser than" attitude toward these alternatives. Hope is hope and comes wrapped with unusual ribbons. People should have the prerogative to refuse to accept the limitations of diagnoses and treatments that aren't meeting their expectations, without being left helpless in their desire to try something new. With pioneers such as Deepak Chopra and Andrew Weil, slow transformation is occurring, as holistic thinking has begun to weave its way into mainstream consciousness. I wished it had happened sooner for Mom and Dad.

I might have appeared to be in denial, but I was not willing to accept that Mom should watch her days ebb away and give up hope. The truth was I wanted her to be a pioneer and look for other paths. In her own way, I wanted to believe she was. Within a few weeks, her leap of faith would surprise me.

Mom and I went to Los Angeles for Mary's birthday. We arrived five days ahead of time. Mary was flying in on the afternoon of her birthday and we planned to drive to San Francisco to celebrate the event. She had lived there for several years while she was married and loved the city. When she heard I was bringing Mom to California, she jumped at the chance to join us. Mom seemed up for the trip, although I was concerned about the eight-hour drive. She had felt better since going off the lavender study and her severe weakness had gone away but she still tired easily.

Our trip to Los Angeles was two-fold. Another extreme cold front was headed for the Midwest with a predicted fifty-below burst of frigid air. The farmhouse was old and not well-insulated, making it a challenge to stay warm even for the healthiest of individuals. It was enough for Mom's body to cope with cancer, let alone bitter cold. Once again, I was hoping the change of environment would do her good.

The main reason for our trip was to see Alex Orbito, a renowned Filipino healer. When the lavender study hadn't worked and there was nothing else available medically, I had prayed for something that could reinstall hope for Mom. The following day I learned Alex was coming to the U.S. I had met him several years before through my friend Jacque and had not only had healings from him but also attended one of his workshops. He was a psychic surgeon who opened an individual's body using the energy of his hands. His type of work was considered quite controversial in our Western culture and had been portrayed skeptically by the media. Had I not had trust in him, I would never have brought Mom to see him.

A couple of years earlier I had told Mom all about Alex and what it was like to have a "healing" from him. She was apprehensive and afraid something might happen to me. So I was totally surprised when she said "yes" the morning after my suggestion she see Alex. It usually took her days to make a decision. This was a huge step on her part. I didn't want to repeat the feeling of pushing Mom into doing something, so I inquired whether her decision was her own choice or if she felt pressured. Her response was, "I don't have anything to lose. You told me to pray about it and I did. I haven't given up on a miracle yet." She never ceased to amaze me and became a valuable study in human behavior. She moved at her own pace, within her own process of what was right for her. My timing wasn't hers and I was learning how to honor that.

The first time I had watched Alex perform a surgery was at a small gathering in a hotel room. About fifty people were present. I stood on a chair for a better view of what was occurring, curious to see what would happen. Because of my nursing experiences, I knew about what went on in an operating room. Everything lay in the balance of the abilities of all the professionals to confidently perform their skills. By contrast, Alex had nothing but a table, a bowl of cotton balls, a bowl of water, a wastebasket, himself and one assistant.

The patient was an older man who had liver cancer. He lay quietly on the table as Alex went into a prayerful state and blessed the body. As Alex placed his hands on the man's abdomen, I heard a pop-like sound and saw his hands enter the body. They went three quarters of the way in and I could see the liquid of this man's blood. A chill went down my spine, my knees became weak and I felt light-headed. There was not a wince of pain on the man's face. He continued to lie calmly on the table with his eyes closed. Alex removed a small piece of tissue about the size of a golf ball and discarded it in the wastebasket. Then he took a cotton ball, wiped a trickle of blood from the open area, moved his hand over the abdomen and the surgical opening closed. My heart was pounding. This was so foreign to what I had ever been taught or experienced. This man had major surgery without any anesthesia or medical technology, lying on a table in a room that could have been anywhere, all in the matter of ten minutes. It was remarkable and profound. The gentleman was conscious the whole time and said he only felt a slight pressure in his abdomen during the surgery. A year later the patient was thriving and his cancer was gone. His medical doctors had given him six months to live.

Later I was able to witness other healings that I watched standing right next to the table. The profundity of what I saw never changed. Experiencing my own healing first-hand and feeling the change in my body lingered with me years later. What impressed me about Alex was not so much his ability to do what he did—which was extraordinary in itself—but rather his spiritual communion with God that allowed him to surrender to the gift that came through his hands. He gave credit to God for all healing that occurred and claimed none for himself.

Within two days, Mom had four healings from Alex, one each morning and afternoon. His fee was a nominal two-hundred dollars. He had a sliding scale dependent on a person's ability to pay and many times treated patients for free. He usually conducted his healings in someone's home to avoid publicity. One room in the house was designated as the "waiting" room, one was where the healings occurred and another was the "recovery" room. Upon entering the home, patients were asked to remove their shoes and were given a slip of paper to list what they wanted treated. Soft music was played and people were asked to remain in a prayerful state. Before the healings, Alex gathered everyone and explained how he facilitated God's work, answered any questions and led the group in prayer. Each person was individually blessed before entering the room to see Alex. Upon completion with him, patients were led to a communal room to rest. Many times people had a release of emotion afterward as the body realigned from the blocked energy that had been removed. It was common for people to cry and others volunteered to hold the person's hand or put their arms around them to offer a gesture of loving support. Individuals were allowed to rest for as long as they needed before leaving, and were encouraged to stay in a reverent state for twenty-one days. An ongoing healing process continued during that time.

While waiting with Mom to see Alex, I found myself comparing the nature of the surroundings with those of my recent experiences. What a dichotomy between the sterile, impersonal environment of the hospitals and doctors' offices and the peaceful ambiance of a home blessed as a healing sanctuary. Both places were dedicated to helping people become well, yet they were vastly different in their approach. How wonderful if a similar environment could be created within the halls of Western medicine.

If Mom were afraid to see Alex, she never mentioned it. Part of me was waiting for her to back out, but she never did. Normally Alex saw patients alone to maintain a trance-like state and to not be affected by external distractions. He allowed me be in the room with Mom for the first healing as emotional support. It was remarkable to watch my mother's body being opened in hopes of restoring it back to a healthy vitality. I heard the same pop-like sound and observed Alex pull tissue from her abdomen the size of an egg. He showed her what he had removed. She was silent and I wondered what was going through her mind. Where would she fit this into her mental framework of what she had experienced with the hysterectomy, the anesthesia and all the hospital proceedings that went with it? I would never know.

After each healing she was more peaceful and relaxed. We rented a hotel room in a beautiful place by the ocean so Mom could be near the water. After each session we would go back so she could rest and take a bath to absorb more of the work that had been done on her. She was quiet most of the time, and I could tell she was thinking a lot. She didn't express much emotion and I became concerned she might be feeling the healings were a waste of money. Although she and Dad had some investments, her main source of income was social security and she worried about how she would get by in the future. She was in uncharted waters because of me and I felt accountable. The last day we both had a healing and I was curious to know what she was thinking.

That evening we had an argument. Sitting on the bed next to Mom, I inquired how she was feeling and her thoughts about the healings.

Much to my surprise, she turned the focus on me. "Susie, aren't you afraid you might be in some kind of cult? You seem to put a lot of trust in your friend Jacque. Don't you think you might be led astray?"

Overly sensitive as a result of the work done on my body earlier in the day, I was hurt by her comment. "Mom, you said you wanted my spirituality. You wanted what I have inside. I lead you through a door that allows you to receive the gift of something new, to see into a part of what I know and you wonder whether I am part of a cult?"

In a gentle voice she responded, "I'm just concerned about you, that's all."

The conversation deteriorated to frustration as my world seemed up for questioning. While she was calm and collected, I became angry. Not so much at her, but at myself for letting my emotions get to that state. We were quiet with each other the remainder of the evening and later, after she had gone to bed, I sat outside on the cement steps overlooking the ocean. As the waves gently crashed along the shore, I pondered our interaction. Somehow my buttons had been pushed and I didn't understand why. Perhaps my defensiveness came from guilt that I had taken her on a wild goose chase and had irresponsibly wasted her money.

The sky was filled with stars as I looked up in prayer asking for understanding. From a quiet place I heard, "Put yourself in her shoes. She has just gone through an experience that is foreign to her comprehension. If she accepts this type of healing as 'real' and not a 'cult,' then her perception of reality as she understands life and her beliefs may be up for reconsideration. That would mean change in a big way for her. She is looking to feel safe right now. Her emotional, spiritual and physical fields have been altered and she is trying to assimilate everything she is feeling. She has been entrenched in the ways of Western medicine. She saw how her husband died. She has the choice to believe it will be the same for her or not. But to choose another way means she has to be willing to let go of old ways of thinking and being. You know how challenging it has been for you to discard attitudes and beliefs in your life. She has many more years on you of habitual patterns."

Glancing toward the ocean, I silently digested what had just been shared.

Minutes passed and I heard, "The exposure to your friends and different lifestyles has not been lost on your mother. She sees what is possible. Her heart is lighter and she is enjoying all the attention and love showered upon her. She has become someone special unto herself and not attached to your father. You are noticing a difference in her. It is as though she were becoming a new woman, and in many ways she is. She may not be able to sustain the newness once she returns because her lifestyle is so rooted at home. It is easy to slip back into old habits if there isn't continual reinforcement for a different way. Even if she does, she will always have the experience and insight from what she has learned on this trip. Remember: for her to be healed doesn't mean in body alone. She may not choose to live physically. But her soul will have a greater understanding and wisdom that will evolve her higher than when she was born. Death of the physical body is not death of the soul. It is ongoing forever. Your society has much to learn about the spirituality of dying and the new life that is awakened in the process. Trust in your mother's process."

Although the night was getting late, I continued to sit in deep thought about my mother and my expectations for her and the trip to L.A..

Our relationship had been tumultuous when I was growing up. From an early age, there seemed to be friction between us. I could never pinpoint the source of the anger; it just was there. For a long time I thought Mom didn't like me, although she claimed she never felt that way. As I hit my early teens, I felt much anger building up inside toward her. Months would go by without any kind of civil conversation. I would only speak to her when I had to ask permission to do something with my friends or to communicate about chores. One day we had a huge argument. To this day I have no idea what our fight was about. Crying, I sought out Dad—which was very unusual. I kept my feelings tucked away deep inside and Smokey, our dog, was usually the safe haven for letting them out. He was happy to have my arms around him and always licked my face to dry the tears.

This particular time, I found Dad alone in the barn pitching hay in front of the cow's stanchions. He wanted to know what we were fighting about. I shared that no matter what I did, Mom got angry with me. Dad was quiet as he continued with his work. Then he stopped what he was doing and shared something that was revealing to my young mind. "After Vern was born, she didn't want any more kids for awhile. Having four each a year apart was enough. She wanted a break. But right away she became pregnant with you." That's all he said and went back to pitching the hay.

I felt a piece of the puzzle about my relationship with Mom had fallen into place. Our tension remained, mostly due to my inability to let go of built up resentment toward her. While insight provided a greater understanding of our dynamics, I had no effective tools to emotionally open my heart to her. It was too scary. However, somewhere inside it was easier to accept the pattern we had created between us.

My relationship with Mom had changed after I got married because my perception of her changed. The geographic distance of living apart afforded me an opportunity to see her in a whole new light and I began to appreciate the qualities I had once judged. Therapy eventually healed old scars and I was able to find common ground on which to develop a healthier relationship with her. She had not been my enemy for many, many years and I couldn't even conceive of ever having thought of her in that way.

As time had passed and our lifestyles had become radically different, I had desired for her to step into the window of my life and experience some of what I believed. Almost all our visits had centered around spending time back at the farm and her life there and I had missed sharing my corner of the world with her. I felt there was so much about me she didn't know. And now we were living together under the same roof. What a twist.

Perhaps my hunger for Mom to become healthy and embrace the possibility of being healed by Alex was a way to make up for time lost during my youth. And also a way to see her become more of the woman she thought she could be, free from Dad's control. But maybe the greater truth was really the reverse: having her become the woman I had always wanted her to be. Had I still not accepted her just the way she was? What expectations did I place on her, even with her illness? Was it unfair to want your mother to live and flourish in new possibilities? What if deep down she was afraid of that, and was tired from the long fight of maintaining strength for her husband and had none left for herself?

I promised myself to be more sensitive and attuned to her fears and quietly returned to our room and went to bed. The next morning I apologized for being upset. Once again I was surprised by Mom's response. "You don't owe me any apology. I really enjoyed our talk last night. I learned a lot about you, how you think and what is important. Your lifestyle isn't what I would have picked for you, but as long as you're happy, that's all that matters to me."

We had been both given a gift of insight about one another and I was grateful for the outcome of the night before. She chose not to talk about her healings from Alex. She said she wasn't ready.

Our excursion to San Francisco turned out to be wonderful. Mom loved the scenic route, oohing and aahing over the rugged terrain of seaside cliffs and crashing waves. We broke up the drive and spent the night outside Carmel. A cozy, rustic chalet nestled next to a little creek rested our weary bodies and we giggled sitting on Mom's bed as we journeyed back into our childhood recollections. Again I had the feeling of happier times when all was right and safe in our world. There was a playfulness and an ease that bonded us closer together. And once again I saw the magic to how things fell into place.

We hadn't booked a hotel but we were able to find a quaint, inexpensive little one in the middle of the city close to everything we wanted to see. The weather was beautiful, sunny and clear. We were told the past two weeks had been nothing but fog. The restaurant Mary took us to for dinner was usually booked several days in advance but just happened to have an opening.

Mom had never been to San Francisco before and was like a child at Christmas. Mary was familiar with the city, and she gave Mom the grand tour. We were like three college women flitting all over the place. The Golden Gate bridge, a ride on the trolley cars and a view of Alcatraz were Mom's favorite attractions. At one point during the trip she turned to us and said, "Now I can say I've been to San Francisco and not wonder anymore what it's like." Then she smiled and became quiet. Sharing this trip with Mom was so different from our time in Florida. She had much more energy and her spirits were more uplifted. It was a precious time.

One experience verified that God was really looking out for us. As we were putting our suitcases in the car after our overnight stay at Carmel, we noticed the hood of my red Toyota was slightly ajar. Mary had taken Mom for dinner the night before and I thought she had accidentally bumped the hood release. She said "no" and there were no marks on the paint to show someone had tried to tamper with it. Thinking it was just some quirk or jarring from bumpy roads, we tossed the moment aside and set our sights on San Francisco. We had only been on the highway thirty minutes when I noticed the hood vibrating. Pulling off the road, once again the release was ajar. I asked Mary if she had closed the hood at the motel and she said, "yes." Thinking nothing further about it, we continued on the trip with no further occurrences. Upon reaching our destination, thoughts about the hood were pushed aside in the excitement of showing Mom the sights.

Because Mary only had four days off from work, we planned to spend one day in the city and the remaining time on the road. Knowing the long drive had been tiring for Mom, I volunteered to drive back alone to Los Angeles. Mary and Mom would fly back allowing them more time for sight seeing together. So, after one day in San Francisco, I headed back. After half an hour on the freeway, a gas station billboard caught my attention. A little voice inside my head told me to check the oil. I pulled off at the exit and stopped at the station. To my surprise, the oil gauge registered empty—not half empty or a quarter empty, but plain old empty. Knowing how easily the engine could have been blown and how twice we had been given a sign, I was thankful for our angels working overtime.

Mom and I stayed in L.A. a week longer than we'd planned because of the weather. It was still bitter cold in the Midwest. Mom was homesick and longing to get back. It had been the longest she had ever been gone from the farm. The trip had been really good for her and I had not seen her this peaceful and relaxed since her hysterectomy. It had been one of the most memorable times I'd shared with her. There were many moments of laughter and silliness, and a lightness filled our hearts from the distance of another world—a world momentarily free from sad memories, entrenched patterns and challenging times. The responsibility of caring for her had eased from my shoulders because the trip felt more like a vacation.

Although the healings had long since passed and we hadn't discussed them, something was different about Mom. She seemed happier and the anger that had been so prevalent since Dad's passing was gone. We had been staying in Sabrina's guest house since the healings and had been in L.A. for three weeks. One morning after running errands, I returned to find Mom sitting quietly on the couch with soft music playing on the stereo. I asked what she was doing. She got a big grin on her face and said in a playful voice, "I'm meditating. I can meditate, you know."

All I could do was smile back in amazement. For all the months of wondering whether we were making any progress toward that end, she was nonchalant, as if she'd been doing it forever. It was a precious exchange and I filed it away in my memory bank of things I loved about my mother.

Just as I had sat with Dad in the bar one night feeling like a bystander as I watched him, so it was observing Mom in my world. Each morning we sat with Sabrina in her kitchen. Mom had her cup of coffee, and I my tea. Mom exuded a grace and sweetness that was so refreshing after her depression and sorrow. She was much more animated and alive. Part of it was due to Sabrina's ability to draw her out. Her zest for life was infectious and her bold directness could not be escaped. It was fascinating listening to the two of them talk. I no longer saw my mother, but a woman filled with wisdom, unmet dreams and pain. She was far more open and revealing to Sabrina than I expected.

One night Mom had a disturbing dream about Dad not loving her and woke up the next morning distressed. Nothing I said relieved her anguish. To my surprise, Mom told Sabrina about her dream.

Good old Sabrina honed right in and asked, "Do you honestly believe he would have married you if he didn't love you? And how many kids do you have? And how long were you together?"

Mom started to laugh. She turned to Sabrina and said, "You're right. He did love me." It was an interesting exchange to watch because I suspected Mom had been carrying around a doubt all these years and wanted to put her mind at ease. In a split second someone who didn't know her very well had helped heal an old wound. How remarkable.

I wondered when she had last felt the freedom or safety to expose her innermost thoughts without expectations or judgments of her? And how long had it been since a stranger showed genuine interest in who she was and what brought her happiness and joy? Her life had revolved around history—with her children, her husband, her brothers, her sisters and people in the community. All had an opinion of one sort or another just because of the nature of those relationships. But now she was no longer that same woman. She was a widow, alone and challenged with a disease. She was vulnerable, seeking answers and direction and reassessing her life.

What a fascinating journey of insight an illness creates. What an incredible trip this was turning out to be for me in learning about my mother.

One day Mom planted Sabrina's herb garden. I watched from the guest house window as she knelt in the ground and delicately placed the tiny seeds in the earth and gently covered them. Julia, Sabrina's six-year-old daughter, was by her side, their voices a murmur through the open window. I felt as if I were observing a grandmother teaching her granddaughter wisdom she had learned from years of tending her own garden. My heart smiled at the priceless exchange displayed before my eyes. I was reliving a similar experience with my knees in the tilled ground and Mom patiently explaining where and how to plant the seeds. The past had merged with the present for a split second and life felt good. In the adversity of Mom's illness, my heart was being healed.

Our time in California had been a real blessing. Mom had a chance to fly a little farther with her wings and see she could do it alone. In learning to let go of expectations, I had seen her take steps into the potential of who she could be. I'd gotten the best of both worlds: knowing my mother as I'd always known her and starting to know her in ways I might not have had her illness not come along. We'd both stepped into new ways of experiencing each other. She had journeyed into my world and had been able to taste life through my eyes. I had come to appreciate her more—her subtle quirks, her sweet innocence from living such a sheltered existence, her tender heart. Our protective masks were coming down with each other, and with that an even greater bond was forged.

My gut told me this trip had been a turning point for her. I was not sure how yet, but change was in the wind. It felt as if her choice as to whether to live or die still hung in the balance.

Chapter Eleven
Longing To Still Make a Difference

After I'd been caring for Mom for six months, the course of our journey together took a new trajectory. My belief she would overcome her cancer no longer existed. She knew it, too, although we hadn't spoken about it. I could see the truth deep in her eyes. While we had been in L.A., Mom had difficulty reading, and the words on a page would become fuzzy. We thought she needed new glasses because it had been several years since her eyes had been tested. Intuitively she sensed it was something more. She was right. We saw her cancer doctor when we returned to Wisconsin. He couldn't detect any problems and suggested she have her eyes checked. So we made an appointment to see her eye doctor. It was a horrible experience.

After examining Mom, the eye doctor told her she had either had a small stroke or the cancer had spread to her brain. She showed no emotion while in his office, but once we got in the car she broke down in tears. Crying, she said, "I knew something like this was going to happen. I just knew it. I always hated taking those depression pills. I knew they were doing something funny to me. I can't handle it anymore, I just can't take anymore."

Instead of being compassionate, I lost it and became angry. It was the third time during my six-month duration with Mom that had happened. The first time occurred a few months after I arrived. My anger toward her lasted a week and we spoke little. The isolation between us ended because I couldn't stand the tension inside. At the time, I wondered how we had endured living that way during my teens. It was awful. The second occurrence was two months later, when her constant negativity built up and I became frustrated. That spell lasted only three days. Both times I brought her flowers and apologized for my behavior. She took the episodes with a grain of salt and said, "You don't need to apologize. I don't take these things personally anymore since your father got sick. I know I'm not easy to live with sometimes."

My anger this time wasn't intended for her, it just came out that way. I was needing to be strong for her and strong for me and, in that particular moment, I wanted her to be strong for both of us. Instead of being sensitive, there was harshness in my voice as I told her the eye doctor's assessment was not concrete and not to fear the worst again. She just sat quietly in the car, crying. By the time we had returned to the farm, I felt awful. Not knowing what else to do, I called my Aunt Mary, a sister with whom Mom was close, and asked her to come and be with her. It was a devastating experience and it took me days to recover from the self-chastisement over my insensitivity. The memory of the incident struck a haunting cord of shame in me for a long while afterward.

Several days later, Mom developed problems seeing out of the right side of her eye. She couldn't focus her thoughts and became forgetful. We made another visit to her doctor in Madison and tests confirmed the cancer had metastasized to her brain. She had a few small spots causing swelling and applying pressure to the areas affecting her eyesight and memory. Medication easily kept the swelling under control, but not before Mom had a scary experience.

The day we first went to have Mom examined, they did a CAT scat of her head to determine the cause of her spells. We returned to Mark's house to wait for the results from the doctor. That evening he called to confirm they had found several tiny spots, but he was not overly concerned about treating them immediately. We scheduled an appointment for the next day.

Early the next morning, Mom started vomiting and was disoriented. Within an hour her symptoms had become worse. I called the doctor immediately and he advised me to bring her in. While it was difficult for me to see her this way, I knew it was even harder for

Mark and Kate because they had gone through similar experiences with Kate's father. We rallied as a family and all three of us went to the hospital with Mom. Her doctor was waiting for us and had a room all prepared to treat her. He was wonderful, tender and supportive, especially to Mom. She was terrified because she didn't understand what was happening to her. When she tried to speak, her words didn't make any sense. He kept reassuring her she would be okay and explained what was going on with her body. She was hospitalized for the night and by the next morning she was fine—just as the doctor had promised.

The incident had a powerful impact on me. It was the first time I had seen Mom so helpless and realized how dependent she had become on me. When the doctor had recommended Mom stay overnight in the hospital, I had driven back to Mark's house to get some things for both of us. Kate and Mark stayed with her. When I returned to her room, Kate mentioned Mom kept asking for me and was restless until I reappeared. It reminded me of when Dad was in the hospital and felt more comfortable when he knew Mom was with him. I felt as if I had become a safety net for her. We had become comrades. I was giving as much to her as she was to me. What a gift.

I also had an opportunity to experience the humanness of Mom's doctor. As we stood in the hall outside her room, I was surprised to hear him express concern that perhaps he could have prevented Mom's episode if he had acted sooner. Never had I heard such candor from a doctor about his decision-making process. He was expressing an accountability and responsibility toward her care that touched me deeply. Regardless of the choice he did or didn't make, I had great respect for his honesty with me. In that one moment, I felt as if the veil over the doctor-patient relationship had been removed and two individuals were sharing their realities and challenges of caring for someone who was ill. He was a gem in my eyes, and I was thankful he was Mom's doctor.

Something more important happened because of this experience. My brother Mark broke the barrier that prevented us from speaking with Mom about her dying. It was very brief, but potent. As much as I desired to talk with her about the possibility of her death, it was something she was not open to discussing. She was going to live and wanted only words of hope that she would. So I was surprised as I listened to Mark speak to her as she was lying in the hospital bed that morning confused because of the pressure on her brain. He was holding her hand as she mumbled about what was wrong with her. He leaned over and said in a tender voice, "Mom you're dying."

My immediate reaction inside to his words was anger. She was terrified. Why in the world was he telling her this? For a split second I wanted to yank him away and chastise his timing for saying such a thing. Yet I knew it was the truth and I had no control over what compelled him to speak it. He was innocent in his love for her and, even though I felt protective of her, she was as much his mother as she was mine. He was entitled to his own process of dealing with her illness. As I stood on the other side of the bed listening, I felt as if his words had spoken to her soul, even though she had no response. Perhaps he was the messenger for Mom that I had been for Dad. A seed from a loving son had been planted. Although she was afraid to admit it, it was finally out in the open.

Mark's gentle display of tenderness was endearing to observe. He was so different from my other three brothers. He never got obsessed with the hunting scene and that set him apart from the others. He was more soft-spoken and, like the rest of us, concealed his emotions. His qualities were similar to Mom's. He had only been fourteen when I'd left home and we'd only seen each other periodically through the years. He was a good father to his kids and a loving husband. My frequent visits with Mom to Madison had allowed me to get to know him better and appreciate his tender heart. He was a good person and added a nice balance to the male dominance in our family.

I still felt disappointment over Mom's healings with Alex. It had felt so right for her to see him. I'd seen others cured through his work and felt she could be one of them. I'd pondered long and hard why some people were healed of their illnesses and others weren't. Why did miracles happen for some individuals and not for others? It was true even during the time when Jesus walked the earth. Where did belief come in, and was it the major factor?

Those healed by Jesus believed they could be. Some were healed just by touching his clothes. If Mom truly believed she could be healed of her cancer, would it happen? She and I had had many, many conversations since I'd been home about miracles and the healing power of God. We both professed to believe in miracles. I'd seen them happen in my life and had no difficulty calling them miracles. It was different for her. She wanted more physical proof.

There had been three incidents in her life that I could contribute to the saving grace of God. Newly married and pregnant with her first child, she was driving on a wintry road when she hit a patch of ice and lost control of her car. It flipped over. At that time cars did not have seatbelts. Yet both she and my unborn sister were unharmed.

When my brothers Johnny and Vernon were small Mom had found them pounding twenty-two gauge rifle bullets with a hammer in the driveway. The bullets had accidentally dropped out of Dad's truck and had gone unnoticed. It was late winter and there was a light coating of ice over the bullets. Mom found my brothers just in time since the hammer hits had fully exposed the unfired, fresh round of bullets. One more slam with the hammer and they could have discharged.

Years later, when John was a teenager, Dad had purchased a 50cc Suzuki motor bike to use getting back and forth to the fields. At that time it was permissible to drive bikes on the highway. One evening John went to a nearby fish hatchery to check on the trout population. On his way back to the farm, a drunk driver swerved over the center line and hit him. His instincts told him to swerve to the right just before impact. Although he was hospitalized, his injuries were minor. Each of these incidences could have been fatal if divine intervention hadn't occurred.

While Mom acknowledged my perspective, it was still just my perspective. What she believed was up to her. I once asked her what a true miracle would look like that would forever eliminate any doubt. She didn't know. Then I asked if God came to her in a dream and said she was cured of cancer, would she believe the dream? She said only if medical tests could prove it. Once again it all came back to her trust in the medical profession. Now they'd shown the cancer had spread to her brain. I wondered if she thought her trip to L.A. had been a waste of time.

Perhaps a physical healing was not her soul's intent. Maybe the importance of her journey was more emotional and spiritual. And maybe the tissue Alex had removed was blocked energy to facilitate greater healing at a higher level. Regardless, Mom chose to make the trip for whatever reasons. In the process she had found out my life wasn't as unstable as she had worried it might be, and that if she were to die, we would all be okay. That trip had been valuable to her. Physically she might not be getting stronger, but emotionally and spiritually she was growing.

Facing the actuality of Mom passing away had lost some of its sharpness. Being with her day in and day out was different from seeing Dad periodically when he was ill. That had been much more dramatic. There was a softness to her evolution. It reminded me of watching my younger brothers subtly transform from babies to little boys. It hadn't happened over night. Neither did her dying. The physical effects from her illness were minimal. Her hair was starting to grow back and she had not lost much weight. Aside from wearing a wig or a turban, she looked much the same externally. Inside, though, her spirit was weary. Caring for Dad so intensely when he was ill and now battling her own disease had taken its toll on her. I felt fortunate I was the one with her all the time. Since her life was ebbing ever so gradually, I found myself savoring moments I had once taken for granted: the sound of her laughter, how she took off her glasses to look at stitching on a piece of fabric, reading from her prayer book every morning. It had become such a rich experience.

When Dad was ill, Mom would sit with him for hours on the couch while he was sleeping, just stroking his feet. She told me nothing else mattered. She just wanted to spend as much time with him as possible. The same was now true for me. I would not have this opportunity again. Moments once chalked up as insignificant had become meaningful. Mom asked me on several occasions how I could put my life on hold to come and be with her. I told her, "This is my life. God sent me to be with you and this is my work now."

Several of my friends commented about my courage to give up everything to be with Mom. I didn't think of myself as being courageous; rather it felt like a gift that had been bestowed upon me. I had a feeling that no matter what else I might do in my life, nothing would be as poignant as this. Mom deserved to be lovingly cared for and to not be alone. By embracing the fragileness of dying and accepting the emotions it evoked in me, I had gained great insight about myself. No emotions would control my life ever again. What had been perceived as weaknesses had turned into strengths. I had become much stronger through Dad's dying and even more so through my process with Mom.

When I broke apart the dying experience into small increments, it was very basic. It became a day-to-day, moment-to-moment exchange of natural human interactions. It was more potent because delicate layers of vulnerability and fear were exposed. Through all the physical ups and downs and the emotional highs and lows, their illnesses had been precious lessons about living. I was given a chance to reassess my life, and what was truly important had become clear. As defenses were stripped away, I gained a greater understanding of how I'd developed my unique personality. I saw how many of my original belief systems, attitudes and ways of being originated from Mom and Dad, and this provided me the freedom to be in new ways. I had a chance to see how unfulfilled dreams create bitterness, anger and resentment. I understood Mom and Dad better and had greater compassion for them because I appreciated the choices they had made.

My greatest challenge was learning how to give love with no conditions attached. This had not been easy for me. I still felt some protective walls around my heart with Mom, although they were more penetrable as each day went by. She was a powerful teacher. It was not comfortable for either of us to accept love and nurturing from others. We both preferred to be the one giving. Hugs from her as a child had been infrequent and it was rare to hear her tell me, "I love you." It wasn't until I married that openly hugging others became less awkward. Our exchange of "I love you" started when I made the conscious choice to end each telephone conversation with these words. Now they were spoken easily between us. I could still feel my hesitancy to let her close physically. We hugged at night but it was difficult to sit during the day with my arms around her. I was getting better but it required a conscious thought to do so. I expected the next phase of her illness would blast away any remaining resistance and teach me the true meaning of "loving someone to death."

The winter had been long and an early spring was not in sight. My body had finally adjusted to the cold and I didn't have to wear long underwear all the time. The newness to being home had long worn off and the days had become more routine. I'd adapted to the frequent sightings of my siblings and really liked having my sister just down the road. Her home was a nice escape when I needed breathing room, and it provided stability. We continued to grow closer and I was enjoying getting to know her kids better.

My brother Johnny stopped by the house each morning on his way to the woods. It had become a ritual and I looked forward to his visits as much as Mom did. When he walked in the door, his first words were always, "What's happening?" He was quite a character. He would give the shirt off his back if you needed it and he and Dave always looked after the house when Mom and I were gone. Most of my interactions with him were done through teasing. He reminded me of a "Gentle Ben," rough on the exterior like Dad and mush inside. He always made me laugh and espoused the quirkiest of sayings. One of his favorites was, "It doesn't matter that the horse is blind, just keep loading the wagon." When we were growing up, his way of showing affection was punching me in the arm. I was close to him and Vernon as kids because we played sports together and they helped me hone my tomboy abilities. I liked him.

Several weeks had passed since Mom's hospitalization and the medication was keeping her from experiencing symptoms from the small lesions in her brain. She had been afraid a similar episode would occur, but with each passing day her concerns diminished. She had never mentioned what Mark said to her that day in the hospital and had not talked about dying at all. She was angry again. She believed the medical profession was in cahoots with the pharmaceutical companies and that they really had a cure for her cancer but just wanted everyone's money. This was not the first time she had expressed her anger about this; it had come up a lot after Dad died.

Her anger was tempered with a longing for more time to live. She often said, "I would be happy if I could have just two or three more years. Then I could do some of the things I've always wanted to do."

She had always desired to become more involved with the Rosary Society, a woman's group at her local church. I knew she would love to work a few days a week in some kind of capacity. She had always enjoyed bookkeeping. We had talked about her going one day a week to the local hospital to talk with other patients who were sick. That was not an option since she was upset with the doctors. That was where Dad had been told he had cancer and should go home to prepare to die. She was frustrated. She had never regained her strength since the hysterectomy and felt she was not capable of doing much. She was hesitant to drive the car because she was afraid she'd have problems seeing. Unless I could persuade her to visit someone or take her to church once a week, she confined herself to the house. With each passing day, I could see her becoming more entrenched in old habits and thought patterns.

A topic that had come up lately was what I would do when all of this was over. Several times Mom had asked about my plans, and it had been on my mind as well. Many nights I prayed for some kind of sign or indication of what was next. It had been a challenge not to go into fear. Having this time with Mom had been a gift to reconsider what that might look like. Having worked for other people all my life, I felt it was time to stretch my wings and risk doing something on my own. While Mom gave me a monthly stipend—one of her stipulations for my coming back—finances were still a concern since I had never anticipated being without a regular income for so long. When I had first moved back to Wisconsin, I had spent my evenings attempting to establish a network marketing business. But after a couple of months, it became clear it was impossible to devote the necessary focus to it and care for Mom at the same time. All I really knew was that I wanted to be able to incorporate my spirituality with a vocation.

I'd been contemplating how to help Mom feel she could still make a difference with her life, even if there were only a short time left. One night after one of our "what do you think you are going to do?" conversations, I was taking a bath. Suddenly the idea popped into my head to interview her. As my mind played with different scenarios, a broader picture appeared. If she weren't able to go to the people she desired to touch, why not visually take her to them. Filming her would be perfect.

That night I prayed for absolute proof I was being guided in this idea by a greater wisdom than mine. The next morning an old professor of mine came into my thoughts. He was an award-winning filmmaker whom I had not seen in fifteen years. Miraculously I still had his home phone number. Much to my surprise, he answered the phone and remembered me. He had met my parents a couple of times and had been to their farm once when he was working on a film. He remembered my father's outrageous nature and my mother's great cooking. Upon hearing about my desire to film Mom and create an uplifting and inspiring story about the gift of dying, he confirmed the idea was worthwhile and could be easily marketed. He was happy to help in any way to get me started. It was my sign.

The next morning, Mom gave me the perfect lead in to present the idea. She was sitting at the kitchen table drinking a blended drink of fresh fruit juices and I could tell something was on her mind. I asked what she was thinking. Turning to me, she said in a concerned voice, "Aren't you worried about what you are going to do down the road? Sabrina isn't going to be able to keep holding your job. You know you can always go back to nursing. Hospitals are always looking for good nurses. Do you have any idea what you will do?"

Oh how I loved God's timing. In the past I would have shared my concerns, but because of Mom's illness and her tendency to worry, I didn't want to create an additional burden for her. Turning to her I said, "Up until now, Mom, I really haven't had a clue. I've been trying to trust that if God paved the way for me to be with you, when the time is right, he'll open the next door. I have been praying about what that might look like and I think my prayers may have been answered in a way that could benefit both of us. You know how you have been wishing to live a couple more years so you could help other people? Well I think there is a way you can do that. How would you feel about letting me interview you on camera?"

Her mouth dropped open and her eyes became very wide and she said, "Exactly what do you mean?"

Mom had always lived a simple existence and saw herself as an ordinary farm wife. Having no college education, she felt she possessed no worldly knowledge or wisdom. I knew she was wondering what she could possibly have to offer with her limited perspective about life. Not wanting to overwhelm her with my idea, I paused to consider an appropriate way to paint a picture with which she might feel comfortable.

Looking at her, the words became clear in my mind. "Mom, there are a lot of people in the world who have cancer. Many of them are of your generation. They are scared, angry, frustrated and looking for hope. They are not that different from you. Whom can they turn to who might be able to understand their fears, their desires or let them know they are not alone? You could be their voice reaching out to be heard. I'd like to film you by asking questions about how you were raised, what it was like for you with Dad—as well as yourself—having cancer, your frustrations with the medical profession not having a cure for your or Dad's cancer, your struggle to find hope—things like that. We could film here at the farm in the security of your own home. You wouldn't have to go anywhere."

She was quiet for awhile and then said, "Susie, I've never been in front of a camera before. I'm not polished or someone important. Why would anyone listen to me?"

Reaching across the table, I held her hand and responded, "Mom, you are important. It's because you aren't a celebrity or someone accomplished in the world that you would appeal to the mass population. You are like them. You have feelings and thoughts like they have. You are facing challenges that many of them may be facing. They could relate to you because you are like them. You're a Midwest farm woman who cared for her husband when he was dying. In the adversity of that same storm, you are struggling with your own life now. You could provide insight to many women of your age, as well as to daughters who have mothers getting older. I think your 'common' qualities would be appealing. What if you could be a voice of inspiration that could touch just one heart and make a difference in one life in some way?"

The more I talked with her the more I felt the power of what could be possible with such a film. Yet I was cautious not to sound too pushy. I didn't want to force her into something she was uncomfortable doing.

Knowing Mom was not one to make quick decisions, I was prepared to wait for her to contemplate my proposal. I wanted her to come to her own decision and know in her heart that was what she wanted to do.

She had more questions. "What would you do with this film and where would you get the money to do it?"

"My initial thought is to have it aired on television and perhaps have a limited release in some movie theaters. That way the story could reach the greatest amount of people. They could watch in the privacy of their own home. I would also make it available to hospitals, schools and educational facilities as a teaching tool. I don't know how much it would cost to do because I haven't done any research. I know there has to be someone out there who would be happy to work on this kind of film for a minimal fee. I don't think it would be that expensive to find a camera crew and the money would come out of my pocket, not yours. I just trust everything would fall into place. Besides you know me and God…"

She smiled. "Yeah, I do know. I've watched you believe something will happen and it does. You're like your father in that way." She was quiet and then continued, "Do I have a choice in what you film? What if I don't like something I've said or your questions are too uncomfortable?"

I could detect a slight trepidation at the thought of perhaps being viewed by millions of people on television. "Not a problem at all, Mom. I promise we'll sit down and go over everything: the kinds of questions I'd ask, the type of shots, and so on. And I promise the film will maintain your sense of dignity and honor and present you in the most impeccable way. If you don't like something or the filming is too much for you, all you have to do is tell me. I give you my word. I'd like you to feel this is a tribute to who you are and a gift to the world. I respect you too much to ever do anything that would portray you in a negative or unkind light. You are my mother and I want you to feel proud about what is filmed and your participation."

She looked at her hands resting on the table and asked one last question. "When do you want to do this?"

"As soon as I can arrange a crew and make all the preparations. Probably in a month if you are up to it." My excitement grew at the prospect of her agreeing to the idea.

She surprised me with her response. "Okay, I'll do it. Just remember I've never done anything like this before and I can't promise that anything I say will be worth much."

In my heart I was hoping for a "yes" but I didn't expect it so quickly. "Thank you, thank you, thank you, God." I put my arms around her. "Mom, I really appreciate your willingness and courage to do this. I know how private a person you are and how difficult this has been for you. I also know your sensitivity about not having any hair. One day, wherever you are, you'll see the contribution you've made in a far greater way than you ever imagined."

Lying in bed, my mind was racing. I didn't know where to begin. There was so much to do to locate a film crew yet not let my care of Mom become lax. We had agreed to keep the project quiet from the rest of the family. I was not ready to deal with possible questions or distractions regarding the intent of the film, nor concern about Mom's frailness in participating in such an endeavor. Whether or not this was the wisest choice, we had made it mutually and it felt right. I had a tendency to rally when I had a specific goal before me, and I was excited by this challenge. I thought the project would be healthy for Mom. It would give her something to look forward to and allow her to focus on something other than being ill. Somehow I sensed this film wasn't just about benefiting other people. There was a gift in it for Mom, as well. Perhaps by talking about her life, the choices she had made and the things she had accomplished, she would realize how much of a difference she had made.

There was a big lesson in this for me, too. Eight months had passed since I'd been home, and I had to trust I would receive some direction regarding my return to the work force. It had been challenging to let go of knowing what that might be or when it would happen— especially with the uncertainty of Mom's condition. Finally I'd been given the first clue of future possibilities. There definitely is a timing to God's wisdom.

I admired Mom's courage not only in her willingness to be filmed, but also her trust in me. It was highly improbable she would ever see the finished product, and she knew that. Yet she agreed to go ahead anyway. She knew we thought and viewed things differently and also that I was prone to asking "deep" questions. She had not always been comfortable with my ability to engage her in a way that elicited tucked away emotions. Perhaps the real reason she agreed was because she felt it would help me get back on my feet. It was amazing to me the length parents would go to help their children. If that were true, it was an extraordinary act of loving on her part to consent. What a remarkable woman and what a blessing for me!

Chapter Twelve

The Unique and Winding Path To God

It was Mom's birthday. She was turning sixty-eight. It was also Easter, one of the holiest times of the year for me. I was in California and wouldn't be sharing the specialness of either one with her. My choice had been the result of considerable contemplation and much prayer.

Once a month my friend Jacque taught a spirituality class in San Diego and the classes for Easter and Christmas were especially meaningful. Since I hadn't been able to attend any of the classes because I was with Mom, my soul was hungry for refortification. Although tapes were sent to me on a regular basis, I missed the connection with my spiritual friends in this sacred way.

It had not been an easy decision. The fact that it was Mom's birthday—and probably her last—made the choice even harder. My intellect and sense of responsibility said to stay. My heart and soul spoke a different message. When I shared my turmoil with Mom, she encouraged me to take the trip. She had never wanted us to make a big deal over her birthday and so she said she would just as soon skip it this year. She had always been a little melancholy on her birthday with each passing year, and was more so with this one.

Physically she was still capable of taking care of herself. Her medication had prevented any further episodes like the one for which she had been hospitalized. We went over her medications and when to take them. Ann would be close by in case she needed anything. I would only be gone for four days. If I had felt my leaving would place her in any kind of jeopardy, I would not have left. The bottom line was that, as much as I loved my mother, God needed to come first for me. Even on her last birthday.

Mom had always been aware of the importance of my spiritual growth. When I had left the Catholic Church many years before, she had been upset and thought she had done something wrong to not anchor me more solidly in my connection with Catholicism. No matter how much I reassured her that my choice to leave had nothing to do with her, she still blamed herself. When she saw my approach to Dad's passing, she acknowledged that perhaps my wandering path hadn't been futile. Although she had come to accept my spirituality, in her eyes the Catholic Church was still "the true way" to God.

Once a week I took her to mass at the Catholic parish close to the farm. Each time we attended, old memories stirred inside. It was the church I had attended growing up, where I was taught Catechism, became confirmed and was married. It was where I first learned about God and where I became disillusioned with the Catholic religion. If I followed certain rules, I would be loved by God. But the only way to get there was through the Church. Fear rather than love was the predominant theme. There was the fear of hell, fear of the judgment day, fear of ever leaving the Catholic faith. I felt restricted rather than free in my expression of God.

Even though the services didn't fulfill me, I enjoyed the priest. He was a dynamic, crust-of-the-earth man who used to be an alcoholic and wasn't afraid to admit it. He was outspoken and witty and so different from the priest who had been the overseer of the parish when I was young. He preached in a simple way that was refreshing. There was a beauty to the rituals, the circular architectural structure and the stained glass windows of this particular church that I truly appreciated.

I had always been spiritual in a natural way. God wasn't complicated. I could easily feel him when I was sitting on the tractor to rake hay or walking in the woods. I could find him in the sunsets, listening to the cooing of the morning doves as they greeted the day, watching a newborn calf take its first breath of life or smelling the sweet fragrance of apple blossoms in the springtime. This was the miracle of life. It was simple. God was present in all things and everything was connected because of God. I knew the experience of God. Where I developed confusion was with intellectual ideology. As a young child, I had asked our elderly priest during Catechism to explain a story about Jesus. Although the meaning had been clear to my innocent mind, I became doubtful after listening to him. I was chastised for even questioning the Bible and learned quickly never to challenge his authority. I didn't realize the difference between the message and the messenger. The Priest was supposed to be the word of God, however what resulted was the beginning of an internal process of discovering who God was for me.

I had difficulty with the rules of the Catholic Church: their position on birth control, not attending church on Sunday constituting a mortal sin, priests not being able to marry and confessing my sins in a dark little closet to the same person who didn't honor my inquisitive nature. Church sermons were dissertations about the Old Testament with little relevance to how to incorporate God into my life. Many times after services I felt little connection to God, and no greater understanding of who God was. For a long time, I believed there was something wrong with me and felt guilty because weekly services became more of an obligation rather than a blessing. It had been my hunger to have a deeper, more intimate relationship with God that eventually caused me to leave the Catholic Church and structured religion. While I didn't know where my path would take me, it felt right in my heart to do so.

I explored Eastern beliefs, New Age philosophy, Native American spirituality and learned how to meditate. I even attended different denominations seeking to feel the oneness I believed could exist. There was a Unity Church in Seattle with which I felt an affinity because of their universal perspectives. I developed a friendship with the young minister whose spiritual search paralleled mine and for a time found spiritual satisfaction. Yet something was still missing. As odd as it may sound, my decision to leave this church centered around its not having any kneelers. A humbleness occurred when I was on my knees that created a stillness that allowed me to connect with God. I realized that not only was that feeling missing, but so was the sense that God existed inside me. Shortly thereafter, I left and continued on my search to find an internal connection. It was to happen in an extraordinary way.

Several years later, I left nursing and began working for a small television production company whose desire was to produce socially conscious programming. I began to feel my life was about to change dramatically. I was both nervous and excited. One night while praying in my apartment, I heard myself speak the following words: "Dear God, I desire to know you through the true intent of who you are without human interpretation. Send me a teacher without earthly bias who is pure and wise in the wisdom to elevate my soul to achieve a oneness with you as I have never known. Fill my hunger to live in union with you always. Amen."

I was surprised at the words that came out of my mouth because they felt as if they had power separate from me, almost as if someone else had said them. A strange sensation came over me and I became light-headed and peaceful.

Two days later, Sheila, a woman I had met through the production company, invited me to a small gathering of people for an evening of spiritual discussion. She later became a dear friend and one of my spiritual sisters. That night I met the teacher asked for in my prayers, whom I would lovingly come to call "Z." He was someone I would have never imagined in my wildest dreams.

It was also at this gathering that I had met Jacque, who would play an integral role in my relationship with "Z." Two months earlier, she'd had a profound spiritual experience. While she was in prayer, the face of Christ appeared before her. As his image became transfixed before her, out of the pupil of one of his eyes a beam of glistening white light pierced the center of her forehead. She said it had the impact of lightning and riveted throughout her entire body and left her weeping with joy. Shortly thereafter she began hearing profound wisdom about God through an internal dialogue. These were thoughts she had never had before during her religious upbringing. She later discovered that a great prophet, Zoroaster, who had lived in Persia, was communicating with her. He referred to himself as Zarathustra. Through her trust and love in God, she was asked to share this information in an unusual way.

That evening, along with about ten or fifteen other people, I participated in learning how this was to happen. It was one of the most remarkable moments I had ever experienced. In laymen's terms, one could refer to what occurred as "channeling." Going into a place of complete surrender, Jacque became the instrument for the wisdom of "Z." Later she became a powerful teacher in her own right.

In the living room of Sheila's home, an overwhelming, encompassing feeling of love embraced me in a way I had never felt before. As I looked into the eyes of this wondrous being, I sensed an instant recognition and connection to what gazed back at me. I immediately felt as if I were sitting with a very wise, very old, very holy, benevolent soul whom I dearly loved and trusted. There was no fear or trepidation whatsoever, only awe over the gift of being led to Sheila and what I found before me. Zarathustra only spoke for about an hour. He said he had come to "teach the teachers and to unteach in us what we knew about God." We were not there to learn about him, but about who we were as lights of God. We would come to know intimately God who lived inside ourselves and to have a rightful, pure relationship with him.

Thus began what would be ten years of teachings by him for those of us who had been led down this unusual path. Walking out of Sheila's house that evening, I knew my search to find God had ended and my understanding of God had begun.

I had never doubted or questioned the unique manner in which my prayer for a teacher had been answered. There was an absolute certainty that what I was being taught was true wisdom because of the place inside where it resonated so deeply. It felt as if my soul had been reawakened to the remembrance and pure connection to the divine. What developed was more of an experience of living God than an intellectual understanding. I felt as if I had returned to the innocence of my childhood relationship with that divine power.

Someone once asked Zarathustra why this spiritual knowledge couldn't be given in another way. His response was, "You would then have the tendency to worship the person giving it and make them the focus of your love and devotion, instead of God. Look at what history has done with all great teachers. They were placed on a pedestal and who they were was confused with what they came to teach. You cannot place a picture of me on your altar because I do not exist in physical form. You are left with what you have come to personally experience as God within yourself. It is far grander that you come to realize God within yourself than continually look to someone else to show you."

While this unique path was not for everyone, it was where my soul and heart had been led. I did not feel better than others because of how they had chosen to worship God since I believed many paths led to God. I had to find the way that honored my own soul. My upbringing in the Catholic Church had been a real blessing. It had provided a foundation to begin to know God. It had created a framework that became the catalyst to explore and expand a relationship that might not have happened if I had been content with Catholicism. It had given me a greater appreciation and understanding of how other people worshipped. I had great respect for them all and saw each as a vehicle to the same place.

I'd had the opportunity to participate in prayer with indigenous chiefs around a sacred fire, with Hindu holy men in their temples, with Jewish rabbis in their synagogues and with Lutheran ministers and other leaders of different faiths. While the style might vary, I found the intent was the same. Members of each faith came together with a prayerful heart to give honor to God and unite in a place of oneness. God was God, no matter what language one spoke or what ceremonies were performed. We all prayed to the same God, regardless of what that was called.

From time to time I have been drawn to sit in an empty church feeling great love emanating inside the structure. Years of silent, genuine prayers by troubled and joyous hearts joined there for a moment in time by a common love. I had yet to find a church that incorporated my unique beliefs, but I didn't feel any less connected to God because of that. Nor did I feel the manner in which I prayed or gave praise to God made me less worthy of his love, guidance and acceptance. All individuals should be allowed to worship in the way that best honored their beliefs and styles. There was no right way or one faith that was superior to any other. At the core of our souls, we are all one.

My constant connection to God was supported by creating sacred places in my dwelling. During my childhood, a crucifix had hung on the wall in the bedroom shared by my sisters. When I became divorced, objects that had special meaning were displayed throughout my bedroom: a pine cone, a feather and my rosary were special items that created a closer feeling with God. Eventually my treasures adorned a specific corner of the room that became an altar where I prayed. When I walked into my bedroom it had the ambiance of a holy sanctuary. I had brought God to me. Before I went to bed, I lit a candle and got down on my knees to pray. And during the day, if something were troubling me or I was seeking guidance, I did the same thing. When I traveled, a mini altar of sacred objects came with me. I was no longer searching for an external place to connect with God because I had come to know and trust that his light existed within me.

Mom and I had many discussions about God, especially after I moved back with her. One night after the funeral of Dad's brother (who was not Catholic), Mom had wondered where his soul would go. She also wondered if Dad had ended up in heaven. We were sitting in the living room in our usual places—she on the couch and I in a reclining rocker next to it.

Turning to her I asked, "Mom don't you think in the end all souls rejoin God, regardless of their religious preference?"

She was quiet and said, "I don't know. I've always been taught that the Catholic Church is the true way to God."

I responded, "Well, look at Dad's parents. They weren't Catholic and neither was he initially. Do you think because he took a vow to practice the Catholic faith and his style of worship changed just a little, he or his parents were less worthy to enter heaven?"

She looked out the window and seemed to be struggling with an answer. After a few minutes she said, "I don't know. I hope that would be the case. I don't know if I know anything anymore. I want to believe that is true."

Since there was absolutely no question in my mind, I decided to give her one of my analogies. "Mom, imagine you are going out to look for a car. There are car lots filled with all different brands: Fords, Chevrolets, Mercedes, and so on. Is there one vehicle that would be more right than the other one?"

She didn't answer, so I continued. "No. You would choose one that appealed to your taste. Perhaps it would be the color, or the look or how it drove. Or maybe the brand of car your parents always drove. It is not different with respect to one's preference for how to worship God. Your mother and father chose the Catholic Church as their vehicle to reach God. That's how you were brought up and that's how you taught us kids. Someone else has chosen the Baptist faith or Methodist or Mormon as their vehicle. They are all just vehicles. One isn't better than the other. It's just a matter of preference."

She chuckled. Smiling, she turned to me and said, "I understand your point of view and I know you look at things differently than I do. It's just hard at this point in my life to question what I've been taught. It's too scary for me and I just have to trust in my own beliefs. I hope God is the way you say and maybe one day I'll be smiling down at you because you were right."

I would not have been able to sustain this journey with both Mom and Dad were it not for my spirituality. It was where I drew strength, comfort and understanding. It formed the basis for my views about dying because I believed we were all spiritual beings first before we took human form. If we originated from God, then we must return to God. If God were truly beauty, love and acceptance, then it made sense to me our souls joined with the same at the completion of this earthly adventure. If I looked to God in living it seemed natural to look to God in dying, because they were one and the same. It was the natural cycle of life. I would never really lose my parents to death because there was a greater Mother/Father to whom I was connected, and I benefited from the best of both worlds.

In spite of my spirituality, it had been difficult losing Dad and watching Mom's health deteriorate before me. What eased my pain was knowing I would never lose them nor my relationship with them. It would just be in a different way.

Even though I did not attach myself to any particular religious affiliation, I garnered strength from the spirituality classes and the wisdom it had afforded me. There was a congregation, so to speak, of individuals who faithfully participated each month and who provided support to each other on a frequent basis. We prayed together, laughed together and spent time together. We just didn't collectively refer to our affiliation as any kind of church. We were all individuals who were committed to a closer relationship with God.

Years before, I had told Mom about Zarathustra and about what I was learning. I had jetted home for a visit while on a business trip with the production company and she had mentioned there was something different about me. I didn't appear as restless nor as hard on myself and I didn't seem to be searching as much. We were sitting in the kitchen, our usual place where many of our in-depth conversations took place. I felt a nervousness to share about the unusual circumstance that was broadening my spiritual realms. I knew Mom had a tendency to worry about my unsettled life. It had been fifteen years since my divorce and I had not remarried. From time to time, Mom would express concern about my being alone and living so far away.

I had been attending classes with Jacqueline and "Z" for two years and had kept this part of my life private from Mom as well as most of my family. To my surprise, she was inquisitive and had no judgment that I had gone off the deep end. She was skeptical yet open. She didn't discourage my participation, although she did ask me to remember my roots in the Catholic Church. While she didn't need to believe the way I did, it was my hope that one day she would be willing to meet "Z." Never did I think that really would occur.

Since returning to Wisconsin, I had maintained a regular dialogue with "Z" over the phone. Every couple of weeks, he provided spiritual counsel to assist with my many questions and concerns about caring for Mom. His loving guidance was the thread that allowed me to maintain a healthy balance in the constant flux of change. He always mentioned taking the focus off Mom's illness and looking for the joy. He inquired what I was learning about both my relationships with Mom and myself. He was the one who suggested I take Mom to Hawaii because of its innate healing energy. He had also encouraged me to take periodic breaks to sustain my own equilibrium and keep a fresh perspective. I had been given much insight about Mom through him. She was aware of our conversations and intuitively knew when I had spoken with "Z." When it felt appropriate and could benefit Mom, I shared his insights. However, much that was provided was for my own spiritual and personal growth. Underneath all his counsel, love was always the predominant factor that came through.

Mom met "Z" during our trip to L.A.. Two days after her last healing he held a class. I told her about it and asked if she would be okay by herself in our hotel suite. To my amazement, she asked if she could come along. I was shocked. I looked at her and said, "Mom are you sure you want to go? I'll only be gone for a few hours. I thought you might want to sleep or walk on the beach and be free of me."

She smiled and replied, "I'd like to. You don't mind, do you?"

With eyebrows raised and bulging eyes, I gasped. "Mind? I'd love for you to come. It would be really great."

Feeling like an excited little kid off to "show and tell," I escorted the treasure of my mother to the monthly gathering. Before we got there, I explained about the class and told her that if at any time she became uncomfortable to let me know and she could leave the room. The class was held in a small suite of buildings that used to be offices. The Church of Religious Science now occupied the space where our class was conducted.

I had a feeling of holiness the minute we walked into the room. In the front was a plexiglass podium surrounded by white burning candles and fresh bouquets of roses nestled among fragrant fern boughs. It looked like an altar. The soft music of monks chanting instilled the feeling that one was sitting in a sacred temple or church. About forty or fifty people were quietly gathered. The minute Sabrina saw us, she put Mom right next to her. On the other side of her was another of my friends, Samantha. Knowing she was in good hands, I sat in front of Mom.

Jacque entered, greeted everyone, asked us to stand and hold hands and led the group in prayer. I had known her for nine years and she had become a dear friend. We had traveled together to Brazil, India and Peru through her non-profit organization called Sacred Life. She had thick, long wavy black hair and had an exotic look about her. She had a beauty and radiance that was captivating, both in her physical appearance and within. But it was her passion for God that exuded beyond her outer beauty. She lived in Seattle and had two sons. In addition to her monthly classes, she had written two books, lectured and traveled abroad. She was an extraordinary woman whose commitment, dedication and service to God was unwavering.

Before every class, the room was blessed, followed by four hours of teaching, usually with a short break in between. The class was composed of a lecture, questions and a discussion. Each class always began with a prayer and ended with a period of reflection and silence. Jacque always taught the first half of class and Zarathustra the last.

The class couldn't have been more perfect for Mom. It centered around healing and miracles. At the end of the prayer, Jacque asked everyone to focus on the divine love of God and the naturalness of health. We were guided to open our hearts to feel the loving energy of the divine and with open palms to place our hands on the areas desiring to be healed. We were asked to hold with a prayer of gratitude the thought to be made well again. Since this was not a regular part of each class, I knew a greater power was at work.

Then Jacque began her teaching by saying, "Miracles are on the increase. We are living in the greatest decade in the history of humanity right now. The time from 1995 to 2005 will be looked back upon and seen as a great transformation, a spiritual awakening of a whole race of people. In the heralding of the time of miracles, it is because the belief and faith of people is increasing. We are learning the power of our thoughts can make us sick or make us well. We are growing in number in our belief and that is why there are so many more testimonials of healings and appearances of angels. As greater numbers believe, it creates a vortex of energy, a vibration to allow even more to happen." I began to wonder what was going through Mom's mind.

Jacque then talked about something I knew Mom had struggled with because of our many talks. She spoke about how God was in every one of us and, since that was so, the healing power of God also dwelled within each of us. I became concerned that Mom might feel Jacque had a New Age bent and was relieved when she talked about how Christ was at the center of her life. She went on to talk about Jesus and that his manner of teaching and ability to heal demonstrated we were all capable of doing the same because he, too, had existed as a human on this earth.

Toward the end of Jacque's portion of the class, the topic arose about how other cultures and people of different religious beliefs viewed the afterlife. Through internal dialogues with Zarathustra, Jacque had asked how different beliefs were accommodated in that realm. He explained to her that it had to do with one's belief that formed the framework for how the person experienced life. Because that belief is still held at one's death—whether it be the belief in Jesus Christ, Krishna or in the tall grasses of the Native American culture—that is what one will experience. While the image of God may be different in various cultures, the oneness is the same. When they cross over from the physical world to the spiritual world, all people experience a connection with loved ones who have gone before them. Someone's mother, father or brother may greet them as their soul walks "into the light." Then that soul reviews its life with the God of their belief. If someone believes in Jesus, Mohammed or Allah, then that is with whom they interact.

He went on to tell her that however great one can imagine the beauty, joy and love of the spiritual world to be, that is what their soul will encounter. An analogy of an elevator was given. If you rode the elevator upward and the door opened to angels and harps playing, and that is what you perceived heaven to be, you would exit there. If you believed there was more, you would keep going until the door opened to your image. What is most important is to be vast in one's perception of heaven and to feel worthy of the grandest expression of God's kingdom.

I sat in amazement at this information and my thoughts went to Dad. He was probably having a blast in the deer hunting grounds he found in heaven. The image of him telling jokes to St. Peter immediately popped into my mind and I found myself smiling at the thought of him slapping his knee and stirring quite a commotion with the guardian of those gates. I had no doubt that however he perceived and encountered heaven, it was wonderful for him.

Jacque finished her portion of the class and we broke to stretch our legs and take a bathroom break. Turning around in my chair, I found Mom sitting content in conversation with Sabrina and Samantha. There was a glow on her face and her eyes sparkled. When I inquired if she wanted to leave, she said "No." She was happy to stay in her chair and was soon surrounded by several of my other friends who knew she was my mother.

Samantha stepped outside the room with me and said, "Your Mom is doing fine. I sense her soul is grasping a great deal of information, even though her mind may think she isn't. Don't worry about her. She is doing great. The attention she is getting is good for her. No matter what may happen with her, she is healing a lot inside. You have a wonderful mother. She is very sweet and has such a gentle nature to her. I bet she really appreciates you."

I hugged Samantha and was comforted by her words. Being so entrenched in Mom's process, it was wonderful to have the perspective of a trusted friend.

I was really curious how Mom would respond to the experience of meeting "Z" and the process by which he appeared. As I walked back inside the room, I looked toward her. She was chatting away as if talking with old friends. Samantha and Sabrina had resumed their places next to Mom, eliminating the opportunity to sit next to her, so I returned to the chair in front of her.

Jacqueline appeared wearing a white, silk tunic—the outfit she always wore out of respect and reverence to "Z" and what he represented. She sat on several pillows in a chair covered with white silk cloth, and crossed her legs. White socks covered her feet. Her long black hair was pulled back and secured with a white elastic band. Her lipstick had been removed. She closed her eyes and began to pray as she went through a ritual of blessing her body. There was complete silence in the room. When she had completed her own surrender to the divine, her head dropped forward. Moments passed as the rhythm of her breath shifted to allow the energy of Zarathustra to come forward. A powerful inhale of breath was heard as "Z" entered Jacqueline's body.

(To make for easier understanding, I will now refer to all movements in the body as Zarathustra.) His head moved upward and his chest expanded outward. His eyes slowly opened as he began to focus in the room. Many times a tear would roll down his cheek when he first blinked. He extended his arms outward and drew them toward his body in a ceremonial fashion as he went through his own ritual of blessing the body and God. He began to look around the room, and tenderly greeted each person with focus and esteem, transmitting the depth and sweetness of wisdom through his eyes. The room took on a different feeling, with a profound, all-encompassing peacefulness and love.

When he finished acknowledging everyone in silence, he spoke. There was a slight brogue to his voice, as if he originated from the Far East. His presence had a kingly quality that commanded reverence and respect. He spoke with a powerful knowingness. At times he displayed a playful nature that gave a lighthearted gentleness to his teachings. He was always loving, inspirational and empowering. He did not engage in fear and damnation.

As he extended his arms outward to the group he said, "Unto you I am here from the light of God of you, to elevate unto you and render you a greater peace. I wish to make manifest in this world wellness, joy and love. All things that are a burden unto your heart, you may leave here with me. There are some of you who have come who have an illness that worries your mind. When we have concluded this day, I will render a blessing. Those of you who, indeed, know in your heart I am communing with you, come and give unto me your illness, your worries, your concern. Leave it here this day. For if not now, when? If not here, where? And I will take it from you if you will offer it."

He then looked at me and smiled. "Be unto you, your mother is here."

I smiled, bowed my head and nodded "yes."

He turned his eyes toward Mom and addressed her. I became very focused wanting to hear every word of his message. He extended his head forward and smiled before he spoke. "Unto you woman, you have already begun to heal on many levels of yourself. You are more alive in all of your life since you have been very young. You have a great more to do in your life. Your progress that is healed in states of your mind and consciousness is assisting greatly all action you are taking to render your body to match your growth. There is a woman that is in angel form now who loves you greatly. You know her. (He was speaking of her best friend Ann, who had died the previous Christmas.) You do not have to join her. Stay. Continue to heal. Amen unto you."

I was deeply honored he had spoken to Mom and was pleased by his words. I yearned to know what was going through her mind. It would have been beyond words to describe how long I had wanted to share this experience with her, and now I finally had. For years I had felt alone on my spiritual path—continually committed to it, yet never knowing where it would take me. Time and time again, I had attempted to explain my journey to Mom when she questioned why I had needed to leave the Catholic faith. Regardless of what her feelings were about the teachings, for one moment she had stepped into my world to experience a broader perspective of her own self as well as mine. She had courage and was willing to walk into that room because I was her daughter. Otherwise she would never have come. Tears rolled down my cheeks as I felt the depth of her love for me.

Zarathustra spoke directly with several other people. One woman in particular must have had family members who had died. His message had great pertinence to my own life. Many times when "Z" addressed someone's concerns or questions, he created a teaching around the issue. He spoke tenderly. "Your loved ones are very close. In the first four days of someone's passing, loved ones are often around. It is called a period of grace where they are burdened and it is hard to feel the loss of the grief of the ones left in form. What is important to know is that they are communing, they are in peace. Often they have a sense of relief. They are no longer in a physical body that may have been diseased or had an ailment. They are still imaging the ethereal body to match. During this time they are often sending great communications of love, and of their presence in particular. It is within their realm to communicate and they do so to many when there are things to find, objects of the one who has departed, and when they wish you to know certain things. In that period of grace, communication is easier during the first four days after crossing.

"After such time they can still communicate with you. Your receptivity is much greater in dream time. In your dream time, you are less of this physical world and are in an alpha space and are in high receptivity and many times out of your body so they can communicate with you and you with them. It is easier for them to send the thought in dream time to give you peace that they are not far. The technique to communicate ... I will teach you. If you have an object that has their vibration, you can hold it but you will then place it in your mind. Your mind is like a projector, you hold a thought and you send an image. That is how they come in on your thought waves. If you do this, then their presence and their communing with you can be known. That is the strongest and highest way I can share with you. And you must do this. Once you start sending the thought to them, then you must hold the place in your mind where you are receiving. Your imagination is both a screen that you put an image on and where you receive an image from. When your soul wants to communicate to you, your soul will place the image on your psyche, the imagination part of your mind. When you are receiving, you receive the same."

Halfway through the class he said something that was addressed to everyone, but could have been directed specifically to Mom and again applied to me. "Many people have a destiny to heal and be healers. I will tell you a great and beautiful truth. Every individual is capable of healing themselves and another. Everyone. Concentration and focus. Discipline yourselves to focus upon God and love and joy and all else will follow."

At moments I still doubted my capacity to heal because I got caught in thinking it was I who was doing it, rather than God working through me. The focus was on my ability rather than God's. If I had these doubts despite the spiritual support to remind me differently, what must it be for Mom? The teaching reminded me to be more gentle in my approach with her as a mother would be with a child and to be more honoring of how far she had come.

My heart felt full and my soul well fed. I prayed that Mom was benefiting from being at the class. As Zarathustra gazed upon the room, the presence of God felt even more powerful than when the class had begun. With a tenderness in his voice he continued, "Many of you who are beyond those in this room feel life-weary and carry the scars of living in the world that has been forgotten. Let your scars transform into compassion and your voice fill the air with laughter because a new era is coming and you are part of it. In the future there will not be those whose hearts feel as you do and all the others who are gathered here and around this world relate to this very well. Soon the place of your dreams will be the place of your dwelling. Amen."

As the class drew to a close he addressed me. "For your mother, create what my woman has taught of a little container that you can put fresh soil from the earth. Better if you go where there is a wondrous old tree. Pray to the tree and ask for part of its domain. Take something and give it back to the earth and take some earth and smell it frequently. It will put back into your field. It is another form of cleansing. Place it in a container where your feet can touch upon it frequently. Take a stone and place it in each corner so the vibration comes up through your feet. For those of you who know people who have had therapy that is called chemotherapy, have them do this and run the energy into that soil or into the earth. Go barefoot. Put it back in the earth, like a lightning rod. What is excess release it and draw in fresh. The soil you would harvest you must put back frequently and put fresh anew. When you do not have your feet upon it or your inhaling of it, set it back out so the moonlight, the stars, the sun refortify the life force for the medicine it gives you. For this is what you are made up of physically. That is your physical part. As you have learned about color, allow yourself to look at all of the spectrums of earth. It is important to keep you also balanced and well.

"The high frequency colors that many of you have been drawn to of the lavenders, the whites, the blues and pinks are very beautiful, but you are also more than spirit. You are human. The browns, the reds, the colors of earth balance your field. As you become more and more awakened, your physical body is also honored to accommodate your dwelling place of God's vibration. There are those who have very dedicated, very high minds, but they have body problems. The body wasn't addressed. They were only thinking of their spirit. But you see the earth is spiritual. Right? We are all one. The earth is spiritual. Love your planet. Connect with it so you can stay on it. Now ... that which is the light of God, that which is called many things by many people, is the Infinite and the Divine that is expressed in honor of this day. Blessed be you who have come to know and remember. Blessed be unto you who have believed before this day so that this day could be. And all there is that will come because you dreamed it and believed it into being. It is unto this light that is all things. So be it. And so it is this day. Amen."

As Zarathustra finished his prayer, he closed his eyes and stretched his arms outward and upward, drawing his hands together as he blessed us. He emitted a humming tone, In the quietness of his ritual for departing, a long, deep sigh could be heard as the energy of his presence was released from the body. His head dropped to his chest and moments passed before the energy of Jacque's life reentered her body. As her life force returned, she immediately took a deep breath, almost like a gasp, and asked for a glass of water. She needed assistance in moving her legs that had become stationery for the two-hour portion of Z's teachings. She had become conditioned to this process and could acclimate to her body quickly. Although she had no conscious remembrance of the information taught, it permeated her field upon return. Since she was in continual dialogue with Zarathustra internally, she received the teachings also.

After Jacque left the room, I was beyond curious to find out how Mom was doing. As I turned around in the chair, she was smiling. Sabrina and Samantha were still sitting next to her and Samantha winked at me with a twinkle in her eyes. People were slow to leave so many of my friends had a chance to meet her. I was sure she must be tired, but to my surprise she was not. As we left the class arm-in-arm, we were both quiet. Driving back to the hotel, I asked Mom what she thought and if she remembered what Z had said to her. She told me there was a lot to reflect upon and she wanted to sit with it all for awhile. She inquired how "Z" knew about her friend Ann, and thought that somehow I had told him.

I turned to her and smiled. " Mom, I have been alone with you ever since we came to Los Angeles. How would I have told Zarathustra? Do you think I called his 800 number in the ether and spoke to him? Sorry, Mom, he doesn't have one, at least not through the telephone company. I didn't even know you were going to the class myself so I couldn't have tipped him off, even if I had wanted to."

"Then how did he know?"

"God."

She grinned at me. Many times in the past she had asked how I knew something. I would always reply, "God told me." That response had always brought a chuckle, and she probably thought I was kidding. But I wasn't.

There is a sacredness about one's experience in a holy setting, whether it be attending an orthodox church service, sitting around a sacred fire with indigenous chiefs or praying privately before going to bed. In the inner sanctuary of a person's heart and soul, God is present. If Mom were never to share about her participation in class, it wouldn't matter to me. Through a fleeting moment in time, we shared the silence of a mother and daughter, connected by the bond of love and respect, regardless of our different beliefs. She had crossed the threshold into my world and I felt honored. My dream had been fulfilled. She would forever carry a spark of my own soul joined together by our individual love of God.

Chapter Thirteen
You Are So Beautiful Without Your Hair

My plans for the movie were arranged. We would be filming Mom for three days. A dear friend of mine, Tom, who lived in Los Angeles and worked in the entertainment industry, had referred me to a Hollywood producer who lived in Wisconsin. Before our initial contact, I had been warned that, depending on my approach, he would either lend his total support or wouldn't want to be bothered. My experience in marketing had taught me the first five minutes in the sale of any idea or product is crucial. If interest can't be engaged in that brief period, the sale is usually lost. My intent this time was not to "sell" a project, but rather "inspire" someone to help me. Making cold calls and meeting individuals through the phone was nothing new for me. I had done hundreds of them. This time more was at stake. Rather than marketing someone else's endeavor, I felt I was marketing God's.

My weakest link was that I had never produced a documentary film. Since my childhood, I had had a fascination with taking pictures. Dad had an old Kodak box camera that I used for my 4-H projects and after that I had a cheap instamatic. When I was married, my husband bought me a good quality Canon that became a cherished friend. I learned the art of taking and developing pictures through a class in college. The same professor who produced documentary films also taught photography. He was with the School of Agriculture and only students with that major were allowed. I was close to graduating and was pursuing joining the Peace Corps because I wanted to combine my nursing skills, my love of photography and travel. I was hoping to be sent to Africa. The day I went to meet him to plead my case, only one space was left in his class. To my amazement, he accepted me.

At one point in my college education, I had considered going into journalism. I had already invested three years in nursing school by then and wasn't willing to start in a new direction. Although I chose not to go into the Peace Corps, photography remained a love. My photography class taught me I had a good eye for capturing an image through the camera lens. My experience with the television production company left me with knowledge about producing. What was lacking in my technical experience for making a documentary film was balanced by my personal relationship with the topic. I intimately knew and was living the story. I was clear about the feel of the film and the shots I wanted and just needed the people who could provide the technical support.

I trusted the right people would come along. Tom had also referred me to several people in Los Angeles. Although they were interested in the project, their cost was too high. Somehow Bruce, the contact in Wisconsin, felt like the right one. The only hurdle was persuading him to assist my cause. While I preferred to meet someone in person to establish whether they were a fit for working together, that wasn't possible with him. His schedule was hectic and left no room for meeting, so everything had to be done by phone.

The night I called Bruce, a gruff voice greeted me. He wanted to know why I was calling and who referred me. Tom's name softened his tone somewhat, but I could tell he was feeling put upon. He was a good interviewer. He wanted to know my background in producing, the vision of my film, my target audience and the budget. Mostly he inquired what I wanted from him. The longer we talked, the more my heart sank. I was sure he was going to tell me he didn't want to be bothered. Even though I had pitched many projects and ideas for other people, engaging someone's support for my own was a whole different ball game. What I didn't realize during our conversation was the impression my determination and tenacity was making on Bruce.

What turned the tide in my favor was when I said to him, "Bruce, whether you are the person to help me or not, all I know and trust is that this project is being divinely guided by God. By all appearances, I am a novice in producing this documentary. But what I do have is the heart and spirit of it. What I am looking for is someone who comes from the same place inside. For Tom to refer your name means to me you are a man with a kindred soul. Your 'no' to me is as good as a 'yes' because, if you aren't the person, it wouldn't serve your time or mine."

He was quiet for a moment and then said, "I get asked by a lot of people to help them. Most are only interested in their own gain. I like your honesty and guts. Fax me your story line and I'll look at it. I can't promise what I can do, but at least I'll give it some consideration."

Two days later he put me in touch with one of his associates, Paul, who turned out to be a blessing and was invaluable in arranging a crew and handling all the details. Bruce remained in the background and proved to be a great mentor. He died unexpectedly many months later and I was saddened he would never see the fruits from his acts of kindness toward me. He will forever hold a special place in my heart.

It was a challenge to coordinate the shoot while staying focused on Mom's needs. Her physical body was beginning to show the effects of the cancer. She was thinner, but not emaciated in appearance as Dad had been. Small lumps had started to develop on her chest that looked like cysts. Her doctor was not concerned about them. Early on, a lump grew on her right upper arm that looked like a purple boil and she had had it removed. At the time when it was done, the doctors had difficulty stopping the bleeding and she ended up needing a transfusion. She was at too much risk to have it removed again. It had grown considerably since then and was about the size of a golf ball. It looked awful. She was extremely self-conscious about its appearance and always kept it covered.

Her appetite was poor. We seemed to go in spells of finding something that appealed to her, only to have it change the next week. She had become like Dad. She didn't care for the food I fixed her. Sometimes I felt I was feeding a child. I had to bargain with her to get her to eat. She was willing to compromise with Ensure for smaller portions of food. I was adamant with her about the need to nourish her body to keep up her strength. She continually tested my limits to see how far I was willing to go. If she had her way, she wouldn't eat at all. One day she told me I was like a dictator. "But a good dictator," she added and smiled.

I wasn't quite sure how she meant the remark so I asked, "Mom, do you feel I am being too forceful or unreasonable with you?"

She looked at me and replied, "No. You push me but I need that. You are only doing what is best for me. You know if you let me have my way, I wouldn't care if I ate at all."

My heart was torn many times about being a task master. I didn't want to dictate her every move or define a rightful way for her to walk through this. It would be so much easier if she hadn't asked me early on to be strong for her. Until she told me she didn't want to keep living, I'd honor her request and hold the space of hope and encouragement.

Mom's anger had diminished and she had become less talkative. Her retreating inside caused me to feel a void between us. It made me a little tentative about how she was going to respond for the filming. I told her a week ahead that I had scheduled a film crew but I purposely held off from telling her sooner to alleviate any stress about it. As much as it felt right to be doing this shoot, I had some hesitancy about her feeling pressured. When I informed her the day the crew was coming she asked, "Do I have to do it?"

I was a little taken back by her response but not totally surprised. Almost two months had passed since I had first approached her with the idea. She had had a lot of time to ponder her participation. It was clear she was in a different space now and less prone to sharing. I wanted to respect the transition she was going through, yet did not want to abandon the project. It felt like treading on thin ice with the possibility she would not be willing to go ahead with the filming.

Sensing there was a fine line between supporting and pushing her not to back out, I inquired what she was feeling. "Mom, does your question have to do with not physically feeling up to it or just being afraid?"

She was sitting on the couch staring out the window. I was in a reclining chair at the opposite end of her. The physical space between us mirrored the emotional distance that had begun to develop. She was pulling back and somehow I needed to respect that. She kept looking straight ahead and spoke softly, "I don't feel whatever I say will matter. If there isn't any hope for me how could I give any to someone else?"

Lately her sense of defeat had become more prevalent. I was quiet pondering the precariousness of the situation. If doubt were the main reason for her hesitancy there was room to bargain. If she physically wasn't up to it, I needed to consider the toll filming could have on her. I took a deep breath and said, "Mom, I don't want to push you into doing this if you really don't want to. I will respect your decision if you tell me it would be too hard on you. I believe your sharing about your life and your struggles would be helpful to others. And I think it would be fun. You can be a shining star. You can have your moment in the sun to say whatever you want as long as your don't tell why my nose has this funny flip at the end of it."

She laughed. Until our school district had been consolidated, we would walk to school a little less than a mile from the farm. During the winter my nose would get cold, causing it to run. I never seemed to have a hanky or Kleenex with me, so I would take the palm of my mitten and wipe my nose in an upward motion. As I got older and became more conscious about my looks, the curvature seemed more apparent. I would tease Mom my nose had this flip because she subjected us to such brutal winters without any Kleenex in our pockets.

My comment at least lightened the heaviness she was feeling. She was quiet for a few moments before she spoke again. "Would you be really hurt if I didn't do it?"

I paused before I answered. I wanted to be truthful but not cause her to feel obligated. "I wouldn't be hurt Mom, just disappointed.

And not for me but for you and others. You see, Mom, in many ways it would be easy to abort this shoot. All it requires is canceling the crew. Not much money will have come out of my pocket and no harm will have been caused. There is more at stake to do the filming. I felt it could be a way for you to give back to society because you kept telling me you wanted that. I believe with my whole heart God is offering you a great gift. It's no accident I dabbled in photography as a child and worked for a production company. Yet, truthfully, I have never done this kind of thing before. I am being stretched and challenged to trust that if I don't know what I am doing, at least God does. If I let myself be afraid or doubt, I will never know what good all this might serve. I think you and I would both lose out and maybe also that one other person who would see this and benefit. Something grander seems to be in place here. That is why I would be disappointed. I will accept whatever answer you give me. The only thing I want you to consider is this. You wouldn't be saying 'no' to me, but I think you would be saying 'no' to God. Only you know deep inside the reason you are hesitant. All I ask is that you honor what is really true for you about being filmed. Don't let my personal feelings influence your choice. That isn't what is important here. You and your health are the priority. And I really mean that with all my heart."

She was quiet and I sensed she wanted to be alone to think. Getting up from the chair, I gave her a hug and left the room to sit on the swing outside.

When I was young, Dad had built a swing for us. The poles to hold it were as large and as high as telephone poles. I loved to swing on it because it made me feel I could touch the sky. It had since been replaced by a much smaller double swing that was attached between the clothesline poles. It was my favorite place to hang out. The motion of the swing reminded me of being rocked in a rocking chair as a child. It was comforting and peaceful. The warmth of the sun felt good. Small shoots on the trees were beginning to bud. It was a welcome relief from the extreme winter now behind us. The air smelled fresh and was soothing to my body. I drew in a deep breath, allowing the sensation of the new season to engulf me. A flock of red-wing blackbirds perched in the huge balsam tree behind me. As much as Dad had seen them as a nuisance because they scared away the other birds, to me the beauty of their unique song always signaled closure of another school year and the start of carefree adventures.

I closed my eyes and thought about Mom. Had I been too confronting and pushy? Was I being manipulative? Was filming her more in my own interest than hers? When this idea had first surfaced, it seemed like the Universe had opened the gates for it to happen. I felt it would be so freeing for her soul. It was only natural for her to be nervous. I would be. Maybe I was just expecting too much of her. After all, she had the right to the privacy of her own illness. Okay God, I thought, it's in your hands. Help me not to hold disappointment if she backs out.

I sat for a little while longer, alone with my thoughts, basking in the fresh air. I watched a robin picking up twigs to build its little palace for the yearly ritual of raising its young. Mom had always been excited by her first sighting of a robin because that meant garden and flower planting were right around the corner. With that came freedom from the doldrums of being cooped up in the house all winter. It also meant she could delegate more household chores to the young women in the family who would be out of school for the summer. She could spend more time doing what she loved rather than what she had to do.

A gust of wind snatched a few remaining dead leaves that had survived the winter from the tree above me and they drifted to the ground. I decided to go back inside. I didn't want Mom to think I was brooding over our conversation.

She was curled up on the couch with a blanket around her. I asked if she needed anything and she said, "No."

I sat back on the reclining chair that had become my space. We were both quiet. I turned to her and said, "Mom, I apologize if I seemed pushy or manipulative about you doing the film. I am really okay if you don't want to."

She looked back at me, as she nestled among her blankets. "You weren't. But you sure are persuasive with your words. I made you a promise that I would do this and I am going to keep my word. But if I get too tired and want you to stop, promise me you will."

Our eyes met and held a gaze. I smiled at her and replied, "I promise. You are really courageous for letting me film you, Mom. I won't go back on my word. I love you."

Her eyes were closed now but I heard back, "I love you, too."

I had never taken on an endeavor like this before by myself, especially one for which I had to wear all the hats. It was a crash course in stepping up to the helm and relying on my intuition and trust. I loved the challenge. My finances were minimal. Two dear friends had given me some money, another provided me with a small loan and the rest was coming out of my pocket. It was enough to get me through the first phase. My crew was not made of award-winning film makers. They were young in their craft, a few years out of college. It was the best I could do within the time and finances. Paul had contacts with the University of Wisconsin for use of their equipment. I was able to get a discount on film stock through friends in L.A.. I decided to shoot in sixteen millimeter film because I had been told the image would be better. It was more cumbersome to set up each shot but it afforded the option of going for both theatrical and television release. Much thought went into assessing the quantity of rolls needed because the film was expensive. My gut feeling differed from Paul's professional opinion. He thought three hours worth of film was plenty. I ordered enough for six.

In spite of the endless decisions that needed to be made, every step fell in place. In the bigger scheme of things, this project was quite insignificant. It was not a multi-million dollar production and I was not accountable to many people for their investments. Because my intent was not to be a money-making venture, it was relatively risk-free. Yet in my little world it was very important. By Mom's willingness to let me capitalize on her seeming misfortune, other people's lives might benefit. More importantly, she could benefit. All I could do was trust. Trust that I would be guided to act on the inspiration of this idea. Little did I know how much the next three days would test me.

It was midnight and I could not sleep. My mind was whirling from reassessing all the details for tomorrow's shoot. There was no room for doubt or trepidation. I had done my homework in creating a story line, preparing questions to ask Mom, establishing the nature of shots and trying to assess any glitches that could occur. My organizational skills had been put to good use. A three-ring binder contained all my research in setting everything up, a thorough outline for the next three days, as well as special proverbs that kept me focused and inspired. I had come to rely upon it so much it felt like a bible.

My major focus the day before the filming had been on apprising Mom of what to expect, making sure she felt comfortable and secure about the invasion of her privacy. We'd gone over the basic nature of the questions and she knew she had the right not to share anything she felt was too intrusive. I did not want her to be caught by the element of unknowing that could leave her feeling vulnerable. I had two surprises for her, though. I had asked one of Mom's sisters, Mary, and a mutual friend, Jerry, to stop by on the last day of our filming. Several years before, Jerry's husband had had a near-death experience that he had shared in a letter to her before he died. Jerry had been a supportive friend to Mom since Dad's passage and they had spoken about the afterlife. The prospect of filming these three women talking together about death appealed to me.

My other surprise was creating a feeling of great nervousness for me. Sensing Mom's birthday would be her last, I was in a quandary about what to give her. Nothing appealed to my heart. Material things seemed senseless. The idea came to write a poem expressing what she meant to me. The last time I had written a poem had been when I was a child. I didn't even remember what it was about, except my teacher never believed it originated from me. I had never written another one after that.

Writing had always been part of my life—letters or cards to family and friends, term papers for school, business documents and my personal journals. Once I had published an article in a nursing magazine about my experience with eating disorders. Somehow, though, I'd never thought of myself as having writing talent. Most of my private thoughts had remained just that.

Lying in bed one night thinking about Mom's birthday, a line had stuck in my mind: "You are so beautiful without your hair." It sounded like a great title for a poem. With anticipation I got up from my warm, cozy bed and started writing. Over the next two weeks the poem was completed. Mom didn't know I had written it. She only knew her birthday present was late in coming. I decided to read it to her as part of the documentary, thus capturing an intimate moment between a mother and her daughter. Even though I was afraid of breaking down while I shared it, it was worth the risk. If I wanted her to be open with her emotions in front of the camera, I needed to be willing to do the same.

At the end of the second day of filming, I felt frustrated. Early that morning, I had learned from my camera person that his lens had been malfunctioning. He was not sure whether the footage he had already shot was in focus or even usable. I was furious, not because there was a problem with the lens, but because I had not been apprised of the situation sooner. When he originally checked out the equipment, he had been aware of the potential glitch but had chosen to use the lens anyway. It was the first test in working with him.

Most of the day was spent locating another lens. That would have been no problem if we weren't in rural Wisconsin. No replacement could be found. Local television stations in the area were unable to help. One station wanted to film us filming, for a local story. Mom wasn't interested and I had my hands full with my own challenges. We finally had a friend of one of the crew members bring another camera from Madison, three hours away. He arrived late at night. The whole day was lost as a result.

I knew everything happens for a reason, but it was beyond me to understand that in the moment. All I could see was that I had missed a vital day for filming Mom. Extending the crew for another day was not an option because my camera person had other obligations. An extra day to capture additional footage was gone. Although everyone else was great, I was not enjoying working with him. Certain types of shots I requested were met with resistance. "That's not possible," or "We'll never be able to film everything you want in three days," were mantras for him. Before we had begun filming, I had sat down and explained my conceptual ideas, to find out if my thoughts were realistic. He had had no problems with what I presented. Somewhere in midstream all that had changed.

He had difficulty when I said I was looking for a certain tone or feeling to the shots. Finally, after hearing one more time "We can't accomplish everything you want," I was convinced an attitude shift needed to take place. I had our little group sit on the floor in the middle of the living room to discuss what had been accomplished, what remained to be done and how the shoot could flow more smoothly. It was interesting to see how people's past history came into play with their expectations. Here was a videographer who really wanted a project of his own and wanted to be in charge, but who had difficulty being a team player. It was payback time for me, a chance to atone for past actions.

Several years earlier, I had been asked to help produce a video for a dear friend. It turned out to be exasperating for both of us. I thought I was in charge only to find out differently. My expectations got in the way of my participation. Now the tables were reversed. I laughed to myself when I realized that "what goes around comes around." Only why did it have to happen during this shoot? I didn't have another Mom I could film down the road. This was it.

Once again I turned to prayer. "Dear God, I surrender. Somehow I got caught in believing I was in control of this shoot and now I have quickly found out I'm not. I apologize for being so arrogant in my thinking. It is in your hands now. Please work your magic. Amen."

Day three, and everything went smoothly. The morning started off on a humorous note. The day before I had asked John, a family friend, if he could assist as a third person with the crew. I had become acquainted with him shortly after returning from the Easter class in Los Angeles. His mother Norma had stopped by to visit Mom and he came along. Her visits were always delightful and both Mom and I enjoyed her company. She had a great sense of humor and was very uplifting. Since Mom had been ill, she had come often, either alone or with her daughter Paula. Although they had lived on a farm next to us when we were growing up, I didn't remembered ever interacting with John. When I had been in my early teens, they had moved to another part of the state. I had been reintroduced to him the winter before Dad died. He was the bartender at the tavern where we stopped on our outing to Turtle Lake.

John led a hermit-like existence in an old farmhouse that belonged to his deceased uncle. It was nestled at the end of a country road overlooking Wolf River. Acres of farmland lay dormant, surrounded by timber land of oak, maple and poplar trees. Deer grazed freely in the open spaces at dusk and a pair of bald eagles maintained residence down the river. He lived about ten miles from Mom. After their visit, much to my surprise, Mom encouraged me to reach out to him because she felt he could use a friend. Since his appearance at the house, we had maintained contact by phone and had visited twice. He appeared lonely and I sensed a hunger in his soul for spiritual sustenance.

John arrived at the house after we had filmed my room and altar upstairs. After the crew left, John asked to see my sacred objects. I brought him upstairs, and shortly thereafter he left.

When Mom woke the next morning, she came into the kitchen and found me going over notes for the shoot. After our usual hug, she said, "Susie, I'm really upset with you."

My mouth dropped open and I said in a surprised tone, "Why?"

The only thing I imagined could be at the base of her agitation was some aspect of the filming. Nothing stuck out in my mind. She seemed to be enjoying the attention and had been in good spirits the past few days.

Her response was shocking and quite funny. I stood at the kitchen sink holding a cup of tea as she said, "I heard you and John upstairs last night and never heard his car leave."

Trying not to laugh, I turned to look out the kitchen window. I couldn't believe my ears. Here I was, a grown woman, and my mother was upset because she thought I might be having sex with a man. Actually, I didn't think the issue was sleeping with someone who wasn't my husband; it was more about doing it under her roof.

After gaining my composure, I turned back to her and smiled. "Mom, you did hear us upstairs last night. John asked to see my altar. We were just talking and he left shortly afterward. He did not spend the night. Remember, you encouraged me to reach out to him. We are just friends. Besides, how could you not have heard his car? The noise from it could wake the neighbors a mile away."

Her whole demeanor changed and she blushed. "I'm sorry. I apologize for making an assumption. It was unfair of me." Then she smiled. It was a precious moment and I felt as though I were back in high school under my mother's rules. Later we laughed about it.

The morning was filled with surprises. Mom and I were being filmed outside on the swing talking about her life as a farm wife, when her brother Vernon drove into the yard. He visited with her frequently and often stopped by to check up on her. When he heard what we were doing, he agreed to be captured on film and share his special memories growing up with Mom on their farm. No sooner had he left when Norma arrived. More priceless footage was shot. It was fascinating to listen to stories I had never heard and learn intimate details about Mom and her younger years. These were tender moments, witnessing the love between a brother and sister and two dear friends.

That afternoon Dennis, the Lutheran Chaplain who had been so helpful during Mom's surgery, agreed to drive two hours to be interviewed with her. They seemed oblivious of the camera as they engaged in a conversation that would normally be spoken in privacy between minister and parishioner. At one point, Dennis asked Mom if she would like to receive communion from him. I was amazed when she said, "no." She wasn't comfortable because he was not of her faith and I was proud of her honesty and ability to be true to her own beliefs. He was respectful of her convictions. It became clear to me that she was very much in control of what was being filmed.

An extraordinary moment came later that evening. Mom and I were being filmed in the kitchen and she was talking about her children. My Aunt Mary and their mutual friend Jerry knocked at the door. Mom was surprised. With their consent, the cameras rolled while these women, all in their sixties, talked about their views of heaven and God. Jerry read the letter from her deceased husband about his near-death experience and their intimate conversation seemed as natural as if they were having a chat over a cup of coffee. None of them was uncomfortable in front of the camera. As I stood in the corner of the kitchen watching them, they seemed less like mothers with grown children and more like giggling school friends. I could have listened to them for hours.

The greatest impact for me came a couple of hours later at the conclusion of our filming, when I read my poem to Mom. Even though I had recited it out loud to myself many times, I felt I was reading the poem for the first time. I felt vulnerable, not just before Mom, but before everyone else in the room. No longer was I producer and director, but a daughter sharing intimate feelings with her mother. I knew then how she felt about wanting to back out of the project. My voice quivered while reading the following words, and I could feel the emotion in Mom's eyes.

You Are So Beautiful Without Your Hair

As I quietly tiptoe into your bedroom
To cover you from the chill of the night,
I am drawn to the vigil candle on the dresser
Radiating a warm golden light.

Your crucifix that sits behind it is illuminated
Filling your room with the presence of God,
Who each night makes a wondrous appearance
To watch over your slumber, a blessing—this job.

There's a soft, gentle glow that tenderly bathes your face
As you peacefully lie curled in your bed.
An inner beauty that emanates from your being
In spite of the turban that surrounds your bald head.

An overwhelming sense of love fills my heart
To see before me this woman—my mother.
Like a newborn child that comes into this world,
There's so much about you to discover.

Do you realize how beautiful you are
In the nakedness of your soul?
Where the spark of eternity comes forward,
That allows you to be whole.

If but for a moment you could look through my eyes
To see pure radiance etched on your face,
In all its delicate richness
Woven intricately like a pattern of lace.

Your deep compassion, your true strength,
The subtle quietness of your ways,

Each unique and genuine characteristic
Simply displayed within our days.

Through the vulnerability of this illness
That has slowly stripped away our masks.
Beyond the mother-daughter trimmings,
To reveal such unconditional love—at last.

Like the caterpillar who with clear purpose,
Spins its cocoon on a branch so high,
The woman you've become
Has taught me how to fly.

If I were to plant a flower garden,
You would be my most cherished seed.
With the graceful blooming of your petals,
Comes a soothing fragrance I most need.

I thank you for the gift you are,
In giving me this precious life.
And allowing me to be there
In your moments of great strife.

I love you and I honor
The sweet nectar of your soul,
For in its constant daily reflection
I have learned how to become whole.

Afterward we hugged for a long time in silence, and then she whispered in my ear, "You have always been very special to me." It was a potent exchange of love between us.

We ended the shoot sharing our evening prayer together. Just as we finished, we ran out of film. We had shot thirty-two rolls of film, six hours worth of footage—exactly what my intuition had guided me to purchase.

Words are so inadequate to describe what it was like to interview Mom. I was humbled and honored. Many times I felt as if we were sharing past conversations sitting on the swing or at the kitchen table. Mom spoke openly about her life as a farm wife, her relationship with her mother, the impact of her parents' deaths, her dreams and aspirations, her children and Dad's passing. She was a great story teller, genuine and down-to-earth. She had no pretenses about her. I hungered to hear her recount stories about our heritage because soon the historian of our family would be gone and a lineage would be broken. I didn't want our filming to end.

I could feel something in her transform. Her life did have meaning. She was able to acknowledge her accomplishments. She had been as integral to the success of a farming career as had her husband, and she had done a wonderful job raising her children. Her feelings of self-worth had been elevated. My hunch had been right. Filming had been good medicine for her soul.

Chapter Fourteen
A Miracle In a Teepee

Almost a month had passed since the filming and Mom was getting much weaker. She didn't want to get out of bed and was depressed most of the time. She started coughing up blood shortly after we finished the shoot. Her doctor thought it was from irritation in her lungs because of the cancer cells. She was scared. There was nothing he could give to treat it. He didn't think it would develop into a major complication, but asked me to keep him apprised if there were any change.

Our regular visits to the doctor had become taxing for Mom. She saw no purpose in going because she heard nothing new. She had become upset at the last visit because she interpreted the doctor as saying she had little time left. What he told her was that her cancer continued to be slow-growing and that she should do things that gave her pleasure in life. She thought he inferred the end was near. I ended up taking her back to clarify their conversation, hoping it would help diminish her depression. During their interaction he said something insightful.

First he apologized for any misunderstanding that might have occurred. He thought she was doing exceptionally well, and reiterated that she could live for many more years. He couldn't give her a timeframe and said it would be unfair of him to do so, because everyone was different. Then he told her that sometimes he was accused of giving too much information to his patients and other times not enough. His quandary was in assessing what was best for each individual because he depended on input from them to learn how to best support their needs. He was there for them and was willing to work with each one because they were equal participants. They knew better than he did what they most needed and unless they shared their desires, he was left to guess.

Many times during our visits when he had asked Mom how things were going, she hadn't been totally honest with him. She wouldn't share how depressed she was or how much she wanted hopeful encouragement from him. Unless I spoke up, he based his conclusions on partially inaccurate information. At times I was concerned I might be interfering in her relationship with him. Yet, if I didn't say anything, my family and I were left with Mom's frustrations and worries that had not been addressed by the doctor. It was a challenge to determine what was responsible care-giving and what constituted stepping over boundaries. It was a question of her health, and I didn't want to be too overbearing and take away what little control she felt she had left.

I was becoming weary myself. It had been ten months and counting since this remarkable journey with Mom began. Caring for her had become such a priority that my own needs had been set aside. I watched it happening yet was not sure how to change the situation. I hungered for the freedom of being carefree and having fun, yet allowing moments of joy created guilt. It was awkward to laugh and be playful when I knew Mom was miserable. She was facing the end of this life while mine loomed fully in front of me. I realized she had a choice in her attitude to embrace the richness of each day or to see it as empty and unfulfilling. I struggled to sustain a positive approach for both of us. I sometimes questioned whether I was strong enough to continue being with her.

In moments I longed for my own place to escape, to be able to shut out the ongoing responsibility that dwelled within me. Leaving was not an option, certainly not in my heart nor in my mind either. It was easier now that winter was over. I loved waking to the sweet, cheerful melody of the morning song birds as they welcomed the day in orchestrated harmony. The echo of their voices floated through my open window and, for a moment each day, all seemed well. It was such a glorious feeling to smell the fragrance of spring from the lilac bushes in bloom next to the house. I had forgotten how refreshing and alive this time of year made me feel. The beckoning of new life compensated for the heavy heart that awaited my footsteps downstairs each morning. I had to remind myself to see the precious beauty of each day, now more than ever.

I had followed "Z"'s suggestion and filled a plastic container with fresh earth for Mom to put her feet in. I had done the same for myself. Even though I thought she considered the idea a little crazy, she was still willing to do it twice a day. I loved the concept and understood the wisdom behind his words. The earth has innate healing abilities. When Dad planted the fields, nature nourished the seeds and the crops flourished. The same elements could be utilized to heal a body. I kept two extra containers filled with fresh soil from the farmland outside and exchanged them every two weeks. Mom wasn't particularly fond of putting her bare feet on the cold earth because she chilled easily. I relished the feeling. It took me back to my childhood and evoked potent memories of times past.

Being back on this land had reawakened the sustenance from my roots. I hadn't realized how living in a large city, especially Los Angeles, had taken its toll. One day, when my cousin Paula and her mother Rosemary, Mom's sister, stopped by, Paula's first remarks had been, "You look ten years younger than the last time I saw you."

My aunt chimed in, "You do look much younger. It must be all this fresh air and Wisconsin life."

The last time I had seen Paula had been in the fall, shortly after coming to stay with Mom. Although I was sure their remarks were intended as a compliment, I felt insulted. Their comments stuck in my mind. There was truth to what they spoke. L.A. was stressful, just from the noise pollution alone. Added to that was the hustle and bustle of constantly being on the go. The body can be affected by such a hectic pace, and I was a walking example of it.

Although life on the farm still held stress, the surroundings added greater balance. I loved the quiet interplay of nature, waking to the morning sky glistening with golden rays of sunlight, frogs croaking in their nightly activities and the impressive silence of the existence of everything and nothing at the same time. I was blessed to have been raised on a farm for all it had offered my soul. I didn't ever want to lose this connection again.

In addition to the containers of soil, I placed a stone in the corner of every room. A large rock pile at the end of one of the fields provided a constant supply of these unusual friends. Each week I took my blue backpack, walked down the road to this island filled with treasures and carefully selected the jewels that would honor the house with their presence. I always left a strand of my hair or some tobacco in exchange. One day my Aunt Mary noticed a rock sitting in the corner of the kitchen and inquired about it to Mom. In a nonchalant voice she said, "Susie put them throughout the whole house. She tells me she is bringing the sunlight and moonlight inside to fill up the rooms with their energy."

I was standing in the living room during their conversation, certain my aunt would begin to laugh. Instead she responded, "Edder (her nickname for Mom), I didn't know that. I should put some in our house. Maybe it might help Joe, too."

Mary's husband had been diagnosed with cancer the year before Dad and had gone through chemotherapy as well as surgery. He had not let his illness get the better of him, had remained active with his outdoor sports and was still enjoying life to the fullest. My aunt had been a strong ally for me in caring for Mom and I was happy to hear her words in support of what could have been perceived as my strange actions.

If she'd had a different reaction, it wouldn't have been surprising. I never considered rocks to be an actual form of life. They were just rocks: solid, dense, useless objects valuable only for skimming on the water or pounding nails. Several years earlier, I had been afforded a whole new perspective. My employment with the production company and the people with whom I worked came to an abrupt halt when financial difficulties forced closure of the business. Lives were thrown into disarray. Out of desperation, I went on a nine-day wilderness retreat at the base of the Cristone Mountains in Colorado. I was led to a man, John, who organized vision quests, designed for people to be in silence with nature. In the Native American culture, this is a sacred journey within to communicate with the Creator and receive visions about the direction of one's life. It is usually an initiation into adulthood for young indigenous boys.

When I arrived at this man's doorstep, he had just finished a group outing. He rarely let anyone go solo because of the intensity of the experience. Although individuals had their own assigned space away from the group, they still had the security of knowing other people were around. I had camped alone many times, but only in areas that were familiar. After explaining my situation and need for reflection, he agreed to send me out on my own. I was led to a lush river bed that wove through a thick forest of towering pine, and a flowery meadow filled with an odd assortment of boulders. Each day I was required to let John know that I was okay by placing a stick upright in an area we designated as a rendezvous point. If the stick wasn't there, it was a sign for him to come and check up on me. My home for the nine days was selected partially because of the magical powers of the boulders. John called them "rock people" and told me not to be alarmed if they spoke to me. I laughed at the time, sure he was pulling my leg. Several days later I found out he was telling the truth.

While lying in my tent one afternoon, after a huge thunderstorm, I heard voices singing. It sounded like a church choir. When I turned my head to the left, the voices became less audible. Shifting my head back to the right, the singing was clear and distinct. I had been fasting for several days and thought my mind was playing tricks on me. Outside my tent, I had built an altar of rocks taken from the nearby meadow, placing some of my special objects there. The closer I turned my ear to the altar, the louder the singing became. It was beautiful. The singing lasted about five minutes. Then suddenly the voices stopped, and I heard clapping—the kind one hears after someone has given a great performance. Going outside my tent, I looked around, thinking a church group had camped nearby. There was no one anywhere. All that existed was a forest of trees as a backdrop to the mountain in front of me.

At the end of my retreat, I told John about my unusual experience. He chuckled and said, "You were very blessed. The rock people came to honor your presence with the healing power of their vibration. They were singing to you. There is no church nearby."

Because my experience on this sacred, indigenous land had been filled with powerful, magical moments, my soul knew he was speaking a truth even though my intellect begged to differ. Yet it was beyond anything I had ever experienced. I walked away with a broader understanding about the mystery of God's communication with me and a smile in my heart. I had been gifted with my own private "rock concert," and never looked at rocks as lifeless again. They had become sacred.

The appearance of Norma's son in my life had turned out to be a blessing in ways I never imagined. His rustic dwelling had become a safe haven to clear my head and relax my tired body. His company was refreshing after the intensity that surrounded my daily life and he provided an impartial ear to my family dynamics.

One afternoon my Aunt Mary came to spend some time with Mom and told me to take a few hours off. I spent the afternoon canoeing with John, basking in the sun and feeling free as we floated down Wolf River. We stopped at a bald eagles' nest a mile down the river and their magnificent presence filled me with renewed strength. He had become a valuable friend and I enjoyed his male companionship.

He usually stopped by once a week and brought Mom wild flowers he had picked on his property. One day he presented her with a poem he had written called, "You Are My Mother's Friend." Her eyes filled with tears as his words reflected the bond between these two women. Mom and I were both deeply touched by the unique display of caring from this unusual man.

Over the Memorial Day weekend, he erected a teepee on his uncle's land near the edge of the river. He had participated in one of my monthly rituals of a sacred pipe ceremony during the full moon and knew about my connection with Native American spirituality. Our conversations triggered his interest in their culture and a subsequent compulsion to construct a teepee. He called it "Namaste," the Hindi word meaning "The God within me honors the God within you." He asked me to bless his holy dwelling and I was honored to do so.

Two days later a miraculous event occurred within those brown canvas walls. There had been a noticeable increase in Mom coughing up blood, which occurred more frequently and in greater amounts. The medical profession's inability to alleviate the situation had left me frustrated and Mom worried. She was afraid to cough and constantly carried Kleenex with her. I had been praying a great deal for answers about how to help her. In the morning, while sitting on the swing, I felt a strong urge to take Mom to John's teepee and to do a ceremony. Initially I pushed the thought aside, thinking the idea too whimsical. The urge wouldn't leave me, even though my rationalization told me Mom would never agree to it. Even if she didn't, in the worse case scenario, she could sit down by the river and be in the fresh air. I told her I had a surprise I thought might help with her coughing that required taking a drive. To my surprise she consented to go.

As we turned down the road to John's house, she knew I had more planned than a simple excursion on a sunny day. I explained my reason for bringing her and asked if she were open for healing on her body. She said, "Yes."

I had asked John earlier for permission to perform a ceremony in Namaste. He waved from the window as we drove into the yard, respectful of our privacy. Maneuvering the car through an old hay field, we drove down to the river bank. Mom sat for a little bit by the river, on a lawn chair I had put into the trunk of the car. While she took off her shoes and placed her feet on the ground, I left her alone to prepare the teepee.

The day couldn't have been more perfect. The sun was warm with a slight breeze and the trees were fragrant with budding blossoms.

The air was poignant with the crisp smell of nature everywhere. It was a glorious day for a healing.

A slight degree of nervousness crept into my body from flickering doubt that relief for Mom's coughing could occur. I had to remind myself of the guidance to bring her to the teepee and trust regardless of my mind chatter. Several years before, I had been gifted with a ceremonial pipe similar to those used by indigenous medicine men and chiefs. I had been taught how to use it honorably and to be accountable for the responsibility that came with such a sacred gift. Most of my pipe ceremonies had been done in private or with my spiritual friends and I had never done one with Mom.

I sat down on the ground in front of the teepee and took a deep breath, embracing the warmth of the sun on my face. At that moment the majestic wings of a bald eagle appeared over the river. A feeling of reverence filled me with awe at the powerful sign of the Creator's presence. I closed my eyes in prayer. "Dear God, thank you for the gift of all life and the beauty of this day. I come before you with an open heart and a willingness to be used as a vessel in this holy ceremony for my mother. Bless her this day so her body, mind and soul may feel your love. Give her peace and healing, especially from coughing up blood. Be the breath of smoke that swirls throughout her and carry my prayers on the wind for her behalf. Bless Uncle Joe that his diseased body may also reap the benefits from this healing. I ask this with love and honor in your name. Amen."

I removed a sage stick from the Peruvian bag carrying my sacred objects. Lighting one end, I walked around the outside perimeter of the teepee, asking God to cleanse its canvas walls. Then I did the same thing inside. When I had finished, I placed the sage stick on one of the rocks forming the fire ring. Taking naturally grown tobacco from a pouch, I closed my eyes, placed the tobacco at my forehead and blessed it. I again walked the perimeter of the teepee, scattering it as an offering. I returned inside and sat cross-legged in front of the fire ring. I smudged it with the sage stick and also scattered tobacco all around the rim. Then I placed a white candle in the center. While I normally built a fire, I was concerned the smoke might cause Mom too much discomfort. I removed my pipe and other sacred objects wrapped in deerskin, placed them on a red cloth next to the fire ring and went and retrieved Mom, who was still sitting quietly by the river.

I placed the lawn chair in a corner of the teepee, behind the fire ring, with a view of the river. I knelt next to her, held her hand and explained what was to occur. The intent was to ask God the Creator to stop her from coughing up blood and provide peace and freedom from worry. I asked her to hold her own prayers in her heart and offer them to God. Then I lit the candle, placing tobacco at its base as a blessing to the sacred fire. I sat down, unwrapped my pipe and other special objects, took the sage stick and blessed them. Then I smudged my body and did the same with Mom. The tobacco was blessed again as I placed it in the green alabaster bowl connected to the stem. Lighting the pipe, I asked that the holiness of the smoke cleanse Mom's body in honor of the divine that resided within her. I did my ritual of offering the pipe to the Creator, the four directions, Grandfather Sky, Mother Earth and the sacred fire. Then I placed a turtle shell in one of Mom's hands and a seashell in the other. I proceeded to draw from the pipe, gently blowing the smoke all over her body.

A week earlier John had given me a beautiful eagle feather he found at the base of the eagle nest. I took the feather and began to fan Mom's body as I continued blowing smoke into her lung and heart areas. The rhythm of the feather back and forth had a swooshing sound like an eagle flapping its powerful wings. I felt a profound energy circling Mom as the wind began blowing against the canvas. I then offered the pipe to Mom, to take its smoke and offer her own prayers. She took a puff and then blew it out her mouth. She handed the pipe back to me and I returned to sit at the fire ring, to finish my final blessing as I drew smoke from the last of the tobacco. I disconnected the bowl from the stem, releasing the power connected with the ceremony. I offered the used tobacco to the fire ring, wrapped the pipe and sat quiet in my thoughts.

Mom had her eyes closed, with her fingers wrapped tightly around the turtle shell and seashell. There was a peaceful look on her face. I got up and placed the eagle feather on her hands and walked out of the teepee, leaving her alone. I went and sat on some rocks next to the river, placing my feet in the chilly water. As I looked up to the turquoise sky, an eagle was soaring high above. I placed my hand on my heart and extended my arm upward to the graceful winged one in acknowledgment of its presence.

An awesome feeling of gratitude riveted my body as tears rolled down my cheeks. I had been used to give a gift to Mom. Whether she believed in the ceremony or not, she had allowed me to return an act of love and caring for all the years she displayed her own tender care. Through this unique journey of her dying, our souls as mother and daughter continued to be drawn closer together. What a fortunate opportunity I had been given within this process.

After the ceremony, Mom did not cough up any more blood. I believed God had answered my prayers. I knew something had happened inside her body. She had noticed a difference, too, although she was cautious to trust her bloody cough wouldn't return. When my Aunt Mary stopped by two days later, we told her about the ceremony. She was pleased. She had also been praying for Mom.

After two weeks had passed, Mom still had not coughed up any more blood. None. Her doctor had no explanation for why it had stopped. Mom had more radiation to her pelvic region plus three areas on her chest. I didn't want her to have it, especially not to her pelvis, because of the excruciating pain she had endured the last time. Her radiologist reduced the voltage and assured us she would have minimal discomfort. While the severity of the pain was less, her bottom was so tender she was not able to sit for more than a few minutes. The narcotic pills made her confused and more depressed because they were not being metabolized in the body. She didn't want to eat at all. One night I spent hours rocking her in my arms because of the discomfort. She regretted putting herself through this ordeal again.

My patience with her was waning. After another day of refusing to eat, I became frustrated and told her I was tired of forcing her to eat. She looked at me with a blank stare and said, "Why should I, when I'm going to die soon anyway?"

I wasn't sure how to respond, and didn't pick up on her cue that maybe she wanted to talk about dying. I had heard derivatives of the same thing before but when I had inquired about her feelings, she had refused to go in the direction of death. Exasperated, I told her I didn't enjoy pushing her to eat and sometimes I just didn't know how to be there for her. I suggested that perhaps she needed to have IV fluids or we should put her in the hospital.

She retorted, "Well, maybe you should."

Trying another approach, I responded, "Mom, maybe I'm just not being effective anymore and I'm not the person to be with you any longer."

Her last remark showed me the conversation was going nowhere. "I told you that you can leave at any time."

I walked out of the bedroom feeling even more frustrated. Since Mom needed more medicine and I needed to regroup, I called my sister Ann and told her I would be gone for an hour, in case Mom needed anything. I left the house telling Mom where I was going.

When I returned she was in the living room. She asked me for water and a piece of toast. I felt awful inside because of our earlier interaction and wondered how to approach her differently. In my phone conversation with "Z" the week before, I had shared my frustration about not knowing what more to do for her. He had said, "What she needs most now is love and tenderness."

Hearing his words again in my mind, I went and sat next to her on the couch. Her fingers were wrapped around the beads of her rosary. I apologized for being harsh. She looked at me and said, "You know I don't get mad anymore since your Dad."

I touched her arm and said, "Mom, I know this is tough on you. Sometimes I get frustrated because I don't want to seem like the bad guy and be the one who is always pushing you. When you get depressed, I don't know what to say to you anymore to help you out. I feel like a broken record."

She became quiet and then said, "I know I get depressed and then spiral into feeling sorry for myself. It's just that since I got cancer I have not had one good day."

Tears welled up in my eyes listening to her and I felt tremendous sadness and compassion for her. I had seen many moments filled with laughter and love among family and friends. How unfortunate she hadn't seen them, too. I turned to her and said, "Mom, how can I be there more for you? I know at times I get short or come across as impatient. It's just that I'm not sure how to be with you anymore and whether I'm giving enough. I question that I'm not providing you with the spiritual strength you wanted from me. What more can I do?"

Mom looked out the living room window as her fingers grasped the rosary beads. After a few minutes she responded, "You are doing more than you realize. I am getting the spiritual strength and you are saying the right things. I just may not tell you. I wouldn't have been able to do this without you."

Tears started rolling down my cheeks. We held each other and I could hear her quietly crying. We both knew her time was getting shorter.

Mom had been having difficulty breathing and was restless. The other night, she had told me she was afraid she was going to die because she couldn't catch her breath. Her doctor had decided to put her on a morphine pump and oxygen to ease her fears. Mary and Ron came home over the Fourth of July weekend and managed all the details. Because of Ron's company, he was able to handle the necessary setup. Mary was arranging for a visiting nurse to come once a week and monitor the medication.

The portable oxygen machine was in the living room, in the corner next to the hallway leading into Mom's bedroom. A long extension of plastic tubing hooked into one end of the machine; the other connected to nasal prongs. The morphine pump was portable and allowed Mom freedom to move about. Her breathing was more relaxed and the medication didn't seem to affect her ability to function mentally. It was hard to see her like this.

Because of the change in Mom's condition, Mary called the hospice at our local hospital. She wanted to inquire about their services in case Mom needed to be hospitalized. We knew the hospice provided a wonderful alternative to being placed on a regular unit because of its homelike atmosphere. What Mary found out was surprising. They would not allow Mom to retain her physician. She would have to be under the care of someone who was not familiar with Mom's history. We also had to participate in their spiritual philosophy regardless of what we were currently practicing. The director of the hospice was adamant about their rules and would not allow any leeway to accommodate our desires. Consequently, they had to be ruled out as an option.

A major shift had occurred in my relationship with Mom. She had begun to withdraw even more. It happened over the Fourth of July. Since Mary was there to care for Mom, she told me to take the day and do something fun. I asked John to go to a Native American powwow that took place every year at this time. It was a gathering of different nations from Wisconsin that met for three days and joined in ceremony and festivities. I told Mom what I was doing and that I would be gone for the afternoon. The powwow was an hour's drive away. She asked me how I was getting there. I told her I was taking the car.

She sat up in bed and said, "That's my car."

I looked at her with surprise. "Mom you've never had a problem with my using the car before. Do you not want me to go?"

Mary was in the bedroom with me and turned to Mom and said, "I'm here with you. Let her go. She can take my rental car. We can spend some time alone together."

Mom was quiet and looked perturbed. She turned her head away from me and replied, "Just take the car and go." She didn't say another word.

I was a little confused because she had never reacted that way before. Mary was certainly more up-to-date in her nursing skills than I was, and Mom would probably be in better hands in case some medical emergency came up. I was torn inside. Was I being selfish about going? Sitting in the living room, I contemplated what to do.

Mary came out of the bedroom and said, "Go, she'll be fine. You deserve a break and may as well take advantage of my being here."

I left but an uncomfortable feeling stayed with me the whole time. On the drive over, John told me he'd had a dream the previous night that Mom died suddenly and I became nervous after hearing what he shared. Maybe Mom didn't want me to go because it was her time. Once we had arrived, I called Mary to see if everything was okay. Even though there was no change with Mom, my nervousness remained. It stayed in the pit of my stomach and wouldn't go away. I found a bench away from the crowd and became silent with my thoughts. What if Mom died while I was gone?

My dear friend Sheila had recently lost her father. She had kept a constant vigil by his bedside in the hospital but when she left for just a short time to run an errand, he had passed away. She had gone into great anguish for not being there. Was that how it would be for me?

I had a strong reaction at the thought of feeling incomplete if that were to happen. I went into prayer. "Dear God, I have come this far with her, please don't let this be her time. Grant me the grace of our farewell."

Still unable to relax, I called Mary again. Mom was the same. Because I was unable to enjoy the festivities, we left. By the time I returned, three hours had passed. Mary was surprised to see me and Mom hardly spoke to me.

Earlier I had mentioned to Mary that I noticed Mom was different around the other kids than she was with me—more friendly and talkative. Mary said she hadn't noticed anything. Later that evening I was in the bathroom brushing my teeth. The door leading into Mom's bedroom was open and I heard Mary and Mom laughing together. Mom got up from the bed, not knowing I was nearby. As soon as she got to the doorway to use the bathroom, she saw me. The smile on her face turned to scorn and she didn't say a word to me. I felt as if a knife had been stabbed into my heart.

In that moment standing in the bathroom, I knew something in our relationship had changed. The void I had experienced between us the month before had become stronger. I pondered why. In one of my meditations it became clear that Mom and I had become like one. In many ways we had become inseparable. She had become totally dependent upon me. She knew she could be herself with me and I wasn't going to walk away. If her time were drawing to a close, she had to begin to disengage from me because I was like a lifeline. She was needing to turn inward to prepare herself for the final journey home. She had to start letting go of her attachment to me and I had to be able to let go, too. Why did it have to feel so isolating?

Chapter Fifteen
Sleepless Nights Curled Next To Mom

Only two weeks had passed since Mom was placed on the oxygen and morphine, and her world was becoming much smaller. She functioned within the diameter of the living room, bedroom and bathroom. Her physical needs were greater because she was weak. We put a commode by the bedside to help conserve her energy. I borrowed a wheelchair from the County Division on Aging to provide more mobility. Over the weekend, Johnny and Ron built a wooden ramp from the front door steps to allow access for taking her outside. She had not been amenable to the idea. Her care was much more demanding. Whereas it once took a few steps to navigate from the bedroom to the living room, now it seemed like miles. We used the wheelchair to get around inside. Mom relied more on me to help her get in and out of the bed, onto the commode and up and down from the couch. Most of our days were consumed with her physical needs.

The portable oxygen unit had become a daily staple for comfort and a constant reminder of Mom's accelerating decline. A few days after Mom started using the oxygen, I found her lying in bed crying. I asked what was wrong, and she muttered, "See, now it's clear I'm not getting any better or I wouldn't need to use this."

I was at a loss for words. Later I wondered if I had missed another opportunity of her willingness to talk about dying. I hungered to be able to speak to her about it, yet I wanted to honor her own timing for when she would be ready. It was not a closed topic of conversation with my brothers and sisters. We all acknowledged she would soon die. I had no idea whether she spoke with them about it. I was amazed she still hung in there, weak as she was. I didn't think it was because she wanted to live. I thought she was afraid to die. Her process was so different from what Dad's had been. When he had become clear he wasn't getting any better, he surrendered and transitioned quickly. Her process was more prolonged. Again, I was able to witness how dying mirrored the way one had lived life. Dad had been much more openly passionate about everything, whereas Mom was much more subtle. Dad hadn't been afraid to take risks, whereas Mom played it safe. Even if Dad had allowed her more freedom, I believed she still would have been content to live in a simple, secure capsule. What would she have done if she had let her heart sing the song of her dreams? I would never know.

The visiting nurse continued to stop by once a week. The young woman assigned to Mom's case was bubbly and energetic and I looked forward to her coming. Ann and I had been discussing having another person come in and be with Mom for an afternoon to give me a break. She had a nurse friend who worked at the local hospital, who also did independent home care. I had been hesitant to consider this option for Mom's sake, because she was self-conscious about needing help with her personal hygiene. She still wore Depends pads because of vaginal drainage and that required changing several times a day. She could no longer go to the bathroom by herself. We had broken through the barrier of her self-consciousness early on, after the first round of radiation to her pelvic area. Narcotic suppositories were the only thing that eased the excruciating pain and she wasn't able to give them to herself. In a moment of extreme intimacy, she expressed her embarrassment over feeling exposed. Compassionate about her sensitivity, I told that when I was a little baby, she had tended to my needs all the time and that I was happy to be able to return the gesture of love. She never had an issue about asking for assistance after that.

It was difficult to watch Mom's health deteriorate and I felt helpless. I still didn't want her to die, although I had accepted she would. Our once frequent and lengthy dialogues no longer existed. I missed them. I especially missed the bond they created between us. Our eyes now conveyed the feelings once shared by words.

I felt more vulnerable. My heart, that had been so protected all these years, had no place to escape. My mind, that was usually clear and focused, had become muddled. Sometimes I felt I was walking around in a fog. It had been like that for the past two months. Zarathustra said it was purposeful and matched Mom's process. The haziness of her mind allowed her to begin experimenting with aspects of the spiritual world and was an essential part of her preparation. My assuming a similar space provided me with an ability to understand what was occurring for her and allowed it to happen without distractions. It also served to keep my own emotional state elevated so I wouldn't feel lower frequencies, such as depression.

During the past two weeks, Mom had mentioned she knew someone else was in the house besides me. While she thought it was Pops or her sister Julie, she couldn't see their faces. I was not aware of any other presence. At this point I was beyond feeling anything. Although she had mentioned seeing Julie every night in her dreams, she said they had no verbal communication. Julie had passed away when I was around fourteen and Mom had always been very close to her. She was Mom's youngest sister.

Mom was going through her life review in her dreams. She told me she dreamed a lot about Dad and us kids. She didn't know what age we were in the dreams, but the events were always situated on the farm. Lately she had been waking up wondering where everyone was. Then, a few days ago, she asked when her sisters Rosemary and Mary would be home. I knew she had retreated back to her own upbringing during her sleep.

There was a great contrast between participating in Mom's and Dad's dying process. With him, I had felt like a bystander. He didn't let me in as deeply. He was more of a maverick. Noble as a king, he quietly and proudly accepted his fate. Mom needed me in the most intimate, basic aspect of human nature, and I cared for her like a mother nurturing a young child. Just as she birthed me into life, I was birthing her into death. I felt I had become a midwife coaching her along, rallying in moments of hope, supportive in the loss of a husband and holding her hand through the pains of learning how to surrender. She had become my teacher in learning about the depth of human emotion, especially my own.

Mary was home again to spend some time with Mom. After her last visit on the Fourth of July, she had called me from the airport and said she wasn't feeling complete and inquired whether she should return to the farm or fly back to Florida. She seemed upset and, after I talked with her, she decided to return to Florida and make arrangements to come back for a few days. Mom responded more openly with her. She was great to have around and picked up my weary spirits.

Because we all knew Mom's time was drawing much closer, the house was never quiet. Ron and Ann came every weekend from Minneapolis. Mark was planning to come for a few days by himself in the middle of the following week, and Vern was going to fly back from Seattle. Although Johnny was back working long days, he made a point of coming after work more often.

It was interesting to watch how we were all coping with the reality that soon both our parents would be gone. Everyone was so different in the unique way they related to Mom. We were all such a blend of sensitivity and toughness and our personalities still carried the same flavors as when Mom and Dad had been healthy. We just were more vulnerable. I could see the weariness in their faces and felt the effect on each of us. It had been a year and a half of constant awareness that our lives were changing dramatically.

I had lost my intuitive edge. I had no sense when Mom would pass. The days felt like a blur. Sometimes I felt I was just waiting for her to die instead of living each moment of the day. I was disappointed in myself for feeling this way. There was a different pace in caring for her and I had slowed down to match her natural rhythm. It reminded me of how Dad had been toward the end: slow, watching, thinking, expressing few words.

Many times we just sat together saying nothing. She was restless. She couldn't seem to find comfort lying on the bed or sitting on the couch. We got up a lot, shifting from the bedroom to the living room. When we had put her on the oxygen and the morphine pump at the beginning of July, we had installed a baby monitor in her bedroom and one in mine. During the day if I were in the kitchen or taking a moment outside, I carried it with me. Her voice had become so quiet that if I were in another room I might not hear her call out. The first week it affected my sleep. I heard her every move as I listened to make sure she was okay. After a few days, I had gotten used to it. I struggled with sleeping on the couch at night to be in closer proximity. Mom told me she was fine knowing I was upstairs and could hear her in the monitor. Several times a night I went downstairs to check on her. Sometimes she was awake and wanted to go to the bathroom or needed a glass of water.

One morning I heard a loud noise as if someone were knocking on the door. It was about 2:30. I had been up several times already hearing her call my name through the baby monitor. I had just nestled back into bed, trusting she was comfortable for the night, when I heard the knock. I hadn't heard Mom move or call out so I thought I was just imagining things. I had a nagging sense I should check on her one more time.

I found her sitting on the floor curled up, looking around. She was wide awake. I don't know how she got there because I never heard her fall. The nasal prongs were resting on her chin and I asked her if she were hurt. She said "no." I asked if she had been calling out for me. She said "no." I asked her what she was doing.

She responded, "I thought I saw a cockroach crawling on the bed and I didn't want it to get on me."

I put her back into bed and sat next to her until she fell asleep. It was one of the few times she seemed confused.

Considering the progression of her illness, she was stable. She had not coughed up any blood since our ceremony in the teepee. She didn't experience any pain and had minimal shortness of breath.

Aside from her thinking she was at her childhood home when she woke in the morning, she was cognizant of everything around her. She looked sick now. She had gotten much weaker, her cheeks were drawn in and she had lost weight. She was not as bony as Dad had been. When she walked, she shuffled her feet just as Dad had done. I bundled her up and took her for wheelchair rides outside. It seemed to depress her.

Earlier in the spring I had talked her into planting a garden. John came over and tilled the earth and Mom re-taught me how to plant it. She laughed when I put potato seedlings together in a clump instead of in furrows. She doubted they would flourish. I hoped the sight of her garden would bring joy to her, to see her labors once again reap a bountiful harvest. It had not. Weeds had taken over her special plot of land from lack of tending. My thoughtful gesture had become a reminder of what she could no longer do. I had also planted the geranium flowers she stored in the basement during the winter and their colorful bouquets now flooded the walkway to the back door. They, too, caused her sadness. The only thing that had brought a smile to her face was the small basket of full-grown potatoes that grew despite my novice hands.

Lately I had been hearing singing. It sounded like children's voices. I knew Mom heard singing, too, because one night as I was tucking her into bed I heard the voices again. Just at that moment Mom turned and looked at me with her eyes wide open. Neither of us said anything and then the voices stopped.

The next morning Mom said to me, "I think your father is coming to get me."

When I asked her why she thought that, she responded, "I just think so." Mom told me that when her sister Julie had passed away, her mother awoke early to a choir of children. She had thought they were kids walking on the street on their way to school. My grandmother was living with my Aunt Julie because of her heart condition. She decided to check on Julie that particular morning and found she had passed away.

I had agreed to let Ann's friend Diane take care of Mom and I felt guilty about it. One morning I discussed it with Mom. She didn't have much to say. She was angry with me even though she had told me she didn't get that way anymore, not since Dad's illness. The look in her eyes was enough to tell me otherwise. I was honest with her and said I needed some time to myself to be able to continue caring for her effectively and that it would only be one afternoon a week. I mentioned that I felt I was becoming short with her at times and didn't like being that way because it wasn't fair to her. She deserved the best from me. I asked her to meet Diane and if she didn't care for her we wouldn't hire her. Although she reluctantly agreed, she didn't speak much to me that day. I felt like a rotten parent and an inadequate daughter.

That night as I was preparing Mom for bed, she told me she was scared.

I inquired what she was scared about. She said, "I don't know."

This had become a common response so I decided to press her for more. "Mom, I bet you do know."

She responded, "I'm afraid of being in pain."

I reminded her that she had not been having any pain for a long time. "Is there something else that is making you afraid?"

She told me I was "pressing and pushing" her too much. Then she said, "I can't take this anymore."

Tenderly looking upon her face, I said, "Mom, I'm sorry if I'm doing that." Not knowing what else to say, I just sat and held her hand. She closed her eyes and didn't speak again. I stayed with her until she fell asleep. Then I went and sat on the couch, feeling as alone as the darkness outside the window. Nothing I did or said seemed to please her and I was not able to find peace, not even with my prayers.

Mark came home for a few days and assumed some of the responsibility of caring for Mom. He was so gentle and tender with her. She was less edgy with him around and there was a noticeable difference in how she interacted with him. I was still feeling sensitive because she had distanced herself from me and hadn't been able to let go of the notion that she was upset over my caring for her.

The day Diane spent her first afternoon with Mom, she stayed for three hours. I took advantage of the warm, sunny day and went canoeing again down Wolf River with John. Trying to lose myself in the current of the river as we floated gracefully with its gentle movement, I had difficulty relaxing. I couldn't get past feeling guilty about leaving Mom with a stranger. What I really wasn't able to come to peace with was my sense of failure in my weariness over caring for her. Why hadn't I paced myself better early on so I would have more reserve left? Now when she needed me the most I was not fully present. My thoughts were random and unfocused. I was susceptible to everyone's energy around me and unable to be centered inside. Not even the peaceful calm of nature rejuvenated me and I couldn't still my mind enough to meditate. So much for my spirituality. Where was my connection with God when I needed it?

I returned home to find Mom in no worse shape than when I had left her. Diane said she was talkative and pleasant. When I asked Mom about being with Diane her only words were, "It was okay."

Something was different about Mom. There was a resolve that hadn't been there before. I thought it was because she felt she had become more of a burden since she needed another person to care for her. Change was in the wind with her and I could sense it. I felt empty and alone at night and missed the fullness of our moments together.

One afternoon something really unique happened. Mom and I were sitting in the living room when a bird flew into the big picture window. I went outside and saw a little robin lying on the ground. It was motionless, with blood coming out its beak. I picked it up and went and sat on the steps. Cupping it in my hands, I closed my eyes and focused on the image of Jesus and imagined the little bird being healed. I found myself gently blowing my breath into the heart area of the tiny winged one, visualizing white light all around it. I sat intensely focused in this way for several minutes and could feel its warm little body nestled in my hands. Mom called out to me, and I placed the robin back on the ground to go and check on her.

About half an hour later, I went back outside. The robin was gone. Worried a stray cat had found it, I began looking for signs of feathers. I searched underneath the window and found nothing. Then I walked around the corner of the house, and saw the robin sitting in some grass. I went to pick it up and was surprised it didn't fly away. When I gathered the little bird in my hands, it offered no resistance. I sat on the swing and opened my hands. It sat there looking up at me, blinking its eyes. I gently stroked its tiny head and kept telling the bird it was okay. We sat this way for a couple of minutes. Hearing Mom call out to me through the baby monitor, I put the little robin on the swing and went inside. When I got into the house, I looked out the window and saw the bird spread its wings and fly away.

I was gifted with another remarkable experience later that night. Mom and I were sitting together on the couch, having finished our evening prayer. She turned to me and said, "I'm scared."

I asked gently, "What scares you Mom?"

She gave her familiar response, "I don't know."

Not wanting to push for an answer, I sat quietly holding her hand. She started to cry. I gently tried to get her to talk about it, mentioning it would help to express her fears.

No answer.

I closed my eyes for a moment and decided to take a new approach. "Mom, if a child is scared before going to bed wouldn't you talk with her so she won't feel afraid and won't have scary dreams?"

She nodded her head but still refused to talk. I gave up trying to get her to speak, and just sat stroking her hand and feeling the fragileness of her weary body. As I was helping her get ready to sleep, she asked me to stay in bed with her awhile. I had slept in Mom's room a couple of times before and was never able to get much sleep, causing me to feel off kilter the next day. That didn't seem important now. I turned off the light and cuddled next to her. The eight-day candle on her dresser flickered a soft glow, filling the room with a warm coziness. I felt Mom's warm fingers enclose my hand in a firm grasp. She was restless. Finally she fell asleep. The humming sound from the oxygen unit in the living room melded with the slow, methodical pace of her breathing. I watched the candlelight dance upon the ceiling, aware of Mom's hand on mine. It felt wonderful. The warmth of her body next to mine slowly edged out the emptiness that had been my constant companion. My inability to sleep was overshadowed by the comfort of being beside her. Her hand never left mine.

After several hours, Mom seemed to be sleeping soundly. I went to retire to my bed upstairs only to wake her. Her quiet voice reached out: "Do you have to leave?"

"No, Mom. I'll be glad to stay if you want me to." I crawled back in bed next to her. She was restless throughout the night, asking several times for her rosary. As I placed the crystal beads in the palm of her hand, she grasped them tightly.

Once, as she turned to check that I was still next to her, I said, "Mom, I'm right next to you. You're safe. You can go back to sleep because I'll be here all night."

Her body seemed to relax hearing my voice. Around three or four in the morning she became more restless, pulling the covers off her chest. I thought she was hot.

Then I heard her voice. "Susie, I'm dying."

I snuggled next to her and said, "I know Mom. It's okay. You don't have to be afraid because Dad, Grandma, Grandpa, Julie and God are waiting for you. It will be wonderful."

She didn't say anything. I didn't know whether what I had said helped or not. Eventually she fell back to sleep.

When she awoke she asked me if I saw the little girl standing out in the driveway.

I told her "no." I inquired what she was doing.

Mom said, "She's just standing there, waiting."

I asked if she knew for whom she was waiting.

In a quiet voice Mom replied, "I think she's waiting for me." She closed her eyes and I watched as her fingers touched the rosary beads intertwined through her hands. She didn't say anything else.

Oh how I wished I could step through the illusionary veil that was connecting Mom with the spirit world. If I could only see this little girl and what she was beckoning Mom toward. If I could only have a glimpse and feel what lay beyond. It must be awesome.

Mom asked me to sleep with her again. She thought someone was in the bedroom. We kept her wig on a styrofoam head, sitting on top of her vanity and at night I thought she sensed it was a stranger standing there. I placed the head under the vanity hoping that might alleviate her fears. She asked to keep a light on in addition to her candle. She was extremely restless. I snuggled next to her and put my arm around her. Gently rocking her, I began humming "Amazing Grace," one of her favorite songs. She reached out and held my hand, stroking it lightly and I could feel her body begin to relax. I kept humming and rocking her. When her breathing shifted to a slower, deeper rhythm, I knew she was finally asleep. There was none for me.

At about two o'clock a soft voice spoke out. "Susie, I'm dying."

I heard the sound of my own voice reply, "I know, Mom."

She was quiet for a moment and said, "I'm going to die soon."

There didn't seem to be any fear in her voice. It came out like a statement of fact. My arm tightened around her. "I know, Mom."

We were both silent and then she turned to me and said, "I need to handle my funeral arrangements." There was an ease to her voice, as if we were having one of our chats.

I stroked her hand. "Mom, you already did that. Remember you wrote everything down on a piece of paper after Dad died and put it in the safe."

Calmly she responded, "Oh, that's right." She was quiet again for a short time and then said, "What about flowers?"

I was amazed by the evenness in her voice. After all the times I had hungered to talk with her about dying, the conversation was finally happening. It was done in her own timing and the security of her own bed and I longed for the moment to go on forever.

"Mom, I'll make sure they are handled."

There was silence again and she spoke. "Maybe some kind of Christmas flowers."

My mind went to "Christmas flowers?" She wasn't particularly fond of poinsettias. Maybe she meant some kind of fall flowers. I waited for her to speak again. She didn't say anything.

I asked her, "Mom is there a certain dress you want to wear?"

She said, "No."

Then I asked if she wanted anyone particular to do her eulogy.

She said, "What's a eulogy?"

Our voices were quiet as we spoke back and forth, almost as if we were whispering special secrets. "Mom, remember how I talked about Dad and the funny things he did?"

She smiled and replied, "Yes."

"We could talk about the time when Uncle Joe smashed the eggs you had in your pocket."

She smiled again and said, "Yes."

Silence passed between us. Her quiet voice spoke again, "Is Ma gone?"

"Do you mean Grandma?" My voice was tender.

"Yes."

"Mom, Grandma has been gone for a long time now."

She was quiet for a little bit and then spoke. "Did she die soon?"

I wasn't sure what she was asking. I waited a moment and then she spoke again. "Did she die soon?"

By now it was around five o'clock in the morning. I thought back to when Grandma had died. It was in July and Ann had called to tell me that she had passed away. I remembered the moment because, as the phone rang early that morning, I had known what had happened before Ann even said anything. Grandma had died at around 5:00 a.m. All of a sudden I knew what Mom was asking.

"Mom, do you mean did Grandma die at about this time in the morning?"

She said, "Yes."

"Yes, Mom she died about this time in the morning. Remember it was Ann's birthday."

Quietly she replied, "Yes," and then dozed off.

The entire time our conversation had taken place, I had been lying next to Mom with my arm around her. I lay there feeling the profoundness of what had just occurred. It had been so natural and effortless. I could never have planned a more perfect setting.

About half an hour passed and she spoke again in a soft voice. "I'm scared."

"Mom, are you afraid of dying?"

"No." Her voice was quiet but strong.

"Mom, what are you afraid of?"

She hesitated a moment and said, "I'm afraid of…."

Then she stopped and became very frustrated. With a crispness to her voice, she said, "Just give me some pills."

She wouldn't say any more. I was curious to know what she wanted to say but wouldn't. I knew better than to push her. It was time for her morning Decadron, so I went to the kitchen to get it. When I came back, she was sitting up at the end of her bed. Her eyes were wide open and with excitement in her voice she said, "Did you see them?"

I looked at her wondering what she was referring to. "Did I see whom, Mom?"

"All the people." Her voice was still excited.

"No …. Are they coming for you?"

"Yes." She spoke in a clear, knowing tone.

Curious, I asked, "Did they have smiles on their faces?"

"No, I don't think so."

"Did you recognize anyone?"

"No." Her face became more of a blank as she stared out the window.

I waited for her to say something more, but she didn't, so I gave her the pills. She asked to lie back down and didn't bring up dying again after that. I stroked her forehead until she fell asleep. I was in a state of wonderment over what had transpired through the early morning hours. Thank God she had wanted me to sleep with her. We might never have had this conversation otherwise.

On my third consecutive night sleeping with Mom, she continued to be afraid. She remained restless and asked for medication to help her sleep. It didn't seem to help at all. I lowered her morphine level thinking that might be the cause of her restlessness. Her breathing became more labored so I raised it back up. There had been no more early hour conversations.

I lay next to her pondering why she had been so uneasy lately. I hadn't been with Dad during the nights before he passed, so I couldn't make a comparison. I had taken care of patients before they died, but hadn't had any kind of intimate relationship with them. My eight-hour shifts were divided among several patients, diminishing my ability to spend much one-on-one time with any of them.

One elderly patient popped into my mind.

I had been working with a nursing agency that sent me to various hospitals. One evening I was sent to a new place. As I was getting a report from the previous shift about the patients who had been as-signed to me, I learned that one of them was an older woman who had been on the unit for several weeks and was terminally ill. Read-ing over her chart, I saw no dramatic change in her condition, except that she had been very restless for the past several days. I sensed she would pass during my shift, so I organized my care with the other patients around her. Since she had no family members around, I wanted to spend as much time with her as possible. Her husband lived several hours away and wasn't able to make the long drive to visit her often.

Toward the end of the evening I asked the other regular nurses on the unit to check on my patients and went and sat with this woman.

Her name was Alda. She was getting oxygen through nasal prongs and had a foley catheter in her bladder. Her breathing was slightly labored and her eyes were closed. She showed no sign that she was aware I was in the room. I moved the chair next to her bed and held her hand. I wondered about her life, her husband and her children. My heart felt sadness that she was alone and I prayed this would never happen to Mom and Dad when their time came. One of the nurses watching over my other patients came into the room and was surprised to find me just sitting with Alda. I told her I sensed Alda was going to pass on my shift and I wanted to be there for her.

She looked at me and said, "She's been like this for the past couple weeks. She's not going to die tonight or the doctors would have indicated that to us."

I asked if my other patients needed anything and she said "no." I asked if she would mind keeping an eye on them for a little bit longer. She agreed, gave me an odd look and left the room.

Turning my focus back to Alda, I found myself quietly telling her it was okay to go. She wasn't alone, she was deeply loved by her family and she was free. I felt her hand move slightly underneath mine at the same time a peacefulness filled the room. Her breathing changed and became slow and sporadic. Then there was a deep sigh and she took her last breath. I closed my eyes and thanked God for the gift of being with her. I sat for a few more minutes in silence, asking that her soul find peace and contentment and said a prayer for her husband. As I did so, there was a feeling of deep agony inside. I realized he had just lost his best friend. It was the only time I was sent to that hospital.

Recalling this image in my mind, I fully understood Mom's restlessness. She was exploring the spirit world and it was a little frightening. There was agitation in her body as she was dealing with the scope of her new life and releasing the old. It had nothing to do with the medication. Her confusion was feeling the reality of both realms and becoming comfortable with what was before her. Oh how I wished I could see what she was seeing. Why was it that some people could and I couldn't? Lately I had been hungry for a book that described the spiritual process someone dying goes through and how to access that world with them.

Dad had been so different. He didn't share about seeing anyone or feeling their presence. Maybe it was because that just wasn't his way. Perhaps Mom was giving me a gift by letting me see through her experience what I had always believed existed.

One day I took Mom for a drive. Around mid-afternoon she had become really agitated. She kept saying, "Get me out of here. Get me out of here. I can't stand it in here anymore. Just take me home."

We were in the bedroom and I had just finished helping her get dressed. At first I thought she didn't want to be in the bedroom, but taking her into the living room didn't help her extreme restlessness.

I said to her, "Mom you are home. This is where you live now."

She looked at me and scowled. "It is not. Take me home."

I hooked her up to the portable oxygen, put her in the wheelchair and took her outside. She didn't recognize anything. So I put her in the car thinking maybe she wanted to see her old homestead. When her parents had retired from farming, her brother Vernon had purchased the property. As kids we had visited there often and sometimes Mom liked to just stop and walk through the house. Not today. As we rounded the curve in the road the house where she was raised came into view.

I said to Mom, "Do you recognize this house?"

She said, "Of course I do."

I asked if she wanted me to pull in the driveway.

She turned to me and said in a curt voice. "No, I don't want to stop. Just keep going. Why did you bring me here?"

Many times she would ask me to take her to the cemetery. She found comfort in spending time at Dad's grave, as well as those of her parents and sister Julie. At a loss of where else to go, I drove to the cemetery. Big mistake.

Mom looked at me in disgust. "What did you come here for? Get me out of here. Just take me home."

I felt awful. So I took her back to the farm. As we drove in the yard I asked Mom if she knew where she was.

She said, "Of course I do."

While she no longer was agitated, Mom was certainly frustrated with me. "Just take me inside."

She did not mention about wanting to go home again.

Thinking back on this incident, I realized a similarity to Dad's passing. Once when I was with him in his hospital room, he was sitting in a chair and he became very agitated. He grabbed my hand at one point and said, "Get me out of here. Just take me home." At the time I thought he wanted to go back to the farm. His doctor wouldn't release him because he felt he was medically unstable. A few days later he died.

My brother Johnny had stopped to see Mom after attending church. It was one of his regular weekend visits. As he walked into the bedroom, I sensed Mom wanted to be alone with him. Later John shared part of their conversation.

As he was sitting on the bed next to her, she turned to him and asked, "What are those builders doing here?"

John responded, "I don't know."

Then she asked, "Do you know them?"

He answered, "No, Mom, I don't."

A few moments passed and she replied, "They are all done now." She paused for a moment and spoke in a soft voice, "It sure is going to look pretty when the water starts flowing." And then she smiled a huge smile and became quiet.

Listening to his story I felt what a cherished, intimate memory she had given him, something he could hold onto for the rest of his life.

Chapter Sixteen

In the Silent Night, Wings Take Flight

It was Monday. Mom's time had come.

I woke to the sound of her coughing. There was a noticeable difference to her breathing. It had become more labored with a deep hollowness. Her lungs were congested and emitted a wheezing gurgle. I looked toward my small alarm clock on the corner of the television stand. It was 1:30 in the morning. She was lying on the couch where she had been since Sunday. She hadn't wanted to be in the bedroom and it hadn't felt right to me either.

I threw the blanket off my shoulders where I had fallen asleep on the living room floor. Curled in another blanket was my friend John. Mom coughed again, waking him up. John quietly tiptoed out of the living room.

Ann, Dave, and John had come over the day before to mow the lawn. Ann brought food and we grilled out. I asked John to stay and watch the closing ceremonies of the Olympics because I didn't want to be alone. We turned the volume down low on the television so as not to disturb Mom. He fell asleep around 8:30. Intending to wake him after the ceremonies were over, I fell asleep as well.

Walking toward Mom, I sensed her time was getting short. My mind quickly considered the possibility of her passing as early as 5:00 a.m., the same time as Grandma. Glancing at Mom's face, one of the oxygen prongs had slipped out of the corner of her nose. As I repositioned it, I noticed a peacefulness about her in spite of the gasping noise coming from her body.

Kneeling next to the couch, my hand stroked her forehead. She opened her eyes and began coughing. Slipping one arm underneath her back and the other around her neck and shoulders, I gently sat her up. She had little strength to assist me. She reached for a crumbled Kleenex lying next to her and slowly covered her mouth as she coughed again. I could feel the boniness of her spine as my hand gently rubbed her back. In the last few days she had become much more frail. My arms tightened around her and my head leaned next to hers. I gently rocked her. My heart felt numb. The soft glow of the living room light cast shadows on her lap as her hands rested on top of each other. Once strong and firm, they had become fragile and thin. My fingers tenderly stroked the surface of her hand, feeling its delicate softness. The kitchen light reflected back through the living room window, illuminating an emptiness in the house.

Mom was too weak to sit up any longer and her body moved sideways. I gently laid her back down and asked if she were comfortable. She slowly nodded her head "yes." I placed the blanket snugly around her shoulders and readjusted the nasal prongs. She closed her eyes.

I went to say good night to John and found him outside smoking. It was a balmy summer evening. The sharp fragrance of freshly mowed grass filtered through the air and crickets awakened the stillness of the night. The sky was peppered with twinkling lights and I couldn't help but wonder which one was Dad. John told me that just as he stepped outside he saw a white light enter the house. Chills went through my body and I felt a sense that God had come to take Mom.

We hugged each other good-night and he told me to call him if there was anything he could do. We both knew what would soon unfold. As he left, I felt a nauseating feeling in the region of my solar plexus. It felt like a gnarly knot signaling what was in store for my body. It created a feeling of anxiety and uncertainty. I took a deep breath and my eyes scanned the horizon of the night sky. My prayers asked that whatever Mom was holding onto be let go. The nausea lessened.

Just as I turned to walk back inside, a shooting star descended from the heavens. For a moment I was drawn to the place where it first appeared. Several lights were shining almost in a circular fashion, creating an opening. Their colors changed from white to green to red and then back to white. A shiver went up my spine. I became transfixed by the opening and felt light-headed. My thoughts raced. Was this a portal for Mom to make her transition? Did such things exist? Was this standard procedure for every soul before it passed over? Deep inside I sensed it was real. I looked toward the configuration of stars one more time and went inside.

My feet echoed on the linoleum floor of the kitchen as I made my way back toward the living room. I could see the reflection of Mom lying on the couch in the large picture window. The humming of the oxygen machine filled my ears and almost sounded deafening. Her breathing was still gasping and her mouth was slightly open. I sat on the floor next to her watching the irregular rhythm of her breath. Suddenly the reality of what was beginning to occur hit me.

A feeling of panic jarred my body. "Dear God. If Mom's time is near let me know I have taken her to the Light." The one constant prayer I had held since coming home to be with Mom was for this to happen. Wanting a clear sign, I laid my head on her lap and closed my eyes. All of a sudden I saw an image of Mom and I standing in a tunnel. I was holding her hand. In front of us was a brilliant, white light. It felt incredibly peaceful. I turned to her and said, "Mom, I can't go with you any further." We stood calmly together for a moment. Then she released my hand and walked toward the light. She didn't look back. The image faded and my eyes automatically opened. My mind questioned what had just happened and I wondered if I had made it up to pacify my own hunger for peace inside.

Closing my eyes again, I said another prayer. "Dear God, show me the truth of this journey with my mother."

The exact same scenario flashed twice through my mind. Rocking back and forth, I started to cry. All the months of wondering whether I had done enough had finally been answered. Zarathustra's words from one of our phone sessions entered my mind: "Don't look to each moment to be shown the gifts in being with your mother. Pearls of insight and wisdom will be given to you the remainder of your life." This was one of those moments.

Mom opened her eyes and looked at me. My fingers stroked her hand and I smiled at her. She closed her eyes. The irregular rhythm of her breathing found a more even pace. Her coughing episode had not reoccurred and she appeared more stable. It was 4:00 a.m. I thought about calling my brothers and sisters. I didn't want to be premature and wake everyone up with one of those dreaded early morning calls. Yet I didn't want to deprive anyone from coming to be with her. All of a sudden I felt very tired and lay down at Mom's feet at the end of the couch and fell asleep. When I awoke, sunlight was streaming through the living room windows. Glancing at the clock, it was 9:00 a.m. My heart started pounding and I looked over at Mom. She was asleep, her breathing unchanged.

I called Ann at work and shared what had transpired. We discussed calling everyone and mutually decided to wait. She thought Mom was going to hold on for a few days as Dad had done. She planned to stop by after work and we'd reassess the situation then. I hung up wondering whether we had made the right decision. I went and checked on Mom again and found her sound asleep. There was a kind of chaotic restlessness going on inside me and I felt very alone. I yearned for a connection with one of my spiritual sisters. I called Jacque and was told she was in California. I called Sabrina, but she wasn't home either.

I fixed a cup of tea and sat at the kitchen table. The sun was shining through the window and it was warm in the house. I thought of picking one of Mom's geranium flowers and creating an altar by the side of the couch. I checked on Mom again and saw that she was still sleeping. Ann was probably right and I was worrying needlessly about not calling everyone. She could go on like this for days.

Walking outside, I took in the fresh air. Everything felt so alive. A small flock of sparrows landed in the balsam tree next to one of Mom's flower gardens. They began serenading back and forth as if they were singing a lullaby. There was a stickiness in the atmosphere as sometimes occurs before a Midwestern rainstorm. I knelt on the ground in front of Mom's geraniums. They were vibrant in colors of white, red, light pink and fuchsia. I touched the petals of the fuchsia flowers and felt their delicate softness. Taking a strand of my hair, I placed it next to the plant. Gently I broke a flower from its stem and held it in my hands, offering it up to the sky. Then I prayed that it fill the house with the sweetness of Mom's essence and the love she had given her flowers throughout the years.

I was eager to linger outside in the warm sun, but felt uncomfortable about leaving Mom alone so I hastened back inside. I found a little glass bowl in the cupboard and filled it with water. Placing my hand over the top, I blessed the water and placed the beautiful geranium flower inside. Then I walked throughout the whole house dipping the fuchsia geranium in the water and sprinkling drops everywhere. I felt like one of the Catholic priests during Sunday services blessing the congregation with holy water. I gentle sprinkled drops around Mom and on myself before placing the bowl on a television tray at the foot of the couch. Aunt Mary had brought one over on Sunday thinking it might be useful for Mom.

Mom was still asleep, her breathing unchanged. It felt sticky in the house so I opened the living room door. A gentle, warm breeze entered through the screen. Then I walked into the bedroom and found the rosary Mom loved to pray with and that had belonged to her sister Julia. It was sitting on Mom's dresser next to her crucifix. The beads were light green, large and illuminated in the dark. I could almost feel Mom's fingers wrapped around them. Also sitting on the dresser was a seashell Mom had been given at the Zarathustra teaching. I took the rosary and shell and walked into the living room and placed them on the stand next to the geranium flower. Then I walked upstairs and took two candles from my altar. One was pink and the other white. I also took the eagle feather from John and walked back downstairs and positioned them on the stand. I was surprised the phone hadn't done its usual Monday morning ringing with everyone checking up on Mom. Oddly enough, it wouldn't ring all day.

The restlessness inside me grew. Remembering that Sabrina had spent the weekend in Santa Barbara, I called her house, got the number from her husband and dialed it. She answered the phone and told me Jacque and Sheila were with her, and that she felt it was Mom's time. Jacque came to the phone and acknowledged the same thing. I asked for guidance. As I listened on the other end, Jacque gathered Sabrina, her daughter Julia and Sheila. They all joined together in a circle around a white candle. She asked me to be quiet, think of the candle and let myself go through its flame and be with them. I closed my eyes and visualized myself going through the flame, sitting with them. Images of each of their faces appeared in my mind. I felt the strong sense of their presence and I started to cry.

Jacque explained I was carrying much of Mom's energy as a result of sleeping next to her and that my crying was releasing the heavy denseness Mom's dying had created in the house. She suggested doing some of the things I'd already done. Since I had been feeling a little lost, like a young child searching for her security blanket, it was great to talk with Jacque. She told me to light incense, smudge myself thoroughly and softly play angelic music. She encouraged me not to speak to Mom about the Light, as it would distract her from going in and out between the spirit world and her physical body. She said that instead my words should be of love, whispered softly throughout the day. I should say how beautiful Mom was, how much she was loved and how much love was surrounding her. She also shared not to overly caress Mom's body because it would be agitating. Her words, "create a very peaceful, loving environment" lingered in my mind.

Then she passed on information from Zarathustra. Mom had already seen the Light and Dad. Her friend Ann, who had passed away the year before, was tending to Mom in the living room as we spoke. She said to call her later and that she would be in prayer with me all day. I was tremendously grateful for her loving and kind support.

As I hung up the phone, a tremendous peace came over me. I went over our conversation in my mind, not wanting to forget any details. When I returned to the living room, I could feel a difference in the energy. There was a deep calm. It almost felt angelic. I sat next to Mom on the floor and lightly touched her hand. She opened her eyes and looked toward me. I didn't speak to her but only smiled. There was a blank stare to her eyes as if she were seeing right through me. She didn't acknowledge my presence. She turned and looked up at the ceiling and her eyes became huge. I looked up with her, hoping some kind of image would be revealed. There was none. I looked back at her. Her eyes were transfixed on the ceiling and seemed even wider. I wondered what she saw and what she was feeling. She stayed that way for some time. Then she slowly shifted her eyes in front of her. As I continued to lightly stroke her hand, she gave no physical response. The only sound in the house was the rhythm of the oxygen unit and Mom's hollow, windy breathing. Occasionally a sparrow's throaty song floated through the screen door. A warm, gentle breeze drifted inside, stirring the stagnant air lingering in the room.

Angel music popped into my thoughts. Gently releasing Mom's hand, I made my way upstairs and searched through my assortment of tapes, looking for something appropriate. I remembered purchasing a cassette when Mom and I were in California. We had gone into a little boutique that specialized in candles and angels. We heard a woman's beautiful voice singing "Ave Marie," one of Mom's favorite songs. We purchased the tape and found, to Mom's surprise, her other favorite, "Amazing Grace."

I was not able to find the tape anywhere. As I continued searching, I opened a box containing two white candles with gold angels wrapped around them. They were a Christmas purchase I had been waiting to use for a special occasion. What a wonderful time. Still unable to find the tape, I went back downstairs. Looking for candle holders, I saw Mom's walkman sitting on a small oak bookshelf in the living room. Something told me to look inside. There was the tape. I walked to the corner of the room next to the screen door and placed it in the tape player sitting on top of a small stereo Dad had given Mom years ago. I pressed the play button and waited to adjust the volume. The sound of dolphins quietly filled the room. I thought it was the wrong tape until an elegant, graceful soprano began singing "Ave Marie." The exquisite nature of her harmony resonated like angels' voices throughout the room. It was the perfect music for Mom and tears filled my eyes. The tape played continuously all day long.

After finding holders for the two angel candles, I arranged them next to the other objects on the stand. The flames from the four candles merged together into one brilliant light, and the television tray was transformed into Mom's sacred altar. The living room felt like a holy sanctuary, fit for a queen preparing to return home. There was an extremely peaceful, blissful quality to it. I was aware that what had once appeared as our different beliefs in worshipping God had finally become joined. I thought Mom would be proud and honored.

I sat on the floor next to Mom. Her eyes were open and I gently touched her arm. She turned and looked at me. I smiled. I longed to speak to her, to connect verbally and reunite in the bond we once shared. She didn't say a word. My curious nature wanted to ask what she had seen as she looked at the ceiling earlier. What caused her eyes to open so wide? What was she feeling and thinking? Could she feel the presence of her friend Ann? I would never know. This journey would remain her mystery, not to be imposed upon by an inquisitive daughter. One day I, too, would experience the private intimacy of the same thing.

I whispered to her how much I loved her, how thankful I was that she was my mother, how special she was to me, how honored I was to be with her, how much she was loved and treasured and how much God loved her. Throughout the day I continued my lullaby of loving words as a prayerful vigil. As I adjusted her blanket, I felt her crystal rosary next to her arm and placed it through her fingers and folded her hands together.

It was close to one o'clock. I was beginning to feel guilty about not having contacted everyone. I called Ann at work. She asked if there had been any change in Mom. I told her "no," that she was resting comfortably. She didn't seem concerned. She told me if I felt adamant about calling everyone to go ahead, otherwise to wait and she would see me after work. Something still prevented me from making the calls. Instead, I went and sat by Mom's feet at the end of the couch, savoring the opportunity to be alone with her.

Closing my eyes, I realized how exhausted I felt. It was the kind of exhaustion that is beyond sleeping. Mom started to cough and as I sat on the floor next to her, I could hear wheezing in her chest. I was prepared to sit her up when the wheezing stopped. She resumed her labored breathing as I heard "Amazing Grace" being sung. I returned to the end of the couch and leaned my head back. I gently rubbed Mom's feet that were covered by her socks, not thinking about what I was doing. She pulled them away. I looked over at her and her eyes were again transfixed upward. Oh how I wished I could see what she was seeing.

There was a slowness to the day, almost as if time had stopped and I was content just to be.

The wind began to blow as I heard the rustling of leaves on the trees outside. The sky had turned gray. Rain drops plopped against the window panes as the wind blew more strongly. As I got up to close the living room door, a bolt of lightning flashed across the sky, followed by booming thunder. I felt excitement and looked at Mom. I wanted to say out loud, "Look, Mom, they are cleaning the heavens for you." But I didn't. A smile formed on my face as I sent the thought to her instead. There was a powerful, yet graceful force to the storm that had a mystical quality about it. Watching the bolts of lightning stretch across the sky like open arms made me realize how much I had missed good, old Midwestern rain storms.

The storm lasted about forty-five minutes. As the wind slowly died down, sun rays entered the living room window, striking the couch by Mom's head. Birds began chirping gloriously back and forth to each other. For an instant I thought I heard children's voices singing in the distance. I looked at Mom and her eyes were open wider than before. As I opened the door, a gentle breeze carried the fragrance of fresh moisture into the room as if it were smudging away the scars of entrenched sadness that had been prevalent in the house. I watched a slender, green hummingbird land on the feeder outside the window, dipping its beak into the red liquid. Its wings fluttered rapidly, reminding me of those of an angel. I pondered how life always gives back life, even in dying. Nature had fed my soul this afternoon, just like the little hummingbird and the sparrows singing outside. I couldn't help but believe that Mom's soul had been nourished as well.

It was 5:30 when Ann's beige car drove into the yard. As she walked into the living room, her eyes glanced at the burning candles on Mom's altar. She looked at me with a slight grin and said, "Cripes, what are you trying to do—burn down the house?"

I just smiled at her. She took a moment and responded lightly, "I thought you'd do something like this."

Ann went and knelt next to Mom. Mom's eyes turned toward her, but she didn't speak. I told Ann she had been like this all day. Her breathing still had a hollowness to it but there appeared to be less congestion in her lungs. While Ann still thought Mom could last for a few more days, I was beginning to sense something different. We agreed to call everyone even if I were wrong.

We split the calls. I made half of them on my phone upstairs and Ann made the others downstairs. No one was really surprised to hear about Mom's condition nor did they seem upset we hadn't called sooner. Johnny had just gotten home from work and planned to stop over after he ate. Neither Mary in Florida, nor Vernon in Seattle planned on flying back since they both felt complete. The only other ones close enough to drive home were Ron and Mark. Neither chose to come. Ron and Ann had been home the weekend before and Mark a week earlier. I wondered whether by not calling sooner I had deprived any of them of the opportunity to be with Mom in the same way I had been.

Ann stayed and we sat in the living room sharing memories about Mom. It had been all day since I had changed Mom's Depends. We were concerned about disturbing her, yet we didn't want her to be uncomfortable. We grunted and groaned as we attempted the difficult task of trying to move her gently. After a few chuckles and smiles she was neatly tucked back into place. She was wearing pink and white cotton pajama bottoms with little blue flowers on them and a fuchsia-colored blouse. She had made both of them. We wrapped the crystal rosary through her hands, folded them on top of her chest and pulled the blue blanket around her shoulders. Her bald head rested to one side on a white pillow.

Johnny came by an hour later looking exhausted. There was a heaviness to his body. He seemed to have been shouldering a lot of internal responsibility since Dad had passed away. Our evening was spent sitting together recalling our childhood. It reminded me of when Dad died and we had gathered in the hospital room, laughing and telling stories. Just as with Dad, Mom was oblivious to anything external. It was so peaceful in the house. The candles radiated a soft glow from the darkness now unfolding outside. The music was no longer playing. Above our voices was the quiet hum of the oxygen unit. As Mom continued to lie motionless on the couch, Johnny occasionally wiped his eyes.

At ten o'clock Ann said she was leaving. I encouraged her to stay because I sensed Mom's time was drawing closer. Just as she couldn't stay when Dad passed, nor could she with Mom. Touching Mom's hand, she left.

Johnny sat on the floor next to Mom, and I walked into the kitchen, leaving him to his privacy. Turning on the stove to heat water to make a cup of tea, I walked to the sink and looked out the window. How many times had Mom pondered her thoughts doing the same thing? This was the window of her life. Now she would be seeing from a new perspective.

I sat at the kitchen table with my cup of tea and looked around the room. So many memories were stored in these walls, so many meals had been eaten at this kitchen table. The mementos told the story: a young couple starting out with hopes and aspirations of a life together; a family raised through challenges, determination and hard work; tiny feet taking their first steps, learning to run and then becoming wings to fly from the nest; grandchildren gracing their aging years with a sense of renewal; the world around them constantly changing, yet theirs remaining relatively sheltered. Moments of laughter, disappointment, sorrow, faith and love became the tapestry that bound them together. They were every couple and no other couple. They were uniquely my parents. They had given me roots, taught me responsibility and loved me the best way they knew how. A chapter was concluding and a new one beginning—starting with a wisp of breath and ending with one. What a mystery life is.

My thoughts came back to the room as I heard the ticking of the clock on the wall. It was 11:15. Walking into the living room, I found Johnny sitting on the end of the couch next to Mom's feet. His eyes were closed and he seemed to be sleeping. I sat on the floor next to Mom. Her eyes were open, staring blankly in front of her. Her hands were warm as I softly stroked them. Johnny opened his eyes and rubbed them. Neither of us spoke. Our silence created a camaraderie, strong in our love for the woman who united us as brother and sister.

My eyes met his and I quietly said, "Johnny, you must be tired. You've been working hard all day. You can go if you want."

He slowly got up from the couch, massaging his right leg. Turning to me, he said, "Do you think I should stay?"

"Johnny, it's entirely up to you."

He looked at Mom, gently touching her hands with the roughness of his. Moments passed. With a catch in his voice he said, "She'd tell me to go home."

He patted me on the back and I sensed he was crying as he left the room. The tires of his truck on the gravel made a crunching sound as he drove out of the yard. Placing my head on Mom's chest, I heard my voice say, "Mom, we started out alone together. I guess it only seems fitting that we end up alone. I love you. Thank you for letting me be here for you. You have been a wonderful mother. God has great things in store for you."

A tremendous emptiness came over me. I went into the kitchen to fix another cup of tea, thinking it could be a long night. Just as I returned to the living room, Mom's breathing changed dramatically. The heaviness was replaced by very short breaths. I was surprised and felt unprepared. I sat on the floor with my hands on top of hers. They felt hot. Her short gasps continued for a few minutes and then stopped. I waited for another breath. There was none.

I felt numb. I looked at the clock on the television stand. It registered 12:45. I heard my thoughts: "Oh my God, it is exactly the same time that Dad died."

I laid my head on Mom's chest, with my hands over hers. My fingers wrapped around hers like a young child not wanting to let go. I started crying, my tears wetting her blouse. An overwhelming sense of responsibility racked my body. I felt an incredible heaviness inside and an aloneness that seemed to fill every cell.

My voice sounded hollow as I said aloud, "Dear God, I don't ever want to go through anything like this in my life alone ever again."

From a place deep, deep inside, I felt I had completed some kind of agreement made lifetimes earlier with Mom. My voice continued through my tears: "God, if this was some agreement I made with Mom, I accept the responsibility and will complete it with honor and grace."

The heaviness began to leave my body. All of a sudden it became clear what to do. I got a basin of warm water and a wash cloth from the bathroom and placed it on the floor. Then I began to bathe Mom, gently cleansing her face. I unbuttoned her blouse and washed her chest and continued down her body. It was still so warm. Her pajama bottoms slipped easily off her legs and I removed her Depends. I tenderly took off her socks and placed the blanket over her body when I was finished. An image entered my mind that seemed ancient. I was with a group of women and we were doing a similar ritual. It seemed to be a ceremony that was naturally performed during that time. There was a holiness and a reverence about it that was transported into the room. As my hands gently stroked

Mom's body, I entered a kind of meditation, oblivious to my surroundings.

I removed Mom's false teeth and scrubbed them. It was difficult replacing them inside her mouth. I took a pair of tweezers and plucked the hairs from her chin that had grown over the past few weeks. I found a brush and scrubbed her fingernails, which were lightly covered with phlegm from coughing. There was still warmth in her hands as I gently cleaned each finger individually.

I thought of wrapping Mom in the fluffy, red flannel bathrobe Mary and Ann had given her for Christmas the previous year. I found it lying on her bed. It was difficult removing her blouse because of the heaviness to her body. Her teeth clattered together every time I moved her head and I found myself smiling and apologizing to Mom over my awkwardness. Somehow I got the bathrobe on and wrapped it tenderly around her. I felt as though I had stepped out of my body and was watching myself.

I took one hand and kissed the palm with a reverence I had known before. I gently placed it on her lap. Then I took the other palm and did the same thing. As I placed it on top of her other hand, I heard inside my head, "It is done."

I felt as though I had just come out of a trance. Sitting on the floor next to Mom with my hands over hers, I felt the last fragment of warmth slowly seep out of them. I closed my eyes and prayed, "Dear God, bless this woman, my mother. Guide her soul to bliss and may she know how much she is loved. Thank you for the gift of being sent to care for her. Bring comfort and peace to my family."

I sat for a while longer with my eyes closed and then began to feel uncomfortable. Looking at Mom, she now had a "death" appearance to her face. Suddenly it felt very cold in the room. I sensed Mom's spirit had left. Unable to stay in the room any longer with her, I walked into the kitchen. The clock ticked 1:30 in the morning. I contemplated calling everyone. Something told me to wait. I placed a call to the funeral home. A man's voice told me they would be at the house in an hour. I felt the urge to phone Jacque.

She had been waiting for my call and the sound of her voice was soothing and reassuring. Her comforting words seemed to float through my body. I asked what I could expect to feel in the days ahead. She responded, "That's your answer. You can expect to feel now."

A profound feeling came over me like wings that had come to set me free. She had spoken an awesome truth. I began crying as if I had just been unshackled from chains that had burdened my heart for years.

We were still speaking when I heard a vehicle turn into the driveway. It was 3:00 a.m. It was surreal opening the living room door. A dense mist made it difficult to see the outline of the hearse parked next to the steps. Two men were dressed in suits. When I told them it would have been okay if they had come in jeans because of the lateness of the hour, one of the men replied, "We dress this way for us, out of respect for what we are doing."

The wooden planks on the steps made easy access for their gurney. One of the directors who had handled Dad's funeral commented on the tranquillity in the room. "This is one of the most peaceful settings I have felt in all my years in this business. How wonderful for your mother to have been able to die at home."

I went into the kitchen to get the doctor's phone number and address. When I returned they had covered Mom with a white cotton sheet. They began to push the gurney toward the door. I asked them to wait a moment. Pulling the sheet away from her face, I tenderly looked upon it. My hands brushed the top of her head and gently stroked her cheeks. I leaned down and kissed them, and whispered, "Good-bye, Mom. I love you." Then I placed the sheet back over her face. As they wheeled her body out of the house, she seemed to just disappear into the fog. Then they drove away.

The candles were still softly burning and I took a moment and glanced around the room. I took an incense stick and smudged the house. All of a sudden I became aware of an odor coming from my body, the kind that dying people emit. I went to take a shower. A weariness came over me as the hot water and steam penetrated my body. I turned out all the lights and left open the kitchen door that led upstairs. I lit a candle next to my bed and lay on the bed. I felt peaceful. The house was extremely quiet and had a soothing effect.

A few minutes passed and then I heard footsteps in the living room. Even though there was carpeting on the floor, they were clear and distinct. I heard them again and they moved into the kitchen. My heart started to pound. I sensed it was Dad. I prayed for him not to come upstairs. It would have been too much for me to handle. The steps stopped and the house became quiet again. I looked at the clock. It was four in the morning. Knowing Johnny got up at five for work I made a mental note to call him. Lying peaceful on the bed, I was no longer tired. Thoughts of Mom and Dad drifted through my head. "They are finally free, God. They are home and they are free."

An hour later I called Johnny. He was crying on the phone as I shared how Mom had passed away. I asked if he wanted to come over and he said, "Yes."

I walked downstairs wrapped in my bathrobe. There was such a tranquil feeling in the living room. I could have sat alone in the energy forever. I knew it was a bit selfish of me to want to absorb the sacredness of what had occurred just hours before, but I knew this moment wouldn't come again.

Johnny arrived at 5:30 am, crying. I sat on the couch with my arm around him, crying also. We talked about Mom's passing. I told him one gift was that they were finally free from their illnesses and were together. I said that we were also free now. We had helped them to die with peace and dignity and now we had our own lives before us. One day we would feel the warmth of all our memories with them and not have sadness. We sat together in silence for awhile.

I left Johnny alone on the couch and called Ann. She was not surprised Mom had passed away. I asked if she could send Dave over because I sensed Johnny's need for a man's energy. I told her I'd call everyone and asked her to come over when she was ready. She was crying as she hung up the phone. By the time she arrived, everyone else had been notified. The quiet solitude I had briefly experienced was quickly replaced with the hustle and bustle of everyone reuniting for Mom's final departure from our lives.

I struggled for several weeks to write this chapter, staring at a blank computer screen for hours on end, but nothing seemed to flow. Instead I felt tremendous agitation. Finally I had the following dream:

I was in some kind of ceremony with Jacque and several other friends. She presented me with the gift of a necklace. It felt very old, like an amulet. A gold, antique-looking chain hung down to the level of my heart. At the end was a grouping of items. There was a turquoise heart, two tiny acorns connected at the top and a smooth half-moon made of a fine metal. The moon was curved at each end. All the items were connected in a circle and each hung separately. As she put it around my neck, I felt peaceful and holy.

After waking from the dream, I sat down and wrote this chapter in half a day. I was in a trance-like state and each moment was vividly relived. When I finished, I walked outside. The sky was filled with big fluffy clouds. In one corner of the sky, beautiful golden rays were streaming down and appeared heavenly. A powerful feeling of love and peace came over me.

Chapter Seventeen

A Loving Farewell and a Ghost Called "Charlie"

Just as birth has its own mystique, the same can be said about dying. I found this especially so after Mom's passing. Shrouded under a veil of intrigue, events occurred that left me spellbound.

The night after Mom passed, I was alone in the house. About two in the morning, a loud knocking woke me. It sounded like someone in distress pounding on the downstairs porch door. I sat up in bed, my heart beating rapidly.

Having heard footsteps the night before, I was pretty skittish. I waited for the knocking to occur again. It didn't. I listened for a car to drive out of the yard. There was none. Several times in the past few months, I had hear a similar knocking in the middle of the night and had taken it as a sign to check on Mom. But the knocking had never been so loud. This one was certainly meant to capture my attention. I was never able to get back to sleep.

The next morning, Ann and I were on our way to see the priest about Mom's service and were drawn to stop at the funeral home. The funeral director asked if we wanted to see Mom. We had ordered a casket from the Amish just like Dad's, but it hadn't arrived yet.

When we walked into the viewing room, Ann and I were greeted by a wondrous sight. Mom was lying elevated on a table draped with a white cloth. A soft, golden light shone down on her body. She was beautiful and looked like an angel. There was a mystical glow about her and she was smiling. My breath stopped for a moment as I gazed at her. I turned to Ann and said, "Doesn't she look wonderful? You can't even tell she was ever sick."

My sister agreed.

Mom looked like a beautiful, elegant queen asleep. To see my mother in this fashion, without the stigma and ambiance created by a casket was awesome. I thought, "Every person who has passed on should be displayed in such a dignified way." It was as though Mom were being presented to the heavens with great honor and glory. Although I wished I had brought my camera to capture the beauty before me, the image would forever be fervently etched in my memory.

As we were standing there admiring Mom, the funeral director came and said Mom's sister Mary had just stopped by. Curious why she hadn't come into the room, we went in search of her. We caught her in the parking lot just as she was getting into her car. We asked her to come and see Mom. It was a precious gift for all of us. It felt as though we were getting ready for a party, doing last minute primping as women do—putting a few strands of Mom's hair into place, smoothing her dress and experimenting with different jewelry. For a moment it seemed Aunt Mary had become our substitute Mom as we giggled and chatted together. My heart was full as she spoke, "Oh Edder, I'm so proud of how you look. John would give you more than a second glance if he saw you now." I savored the moment, drawing strength from the loving bond with my sister and aunt.

Later that afternoon, I returned to the funeral home, this time with my other sister. I wanted to bless and smudge the viewing room just as I had done for Dad, and Mary had asked to come along. When we arrived, the room felt heavy and void of life. Lighting the sage stick, I circled the room once. Then I took the geranium flower that had been on Mom's altar and circled again, sprinkling drops of water. In my thoughts I asked that the essence of Mom be felt by every person as they entered to share in their farewell of this gentle and kind woman who had graced all our lives. When Mary and I finished our individual prayers, we both could sense a dramatic change in the room. It felt peaceful and light.

We went to the florist to pick out flowers and to find something uniquely like Mom that we could display at the funeral home. When Mom wrote letters, she would always draw a smiley face after she signed her name. Browsing through the shop, we saw a yellow balloon with big black eyes and a large black smile. We started laughing and knew we had found one of the special qualities of Mom. Because of Mom's love for flowers, we also decided to have arrangements of little bouquets in baskets that people could take after the service. These things added that special touch Mom would have appreciated.

I had offered to give Mom's eulogy. That evening I drove to John's home to sit by the river and begin collecting my thoughts. The funeral would be in two days.

I found myself on some rocks in the same place I had gone after Mom's healing ceremony in the teepee. Words to a poem started flowing onto the paper as the warm, late afternoon sun shimmered on the gently moving river.

Mom, you have been a remarkable teacher.
You taught us how to love and to laugh,
To believe in ourselves and be who we are.
For in your illness, we sought strength.
In your pain and sorrow, we hungered to have peace and joy.
Amidst your darkness, we looked for light.
As you struggled to become free, we became whole.
You gave us our wings and taught us how to fly.

We will listen for your laughter on the wind,
And smell your sweet essence in every flower,
Feel your warm embrace from every sunrise and sunset,
And sense your magical presence, as we embrace each new day
With the fullness of having felt the love of God through you.

Enjoy your bountiful freedom as you soar the skies of heaven,

And tend to your precious garden.
May you finally know the true beauty and sweet nectar
of your soul,
And bask in the light of God.
And may you realize how truly loved you are.

As I finished writing, a bald eagle circled above me. Suddenly there was a pounding sensation in the back of my head and a feeling of nausea overcame me. Thinking it would help, I took my shoes and socks off and placed my feet in the cold water. The pounding got stronger. I forced myself to focus. For a brief second the words "prayer of farewell" popped into my head. I thought, "Great, that's what I'll call this. But I still don't have any kind of eulogy."

The more I tried to concentrate, the worse I felt. Finally I couldn't focus at all. I had the most incredible migraine headache. The first time I had ever experienced one was in college, and they occurred occasionally after periods of stress. None had compared with this. Wanting to finish the eulogy, I went and sat inside the teepee. It didn't help. Making my way back up from the river to John's house was agony. One step felt like a hundred miles. Every time my feet touched the ground, my head pounded harder. When I finally arrived at the house, I could hardly function. I asked John to drive me home.

By the time we got there, it was difficult for me to even walk. The house was filled with relatives but I was unable to speak to anyone. With John behind me, I practically crawled up the stairs. To lie on a pillow felt as if my head were resting on a rock. All I could do was sit up and rock back and forth.

My sister Ann came upstairs and looked concerned. She asked what had happened and John explained. Afraid I was having some kind of "coronary," she inquired whether I should go to the hospital. Mumbling that I would be okay, I told her to leave me alone. By this time my whole body was writhing in pain. I asked John to call Jacque. She wasn't home. I asked him to get me a cold wash cloth. It didn't help.

The migraine had now penetrated my whole body and I thought I was going to die. I thought, "If this is what Jacque meant by being able to feel, I prefer the other way."

Even though I knew my body was releasing pressure that had stored up from caring for Mom, it didn't ease the intense pain. I was unable to think clearly and didn't know what to do. All I could do was rock back and forth and moan. I kept asking John to call Jacque. No answer.

After about an hour and a half, I crawled from the bed and called Jacque myself. She picked up the phone. Her voice was a blur through the receiver. I asked if she knew this would occur and why hadn't she warned me. She said she didn't want to alarm me about what might happen. She confirmed I was releasing a great deal of Mom's energy, especially from sleeping next to her. Although she reassured me I would be fine, it didn't feel that way. Wanting suggestions about how to ease the pain, I gave the phone to John because I was no longer able to endure talking.

When he hung up the phone, he went outside and came back with a bowl of soil. He told me to smell it and that it would ground me in my body. I asked him where he had gotten it and he said from the base of a tree that had split outside Mom's bedroom. It must have occurred during the thunderstorm the afternoon before she died. I hadn't heard it happen. The earthiness of its aroma soothed my body somewhat. Then he began rubbing his hands on my legs, rubbing downward toward my toes and pulling energy out of my body. He did the same thing to my arms. All I could do was lie still and groan. While I was normally not one to display pain or complain, I was unable to control myself.

At one point, my brother Mark came upstairs to check on me and in my irritation I sent him away. Ann came back upstairs but quickly left after hearing my moaning. She had never been able to handle the physical aspects of someone not feeling well.

After what seemed like hours, John stopped. The intense pain had subsided, but I felt weak and drained. I went downstairs to take a warm bath. Embarrassed to be seen so "out of it," I mumbled my way to the bathroom. The warm, soothing water pulled more tension from my body. By the time I returned upstairs, I was physically and emotionally exhausted. The headache had lessened. John shared that Jacque had said he was to lie next to me all night to stabilize my body. Too tired to complain, I finally fell asleep unaware he was there.

The next morning I had only slight remnants of a headache. I had begun my own process of cleansing and wondered what else was in store for me.

The viewing for Mom was similar to Dad's. Laughter from friends and family filled the room and I could sense Mom's presence. Mom always worried no one would show up at her funeral because of her secluded life. More came than for Dad.

Still drained from the night before, I felt like a zombie and deficient in interacting with people. Every now and then my eyes would catch the face of a smiling yellow balloon swaying from the breeze of the air conditioner. It warmed my heart and helped ease the tiredness in my body.

Late that night I lay in bed and faced the task of completing Mom's eulogy. It was midnight and the house was quiet. Margaret and Vernon had arrived earlier that morning. They were sleeping in Mom's and Dad's bedroom. In the room next to mine were Ron and Ann. Mary was at Ann's and Dave's house. Mark, Kate and their kids were staying nearby at a cottage her parents owned.

Again I felt the heaviness of responsibility. Numb and tired, I pondered setting the alarm clock to get up around six and write then, as I had done for Dad's eulogy. But my intuition told me to hang in there. Weariness caused me to question my ability to write it. For a long time I had nothing but blank thoughts. Closing my eyes, my mind drifted to Mom. I prayed, "Dear Mom, let me do justice to you when I speak tomorrow. Guide me in what you would like shared. Help me to inspire and uplift everyone. Let the grace and beauty of your soul fill the church. Give me the appropriate words to write."

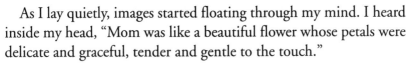

As I lay quietly, images started floating through my mind. I heard inside my head, "Mom was like a beautiful flower whose petals were delicate and graceful, tender and gentle to the touch."

The words started flowing on the paper. Each time my mind became blank, I would close my eyes and reflect about her. More images would come and with them words. When I had finished, I felt peaceful. I looked at the clock. It was three in the morning. Just before I turned to blow out the candle at my bedside, I felt a distinct kiss on my forehead. It was gentle and soft, lingering for a moment and no different from when I would kiss Mom good night in the same way. My eyes filled with tears. Mom had been in the room with me assisting with my final vigil to her memory.

The day of Mom's funeral was beautiful, warm and sunny. The sky was clear with a few white, puffy clouds, the kind she always loved. There was another viewing at the funeral home before the service, which was held at the church she had attended all her life. I would have preferred time alone just for my family. Mary felt the same way. But it was such a standard practice in the community that even if we had requested privacy, people would have still shown up. It had become a ritual for final farewells.

I was feeling trepidation about giving the eulogy. I had been so strong for Mom for so long, I was concerned a rush of emotion would finally surface and leave me unable to speak. I wanted the service to be one of celebration and not tremendous grief.

When only our immediate family remained in the viewing room, I sat staring blankly in front of me wondering why I hadn't been able to cry. All of a sudden, a flood of sadness welled up in my body. I began to sob, my body shaking. Just as it seemed I would lose control, my sister Ann sat next to me and held my hand. She turned and said, "Come on, we'll do this together."

For a moment I felt like a little girl with my mother comforting me. My emotions subsided and I knew I would be okay. My brothers and their families said their good-byes, leaving Mary, Ann and me alone with Mom. I thought, "How fitting. We were the women in Mom's life. We represent who she was in all our unique ways."

We stood by the casket and gazed at Mom. She had an angelic look about her. Mary had wanted Mom buried with yellow socks on her feet and she asked the funeral director if she could see them. He looked a little surprised but graciously lifted the white velvet cloth covering Moms' legs. We all smiled at the sight of the socks. The little girl who had grown up to be a graceful, caring, loving mother would forever remain young at heart, thanks to my sister.

Glancing down at Mom, I saw her crystal rosary was wrapped between her delicate fingers just as she had requested. An angel pin was attached to the lapel of her jacket. Looking at her, I thought something was missing. Removing a yellow rose from one of the bouquets, I hooked its stem through one of the button holes on Mom's jacket. For me, she was now complete. We said our final good-byes in silent prayer and left the room. Outside my brothers inquired about our delay. Staying true to form, once again the women had kept the men in our lives waiting.

It was an odd sensation being in the church and listening to the service. An era was ending and a new one beginning. Although it had been a year since Dad had passed away, it felt as if it were happening all over again. Only this time Mom wasn't sitting with us. The strong, yet fragile, gentle glue that had bound us together was gone. There was something different about giving her eulogy. The intimacy of sharing the past year together had softened my heart, that had beat so strongly in the adversity of Dad's illness. Gone was her face to lend courage as I spoke. I felt like a little girl again, only now all alone.

As the moment came closer to speak, my heart started pounding and emotion filled my body. Taking a deep breath I looked to one side of the altar and saw the yellow balloon bobbing back and forth and it caused me to smile. The image of Mom standing there looking to see who had come and what they were wearing, flashed in my head. I saw her grinning. It gave me the impetus to step forward. Standing at the podium, a rush of nervousness left me struggling to maintain composure. I searched for the words to begin. My eyes caught the face of my friend John and he smiled at me. All of a sudden, I felt a tremendous anchoring inside my body and heard a voice in my head say, "It's okay to begin now."

The voice that spoke was not mine and I felt God was talking through me. Gone was the extreme nervousness. It was replaced by a grace that mirrored my mother. It was so quiet in the church I could hear the birds outside singing. I felt honored to be representing my family as we celebrated the life of this beloved woman. As the eulogy ended, I asked everyone to rise and join with me in a prayer of farewell and celebration. It was not a part of the written script but was spontaneous. It seemed to be God's final crown of completion.

When the service was over, we left the church and walked to the grave site. Mom's grandchildren, both male and female, carried the casket. That had been her desire and was her way of acknowledging the deep love she had for them. I stood next to Mom's casket, and my sister Ann was next to me. As the priest was saying the final prayer, a little bird started sweetly singing behind us. Both Ann and I turned toward each other and smiled. For a fleeting moment, I thought of the robin a few days earlier. What a wonderful tribute to Mom.

Earlier that morning, Dave had dug Mom's grave. I had asked if I could join him to help with the digging and do a blessing of the earth. Accustomed to my idiosyncrasies over the years, he graciously and teasingly accommodated my request. It was a rich experience. Dave had a big heart and dearly loved both my parents. I had tremendous respect for his emotional capacity to carry out these preparations. He was quiet as I blessed tobacco and spread it over the ground. Then he went about the task as if it were a natural thing. Knowing how much love Mom had put into tending her flower and vegetable gardens, it was fitting to give the same love to this endeavor.

After the service and the meal that followed, I quickly went back to the farm to change my clothes and participate in covering the casket. Upon my return to the cemetery, I was disappointed to find Dave had already finished. I asked why he hadn't waited for me.

He replied, "Your mother didn't want you throwing dirt on her like you did with your Dad. You know, you can't have everything your way."

Feeling sensitive to his words, I asked what he meant.

"Nothing."

Although he didn't sound angry, his words stayed with me. I wondered if somehow through Mom's process of dying, I had been too controlling. It was something I pondered for a long time afterward.

The day after the funeral, we had a family meeting. Everyone from out of town was leaving the next day and many financial issues needed to be discussed. The meeting was comprised of all the brothers and sisters, as well as their mates, and was the first time such an eclectic group had met alone without any influence from Mom or Dad. It felt like a board meeting at which we were coming together and learning how to effectively communicate with one another. We represented different life experiences and perspectives and had different relationships with each other. I knew families that had suffered gaping wounds after their parents died as a result of unresolved bitterness. I didn't want that happening to us. Yet this possibility existed if we didn't discuss matters. It was risky bringing our emotional rawness to the table to discuss sensitive matters a day after Mom's funeral. The geographic distance that separated us limited the time when we could all be together.

Johnny and Ron, executors and trustees of Mom's will, led the meeting. It turned out to be a lively and enlightening experience. We had always been a feisty lot, each strong in our own opinions. Toes had been stepped on from blurting out comments, innocently spoken without regard for the sensitivity of others' feelings. Because we had been burned by one another at some point in our lives, many of us were protecting old hurts. There was caution and nervousness in the air as we gingerly mingled and waited for everyone to arrive. We decided to have the meeting outside and chairs were placed in a circle. We lit a candle and set it in the middle on a stump. Everyone was smudged with burning sage using my eagle feather. We joined hands and I led everyone in prayer: "Dear God, we come together today asking for your guidance and strength to lead us in a rightful path to discuss the matters before us. Let all decisions be made for the highest and greatest benefit of all. All feelings and thoughts are accepted and honored within this circle. We agree that issues we are unwilling to express in the sanctity of this group will not be bantered back and forth among individuals and left unresolved. May our choices reflect the integrity and honesty of Mom and Dad. Bless and help us toward healing our hearts and building a new foundation. Amen."

I was curious to see how Johnny and Ron would conduct the meeting. Late the night before, they had cornered me in the kitchen to discuss my needs. In Ron's unique nature, he blurted out, "We want to know what you want."

I was exhausted and had no idea what he was talking about. Feeling most of my responsibilities were complete, I had no reserve energy left to engage in any kind of conversation. Feeling slightly irritated, I joined them in conversation, expecting it to be a few minutes of dialogue. It turned out to be several hours and very insightful. Gone was the superficial chit chat that had kept us safe throughout the years. Instead there was an emotional vulnerability and sensitivity. As trustees, I inquired how they planned to run the meeting. They asked what I meant. I explained that the tone they initially carried into the group would dictate how safe everyone felt in interacting. As representatives of Mom and Dad, it was important to use wise counsel in how things were presented so we could work together as a team and utilize our strengths. Ron had strong business acumen but was short on sensitivity. I cautioned him about not coming on like a bull dog just to get things settled, and disregarding people's feelings. I told Johnny his fairness could balance the emotional rawness that was certain to surface. What was vital was that all voices be allowed the equal right to be heard. Then I asked them to pray for guidance because of their responsibility. Afraid they might take offense to my input, I was surprised to hear words of thanks for posing possibilities they hadn't considered.

My brothers came to the circle prepared, organized and tempered in their approach. As each matter was discussed smoothly, my optimism for a peaceful meeting soared. It would soon be put to a great test. Sitting outside was perfect. It was neutral ground and it was healing to smell the fresh air and feel the gentle breeze on our faces. As meatier issues came up, dominant personalities emerged and, with them, strong emotions. The flood gates were opened, and wounds were exposed. Just at the moment when things really started to heat up, Aunt Mary and Uncle Joe drove into the yard to drop off a casserole she had fixed. In a fit of frustration and anger, one of my brothers kicked a chair and stormed away from the group. I was embarrassed for us all that a family outburst had been witnessed by relatives. I quickly went to their vehicle and explained we were in the middle of a family meeting and it was not a good time for visitors. With the silent understanding that at the best of times families have their disputes, they were unfazed by what they had seen. Smiling, my aunt handed me the warm dish and said to call if we needed anything. Their unexpected appearance turned out to be a welcome break from the tension in the air.

As a result of my brother's outburst, we all learned about the importance of holding the space for dialogue to continue. The remaining siblings sat together outside, looked at one another and said, "Now what do we do?"

We all agreed to hold strong to our initial commitment out of respect and love for Mom and Dad. I volunteered to go and talk with my brother. It was challenging for both of us. Tempers flared and finally after several hours we all reunited in the sacred circle. Even after establishing ground rules that all feelings were welcome, it was difficult to listen to sentiments directed with passion and intensity. As uncomfortable as it was, the intent of our prayer held its power. We walked away from the meeting with a greater knowledge of each other and with our family still intact. A new foundation was being built that would require patience, understanding, love and the willingness to walk together into the unknown. Over the next few months, more meetings continued to expose the fragments of scars formed around our tender hearts.

We were slowly learning how to work together and listen with greater compassion to the sensitivities that still lay within us. We were stronger individually and collectively and would always be bonded by our blood connection. We still weren't clean with respect to some of our individual issues, but at least there was an open door to eventually resolving them.

Everyone's departure on Sunday was bittersweet. While I looked forward to finally having some time alone, I would miss the uplifting, familiar flutter of activity, as well as the camaraderie of my siblings.

Mark, Kate and their kids were the last to leave. As they walked into the house on Sunday afternoon, Mark was holding their white cat Farley in his arms. As soon as I saw their cat, a dream from the night before flashed through my mind. I turned to my brother and said, "Mark, would you mind leaving Farley with me for a few days?"

"Sure. Kate's Mom is coming down at the end of the week and she can bring him with her. Why do you want him?"

Looking at him in surprise, I said, "When you just walked in with Farley, I vividly remembered having a dream about him. You had left him with me for some reason. I don't recall why. But I think he is supposed to be here. Animals have a natural tendency to provide comfort when someone is hurting and I think his energy is supposed to bring some healing to the house and to me."

Mark grinned at Farley and said, "Hey, Farley, did you hear that? Do you want to stay with Suzane?"

A few hours later, minus one family member, they left. As the evening darkness set in, the quietness of the house became extremely uncomfortable. Memories of knocking at the door on the previous nights left me edgy and I called John and asked if he would spend the night. He was happy to oblige my request. Two interesting things happened. As I was standing in the bathroom brushing my teeth with the door open, I felt the presence of someone and heard voices in the kitchen. Thinking someone had come over, I stuck my head in the kitchen doorway. John was sitting alone at the kitchen table. I asked if he said something to me. He replied that he hadn't spoken a word. I questioned him again and he said, "No, I didn't say anything at all. I've been reading the paper." And yet, I had distinctly heard a conversation going on and felt other people present in the kitchen.

Before retiring for the night, I went to retrieve Farley from outside and couldn't get him to come into the house. After half an hour of exasperated attempts, I left him alone to fend for himself.

Around five in the morning I had to go to the bathroom. Used to maneuvering the dark hallway to the steps downstairs, I walked out of my room without turning on a light. In the corner, just at the foot of the steps, I saw what appeared to be a white glowing cat. Groggy from sleepiness I thought John had brought Farley into the house. As I went to pick him up, the white form moved upward in the air, directly in front of me. It caught me by surprise and I gasped. There was a peaceful feeling about the form and I didn't sense any fear or need for alarm. My nerves were still edgy and I thought my exhaustion was creating the illusion before me. So I put my hand out and it went completely through the whiteness. I immediately thought, "I can't handle whatever this is right now." I quickly turned on the light, and the form disappeared.

Making my way downstairs, I went to the back porch. Farley was sitting outside waiting to come in. In disbelief over what had just happened, I told myself, "Okay, I'm just having a dream, that's all this is."

Leaving Farley to his food dish in the corner of the kitchen, I went back upstairs and crawled into bed. After a few minutes, I could hear him downstairs. "Raaaarrr, Raaaarrr." The sound was similar to that of a cat defending its territory from a predator. He made the sound one more time. I went back downstairs and he was sitting in the corner of the room looking upward. Although he was not always eager to be picked up by me, he had no resistance this time and I carried him upstairs and put him on the bed next to me. Unable to fall back asleep, I realized both Farley and I had seen a ghost.

I remembered the loud knocking at the door a few days before, as well as in previous months. Was someone trying to communicate with me? Were Mom or Dad trying to get my attention? As thoughts went through my mind, I recalled them telling the story when we were younger that one of the previous owners of the farm had hung himself in an old garage that had been torn down when I was little. I had never liked going inside it because it gave me creepy feelings.

Later that morning, I asked John whether he had seen or felt anything unusual. He hadn't.

That afternoon, I talked with Samantha, one of my spiritual sisters, and relayed the incident and the memory from my childhood. She felt the soul of this man was still lingering around the homestead and had been trying to get my attention so he could be released from bondage to his demise. As bizarre as it sounded, her voice rang true inside my body.

Later, while mowing the lawn, I kept thinking about the white image in the hallway. Who was this spirit? Was he really trying to contact me? And why now? The name "Charlie" kept popping into my mind. That night Jacque called to see how I was doing and again I shared the story. She confirmed Samantha's hunch. She told me to do a pipe ceremony to send his lost soul back to the Light, and described in detail how to do it. She said what I was being asked to do was a great honor. She shared that because of my connection to God and my having assisted Mom with her passage, this man's spirit recognized a window to achieve final peace.

I knew my family had always thought there were a few screws loose with me, but this would really validate their suspicions. I had no idea when to perform the ceremony, but I thought it would probably occur late at night. I was in no hurry to do it, and questioned my own abilities to partake in such an unusual request. When Ann and Dave stopped by after work the next day, I told them about the ghost adventure. They glanced at one another with a funny look in their eyes. Much to my surprise, my sister didn't doubt my sanity, but I couldn't tell about Dave.

Two days later, around sunset, the ceremony took place. While I was working outside, I felt a sudden urge to prepare the fire ring Mom had used for burning small brush in the yard. I placed it in the driveway with tinfoil underneath and blessed it with tobacco before placing wood inside. Looking up at the sky, I noticed spectacular rays of reddish light streaming downward. A chill went through my body and inside I heard, "Go and get your pipe. The time is fast approaching when this man took his life many years ago."

I ran upstairs, grabbed my pipe bag and ran back downstairs. Kneeling next to the fire ring, I quickly unwrapped my holy objects. I was wearing shorts and sat on a swatch of carpet to protect my legs from the gravel. After lighting the fire, I began preparing myself and the pipe in a sacred way. I glanced upward. The sky was a brilliant reddish orange and looked as if it were on fire. I closed my eyes and prayed, "Dear God, please guide me in returning this soul back to the Light. Use my body as a vessel in honor of this sacred journey. Help him be released from his agony and heal his sorrow. Thank you for bestowing this gift of assisting him. Amen."

I was nervous and had to focus on stopping the chatter of doubt going through my mind. After a few minutes of silence, I asked for a sign to know when this man's spirit was present. All of a sudden, I felt a gentle stroke across my leg that felt like a feather. In my mind I asked the spirit's name.

In my head, I heard very clearly, "Charles, but my friends called me Charlie."

It took everything to control my excitement. Then an image appeared in my mind. In the distance a man was hanging from a rope in an old, dark garage. I couldn't see his face. In my mind, I began a dialogue. "Charles, I have heard your cry for help. I am here to assist in freeing your soul to return to the Light. I come with pureness and love in my heart and am honored to be of service to your soul."

I heard, "Thank you. You can call me Charlie."

I felt more peaceful knowing we had made a connection. I asked, "Charlie, do you care to share what happened?"

In a voice that sounded like it came from a person sitting right next to me, I heard, "My mother and I purchased this farm. I didn't know much about the financial business of running it. I made some bad choices and was afraid to tell anyone. We kept going deeper in debt. My mother never knew. I was too ashamed to tell her. Out of desperation, I hung myself."

Then I heard sobbing.

I waited quietly until he had stopped weeping. "Charlie, you have been holding onto this pain for a long time. It is from not forgiving yourself. Your judgments about your actions have kept your soul from moving on. It is what has kept you in bondage here. God loves you very much and holds no judgment upon you. I will help you to let go."

There was just silence in my head, so I continued: "I want you to imagine when you were younger someone who loved you very much and whom you loved, someone who has already passed on."

Within a few seconds, I saw the image of a head bouncing up and down. Then the picture expanded to a little boy being bounced on the leg of an elderly man. In my mind I asked, "Do you have the person in mind?"

His voice was clear as he responded. "Yes. It's my grandfather. He loved me very much and I loved him, too. When I was little he used to bounce me up and down on his leg."

It felt as if we were sharing the same experience and it seemed very real. I felt as if I were in a trance and totally oblivious to anything external. He didn't say any more so I said, "Good. Now feel all his love filling you up inside and all around you. Just stay in that loving emotion for a moment."

Time passed as I remained focused in prayer with him. "Charlie, do you feel all his love?"

He responded quietly, "Yes."

"Okay, now imagine a time when you were happy. You were so happy you almost couldn't contain yourself."

Another image flashed before me of a young man on a bicycle. His voice said, "I'm going to see my girlfriend. I am in high school and I visit her every day on my bicycle. I really like her."

He became quiet. A few moments passed and I said, "Stay with that feeling and let it swirl all around inside. Let yourself feel how happy you were and let me know when you are finished."

More time passed. Eventually he responded, "Okay, I'm done."

"Now, Charlie, feel all the loving energy around you and let your soul drift upward."

Another image appeared. I was standing with a man and a brilliant light was shining in front of us. He was holding my hand and it felt peaceful. In the distance, an image of someone appeared. It came out of a bright light and walked toward us.

We were both silent and I felt as if I were right there with him. As the image of the being surrounded by light came closer, I said, "Charlie, you are free to go now."

The man held my hand for a few seconds and then released it . He started walking toward the white being. I watched for a few seconds and then Charlie turned back to me and smiled. Bowing my head, I placed my hand in a fist over my heart and extended my arm toward him as my fingers open upward. He repeated the same action and then turned and walked side-by-side with the being into the glowing, bright light.

I sat for many moments in silence. Then I felt pulled off my feet. Taking my ceremonial pipe, I walked around the house, releasing smoke upward in prayer. I asked that the remnants of Charlie's energy be released and the land of my parent's property be cleansed. My voice spoke aloud, "Let only joy and happiness dwell within this home. Bless this house and the land that surrounds it. Amen."

Then I returned to the fire ring and sat back down. An incredibly peaceful feeling circled around me for about five minutes. Then the energy shifted and I felt pulled out of the trance. Just at that moment, a car drove down the highway. By now it was dark. The ceremony had lasted two hours.

The next morning, I called Ann at work and told her what had happened. She said Mom and Dad had kept copies of old deeds in the safe and to go and look through them. With papers in hand, I sat at the kitchen table drinking a cup of tea. I was excited to come upon a man named Charles who had purchased the farm with his mother. Several years later, the farm had been sold. Only the mother's name was on the deed. Her son was deceased.

A couple of days later, Dave stopped by the farm. He had been to his aunt's house to help fix something and he had told her about the sighting of Charlie.

She had told him, "Don't you ever think your sister-in-law is crazy. That stuff is real. Because it happened to me, too. Years ago when my sister was sick, she was in the hospital. Her daughter was staying at my house. Late one night, I was asleep and woke up to the image of her standing at the foot of the bed. I thought she needed something. I called out her name, but she didn't answer. Then she moved to the side of my bed. I reached out to give her a hug, and my arms went right through her. My sister died early the next morning. Don't you ever doubt this stuff."

What a glorious mystery death is.

Chapter Eighteen
Endings, Beginnings and a Sacred Letter

It had been two weeks since Mom passed away. I awoke from a disturbing dream to the sound of my own voice crying:

I was on a large ship that looked like an ocean liner. It was surrounded by miles and miles of water. The sun was shining and it was a balmy day. I was standing next to an older man who seemed to be very holy. Unable to see his face, I sensed a presence about him that was profound. While I didn't know who he was, I felt safe and comfortable being with him. We stood quietly next to one another and he said to me, "You are going to die from cancer."

Shocked by his words, I replied, "That's impossible. I've been taught that no one ever has to die from an illness. I know what you're saying can't be true."

He spoke the same words again.

The scene changed and I was by myself looking out a porthole at crystal blue water. Thinking about what the holy man had just told me, I was in disbelief. I knew he was wrong, I returned to find him. He was not there. Instead I saw another man dressed in a brown robe who appeared to be a monk. His face was covered by a cloak. He walked up to me and repeated the words of the holy man: "You are going to die from cancer."

My response was still the same.

The scene changed and again I found myself looking out a porthole. As I stared at the ocean, tremendous emotion filled my body, and my life flashed before me. I thought to myself, "I can't die from cancer. My life isn't complete. I have too many things to do yet."

I began sobbing and sobbing and my voice inside screamed, "No, it's not true. It can't be true. I'm not ready."

I searched all over the ship for comfort from one of the holy men. But they were gone.

Lying in bed, I was visibly distraught and I couldn't shake the feeling in the pit of my stomach. Never had I had a dream as riveting as this. I was not a stranger to interpreting dreams, but this one had me perplexed.

The phone rang and it was Samantha. "Are you okay? You've been strongly on my mind all morning."

I told her about the dream and started crying.

Her voice was soothing. "Suzane I think it applies to your mother. You are still releasing some of her energy. That was probably how she was feeling when she began to accept the reality of her dying. You are still very connected to her." She encouraged me to spend time at the eagle's nest near John's house, ground myself in the strength of their energy and ask to release what wasn't mine.

As I hung up the phone, I thought of Mom and how she came to terms with dying. A deep emptiness and sorrow filled me. How difficult to feel you were not complete with your life, only to realize it would soon be over. I heard her words in my mind: "You don't know what it's like." What a gripping feeling it was to accept the truth of your own mortality. I wished I had been more compassionate and sensitive to what she must have been going through.

I decided to follow Samantha's advice. I called John and asked whether I could come over. Borrowing his canoe, I paddled down the river and anchored a few hundred feet from the nest. I asked for permission to enter the eagle's sacred space. Then I sat on an old log directly underneath the nest, which was at the top of a tall tree and was about six feet wide. Removing my shoes, I placed my bare feet on the ground and looked out at the river. I took some deep breaths and tried to focus on the energy flowing from the top of my head down into the earth. I prayed that my body be cleansed from the emotional effects of the dream.

As I sat quietly for about half an hour, my fear and edginess slowly left. Across the river, I could see one of the eagles perched on the branch of a dead tree. Glancing around the landscape of the forest, I noticed an opening through some trees and was drawn to it. Replacing my shoes, I made my way through a path amid the thick brush and discovered a large clearing filled with clover. The clearing narrowed at one end, which led to a grass-covered road. Curious where it went, I started walking down it and continued for about half a mile. Aware that it led into private land, I turned around and started back toward the clearing. The closer I got, the more I felt I should be quiet and walk slowly. Just as I reached the edge of the clearing, I saw two deer grazing side-by-side in the corner of the opening. I was amazed at the sight. Immediately, I thought of Mom and Dad. The deer kept grazing and seemed oblivious to my presence. About five minutes passed and a gentle breeze started blowing. Just then they looked over at me. For a few seconds they just stood there and then they began to leap toward the same opening through which I had walked. Sensing they were motioning me to come, I followed their guidance.

I made my way back to the eagle's nest, and was drawn to sit and pray among some evergreen trees. I asked for a sign that all was well with Mom and Dad, that she had received the best possible care. I asked for clarity that my dream pertained to her rather than me. I was feeling peaceful and protected under the towering trees, when the image of a feather popped into my mind. Sensing one was close by, I began looking around. I lifted up the branches of a small evergreen branch where I was sitting, but there was nothing. I started walking in a circular fashion around the nest trying to anticipate where one might have fallen. It was difficult to find anything in the thick underbrush, let alone an imaginary feather. I gave up and went to sit once again by the small evergreen tree. Something told me to lift up the branch where I had looked earlier. Doing so, I saw a beautiful, long, elegant bald eagle feather sitting as if someone had gently placed it there. It was about seventeen inches long. At the base on one side, it fanned out like a wing. I sat in complete amazement knowing it had not been there the first time I had looked. Overwhelmed with emotion, I started to cry. Mom and Dad had gotten their wings and so had I.

In the Native American culture, eagle medicine is the power of the Great Spirit, our connection to the divine. It is the ability to live in the realm of spirit and yet remain connected and balanced within the realm of earth. From the heights of the clouds, eagles are close to the heavens where the Great Spirit dwells. The eagle represents a state of grace achieved through hard work, understanding and a completion of the tests of initiation that result in the taking of one's personal power.

I will never have the appropriate words to express the profoundness of this experience. Sitting in the woods, I wondered if all along I had been guided to come to this place and the dream had been a catalyst for the healing gifts that awaited me. When I returned home, I placed the feather next to my other one and bowed in blessing over my incredible fortune.

Over the next few days, phrases ran through my mind about the night Mom died. Not wanting to lose the potency of the experience I found myself writing a poem.

One Last Time

As you gently breathe a wisp of your last breath, I am
    unprepared.
It came so quickly as I left the room for just a minute,
To make a cup of tea and lovingly sit with you—one last time.
But you knew your hour had arrived and that's what you
    preferred.
Only I returned sooner and was gifted with that last moment.
I knew it was for me.

An overwhelming sense of responsibility fills my heart,
As I lay my head upon your chest.

And I weep as I feel the warmth of your body.
For I know my work is not yet complete.
The commitment made lifetimes ago of a daughter to a mother,
A ritual, so to speak, that was once passed down from
  generation to generation.
The mother giving life and the daughter returning it.
Back to the light where it once began.
One last time.

I tenderly bathe your body like a newborn babe,
As you so lovingly did for me.
Brushing your teeth and cleaning your nails,
Like a sculptor crafting his art.
Your red fluffy robe caresses your body,
As I gently wrap you in its warmth.
While you quietly lie upon the couch in graceful receivership
For all the love you once gave so unselfishly.

Your hands once worn and rough from hardened years of
  farm life,
Have become delicate and soft with the months of enduring
  frailness.
I bow my head in reverence as I sweetly kiss the center of each
  palm,
Where the indented lines now define the wisdom of your years,
And I gently fold them in solitary prayer across your lap.

A prevailing sense of peace comes over me,
As I softly stroke each cheek.
Allowing my eyes to slowly gaze upon your face as you transform
Your weakened form into the woman I always knew you to be.
The queen prepared for her throne in all her grace and glory.
A chosen one returning back home.
One last time.

Early the next morning after writing this poem, I went outside and knelt in the ground that had once been Mom's garden plot. Letting the soil run through my fingers, I felt a loving, sweet presence all around me. It circled like a warm, gentle breeze and had the slight fragrance of a rose. I knew it was Mom. The feeling lingered for several moments and then disappeared with the graceful breath of the wind.

We sold the homestead to my brother Johnny. Everyone was excited he wanted to purchase it. The thought of being able to return to the sustenance of our roots was comforting. I thought it would have pleased Mom and Dad to know their sacred piece of land had been honored and would continue to be lovingly preserved.

Alone in the house, I felt both a richness and a haunting feeling. My interpretations of what I saw and felt now were filtered through a new set of eyes and a more delicate heart. Being ensconced in the history of memories had been freeing.

As I packed and sorted through things, I felt as if I were cleaning the cobwebs out of my life. By facing the physical evidence every day that both my parents were gone shattered any illusions and had a healing effect. The days were busy with endless things to do in preparation for my brother moving in. Mom had been a packrat accomplished in the art of filling empty spaces. It was precious to discover the treasures she had collected over the years, such as special cards from her children or Dad, hankies that belonged to my grandmother, a white scarf with her initials she had given Dad before they were married. Each of these things had been made more endearing by the woman who was my mother.

The challenge of dividing things up had been made easy. Mom had left all the household items to the "girls," while Dads' tools, guns and other manly belongings were given to the "boys." There was no disharmony between my sisters and me over our preferences. I didn't really care for much, only a few things that had great sentimental value. I asked for Mom's turquoise turban, and was gladly gifted it.

Having more would not bring Mom closer to me. To decide on pieces we all liked, we assigned ourselves each a number, put them in a hat and picked. We also decided to give our brothers some of the things in the house and asked them to make a list of what they would like. Many of Mom's clothes we gave to her sisters, and each sister-in-law plus the grandchildren received a special memory. The process was more tedious than painful because of the short timeframe in which to accomplish it all.

Two dear friends came to visit and their company was refreshing. One experience was especially meaningful. One day Sharon, whom I had met through spirituality classes and who had become one of my spiritual sisters, drove into the yard and parked her truck in front of a large shed-like building that housed Dad's farm equipment at one end and his garage and work bench at the other. As she got out, she asked, "Where did I just park?"

I told her and then inquired why she had asked.

She said, "As I drove up, I was told to leave some tobacco in front of the doors and I saw an image of a man leaning on the tree next to that shed."

I knew she was talking about Dad. Later that day we took a canoe ride down to the eagle's nest and encountered a huge rain storm on the way back. That evening, concerned it might rain again, she asked to put her open-bed truck in Dad's garage because she had valuable artwork in the back. The next morning she noticed the back was wet. We were sitting outside on the swing and she mentioned that Dad's garage must have a leak. I told her that was impossible because he had been very particular about the things in it.

All of a sudden, she started to laugh. Looking at her, I asked what was so funny.

She replied, "Your father just corrected me. In a distinct and indignant tone I heard, 'My garage does not leak. My garage does not leak. Where did you park your truck yesterday during that storm? It isn't wet because of my garage.'"

Because of the unexpected rain, she had left the truck outside, uncovered. Then Sharon said, "I was told to tell you to spend more time in your father's space. There is a gift for you somewhere."

Days later, I was poking around Dad's garage. We used to store grain above its ceiling when we grew our own wheat. Not really searching for anything, I heard some kernels of oats hit the cement floor. I thought it was mice. Then I saw a few tools Dad had used when I was little, and a broken deer horn none of my brothers had taken. Smiling, I wrapped them in one of his old work rags, and walked out of the garage.

I made a trip to India in honor of Mom. Earlier in the year, my friend Jacque had been given an ashram by a Hindu leader, who gave it for her foundation. She organized the trip to prepare the sacred land, which she called Shangri-La, for people of all denominations to come and worship God. The main reason I went was to bring some of Mom's and her friend Ann's geranium plants. In light of my promise to her about making a difference, the idea of spreading love through her flowers felt like a great place to begin. I was a little nervous about bringing plants abroad, but I was assured there would be no problem at customs. A local florist prepared them for the lengthy journey.

Checking the box at the Minneapolis airport, I noticed water had seeped through the bottom. The ticket agent was hesitant about taking it. After explaining the story behind my trip, the agent secured the bottom with extra tape. Then I asked if she would hold the box while I blessed it. Although she was unable to assure its safe arrival, she smiled as I told her there would be no problem because God would watch over the plants.

Seventeen hours later, I gathered my luggage at the airport in India. Although the box was fairly well squished, it was completely dry on the bottom. Going through customs was still a concern. The man at the gate looked curiously at the box and back at me three distinct times, never saying a word, and let us pass through. It was four more days before the plants were removed from the box and planted. By that time they were in pretty poor shape. Many of them were brown and shriveled. Not knowing much about the durability of geraniums, I was concerned they wouldn't survive.

When we arrived at the ashram, a young Indian man helped me pot them. While neither of us could speak the other's language, I felt he knew the plants had special meaning and was tender in his handling of them. It required ten ceramic pots to accommodate all the cuttings.

The next morning after they had been transplanted, little green shoots had already formed. By the time I left India, they were thriving. The story of the geraniums spread among the ashram workers and they gave them special attention. They were left in the good hands of a woman, Kay, who remained at the ashram caring for the grounds of Shangri-La. While I was writing this book, Kay returned to the U.S. and informed me the plants had survived the monsoon and heat of the summer. With her tender nurturing, they flourished with beautiful pink, red and white flowers. Mom was starting to make a difference in ways she probably never imagined.

I was beginning to feel it was time for me to leave the farm. Although my brother had encouraged me to stay for as long as I wanted, I felt a stirring to move on.

I was sad at the thought of returning to Los Angeles. It would be hard to say good-bye to my family and relatives to whom I'd grown closer. And to John, the mysterious man who had walked into my life and touched my heart deeply through his kindness, love and support.

It was nearing Christmas and my brother Vernon had asked me to spend the holiday with them in Seattle. I planned to drive back in Mom's and Dad's Oldsmobile, a gift from my family. I wanted to be in California by the start of the new year.

I took one last journey down the country roads that held so many memories. My mission was complete. A huge chapter of my life was over and it was time for a new season to begin. Never had I imagined it would entail losing both Mom and Dad. The place I had always called "home" would never be the same.

The day of my departure was gray and dismal, matching my feeling inside. My good-byes were tearful, signaling the end of the past one and a half years. Before getting on my way, my last stop was the cemetery. I had bought three reddish-pink silk roses and planted them in some soil in a can wrapped in tinfoil. I had put them outside for a few days to let the soil freeze around the stems to make the base sturdy. The car was packed full and I placed the flowers on the floor of the front seat. As I drove out of the yard, the house was empty and the familiar crunch of the gravel imparted one last farewell. Arriving at the cemetery, I broke down with emotion as I got out of the car. The snow was knee-deep and I plodded through it, weeping. I scooped the white powder away from their headstone, and nestled the tin can to one side. Amidst the dreariness, the reddish-pink roses made the white landscape seem vibrant. Flowers always come alive and return to bloom after a sleepy winter and that was how I wanted to remember Mom and Dad. Driving away from the cemetery, I glanced out the window to see their dramatic color standing proud above the snowy mounds.

My trip back to L.A. was broken in three segments and matched my emotional state. As soon as I left Wisconsin, I encountered bitter cold weather, hitting fifty degrees below in the Dakotas. I stayed ahead of a major snow storm for most of the trip. I was able to get through the passes in Washington and into Seattle just before the roads were closed. I drove for at least twelve hours each day and layers of emotion fell away with the passing miles. The more I drove, the more cleansed I felt. The silent time alone allowed me to reflect on the past year, all that I had learned, all that I had given and all that I had received.

Remnants of the past felt as if they were being discarded, like the shedding of old skin. I could never return to who I once was. I had been changed forever.

I arrived back in L.A. on January 7th and went to stay in Sabrina's guest house. It was difficult being back. I didn't feel as if my old life fit me anymore and I was not ready to see my friends. The pace of L.A. was hectic and disturbing to my body. I missed the quiet, peacefulness of the farm and its cocoon of protection. I didn't quite know where or how to start over.

Part of me also didn't feel complete about Mom, and a deep sadness nagged at me. Since I had found peace with Dad's passing, I thought the same would be true with Mom—and even more so because of the intimacy we had shared during her last year. Looking for guidance, I sought the counsel of Solano.

His input was both comforting and enlightening. As I shared my feelings, he responded tenderly, "That fragment of sadness you feel is important. Sadness is the way the soul acknowledges yearning. You see, all relationships that move one deeply are complex. In that complexity, you are more available to greater understanding of your own soul. Relationships that are very simple, in which you have an encounter with someone in passing, also serve a purpose. You serve a purpose. These relationships go on without much depth. The relationship with your mother hits on many, many, many cylinders. Those different aspects that are hit upon will grant you much in the way of thought and feeling over the years. You will be processing this event in your existence for the rest of your lifetime. You were given many, many tools; and you gave many tools. There were various tools you did not get that you will have to get from another source. And that is as it should be.

"In your culture, people feel they are supposed to be able to manage their feelings all the time. One of the things that is not understood is that the soul inside each person has so many things to communicate to them. The way in which it communicates is not singular. It is not simply to grant unto you a message in words, or a gift from a friend. Nor even an understanding of a sign that comes from the weather, from the wind upon your cheek, or a communication that comes from a loved one. The soul's voice is all of the aspects within your life that bring unto you the depth of your being. That means that if a single source, like your mother, brings unto you joy, sadness, yearning, longing and all the various things you experienced with her, then that voice of your soul is a voice you can listen to and listen to and never grow tired of it. This fragment of sadness, do not try to eradicate it. Listen to it. Let it into your being. Let it be a part of the depth of you. Allow this to happen with all of your emotions because your feelings constantly teach you about yourself."

He stopped. Understanding more about the nature of my sadness was freeing and left me much to ponder. I asked how to move forward with the uncertainty of starting anew.

"I am pleased you have asked this. Simply know that where you are right now is a juncture point of moving from a time of no focus into a time of great focus. Do not be in a hurry to leap back into the fray of life. I urge you at all costs not to design your life in that way. The mystical aspect that you have engaged within yourself, the dialogue with your soul's understanding of the mystical, is the most fulfilling thing you will ever know. Furthermore, it is one of the most powerful resources for achieving your aims. The thing that is an utter and complete paradox is how to be in that mystical flow and try and take care of yourself. For it seems that the energy needed to care for yourself is the energy that is ambitious and driving and concerned with the world of things. The greater providence comes from the aspect that connects with mysticism, the mystical within your being. To achieve this, simply make no move in any of your days until you have connected with your spirit and been guided about what action to take that day. For, in connecting with God, all guidance is available and all action is subsidiary to that guidance."

He paused to allow his words to sink in and then continued, "The important thing to know is there is no thing, no action, no achievement that is out of the scope of God. In every moment ask, 'How should I spend my energy now?' God will most assuredly answer you. In some instances the answers will be extraordinary and seem to be completely without logic. Take the action that has been spoken. For the action that has been spoken is the most direct route to achieving your goals. You must listen first for guidance and when it comes, then you must act. In that way, God will often say to step out of your ordinary realm of behavior and do things you may consider to be outrageous, unsafe, unwise or even illogical. God knows the straightest, clearest and quickest route to accomplish what you are wanting to accomplish. If one is willing to throw aside their logical mind, to be a babe and step out into the world that way, then God can guide you in the most remarkable ways. God knows how to take you where you want to go. It requires balance to do this. Your balance has come from the experience of the reverence of death, the splendor of death and the juxtaposition of the splendor of life and love. That balance grants you the availability to be reverent in your approach to God in each day and listen and act and listen and act. For what is the point of being in a place of mysticism within yourself, if not for the purpose of achieving something that demonstrates it, so others may see for themselves the value for living a life in that way."

I was comforted after our conversation and grateful for his insight. I was relieved to know it was okay to go slow and not be in a hurry to leap back into the seeming chaos around me.

Sabrina, Richard and Julie were gone for the weekend and I was house-sitting. The quietness was rejuvenating. While I was alone in the guest house, my eyes were drawn to one of the boxes containing my belongings from Wisconsin. Inside was Mom's wedding dress. It was still in incredible condition, except for a yellow discoloring from aging. My sisters and I weren't sure what to do with it, so I had decided to bring it back with me. All the while I was growing up, Mom had it stored in a box in one of the upstairs closets. I had never had a desire to try it on. For some reason, I did on this night.

As petite as I was, Mom must have been more so when she married. Buttons ran up the entire back and the train unfolded from the dress as one entire piece. The front had a see-through bodice. It was elegant and stylish and Mom must have looked stunning in it.

Slipping into the dress, I felt transported back in time, as if I were Mom. Swirling in front of the mirror, I felt great pride about being her daughter. In the mystery of her dying, I had learned so much about her, more than in all the years combined. She had given me freedom in more ways than either of us could have realized as I journeyed back to care for her. She had taught me how to fly.

Gone was the role of feeling like a mother tending to a sick child. I had been transformed back into being her daughter. The image in the mirror no longer was of her and a life gone by. Instead, what was reflected was a unique woman who was also filled with hopes, dreams and aspirations. A woman who also wanted to make a difference in the world, spurred by inspiration from another one who'd thought she hadn't.

As I sat on the couch in her wedding dress, I opened another box. Inside were old letters and cards I had not looked at for years. They had been stored with my brother in Seattle and forgotten. Several were from Mom. One in particular was priceless. The envelope was postmarked April 2, 1985. Tears streamed down my face as I read the contents. At that time, I had been going through a rough period in my life and had reached out to her.

The beauty and wisdom of her words were timeless and could have been written by any mother to one of her children. In acknowledgment of her essence, I share it with you.

Dear Susie,

It really was good talking to you and in this letter I'm going to continue on with our talk. I'm hesitant because there may be said some things you don't care to hear and the bad part about putting one's thoughts in writing is that the reader may interpret things as they weren't meant to be. As I said, I wish I knew the magic words to tell you to make all things well but that's impossible. This is life and life is a mystery and will always be so and it's far from my humble mind to explain it. As I've told you many times, I know and understand your feelings far more than you realize but I don't have the power to make all the bad things good or have the magic words to pretend to do so. Life is just not so. Life can be very cruel and we have no power to change many things, but we've got to have faith that Someone is guiding us and testing us and I always look on this life as just a testing place. Would that we had the simplicity of little children to look at things and deal with them.

I sense in your talk the questioning of love in your childhood. I see and hear you trying to put your life in neat little boxes and resolve every problem—in my way of thinking this is impossible as life cannot be resolved and put in retrospect as we would like to. There are too many uncertainties we have no control over and never will. I firmly believe we are made stronger by our hurts, mistakes, etc., and by which we cope with living. I see your childhood as being no different from that of your brothers and sisters or other children. As a child you were as normal and caring as anyone else and we would never have thought of you as an angry child, but with your own personality traits as you each had. I saw anger in your teens as well as all the other normal feelings and actions in those so-called sometimes difficult years. I feel each of us dealt with these feelings in our own ways—just a process of growing up. In all openness I must say I feel hurt by the intense hate you had for me for so many years. I've always thought it was so easy for someone to say "I love you" and easy hugs and kisses—to me true love is lived and not just surface actions.

Now let me tell you my concept of love. Love is many everyday things. In having children, it's wanting them not only when they're at their most desirable but all times. Love is working your fool head off so these children have food and clothes. Love is getting up night after night to feed and change these babies. Love is making special Sunday dinners for the family. Love is sleepless nights, hours of rocking when these children are sick. Love is caring enough to take an interest in all their school activities, being so proud at *graduations, communions and so forth. Love is seeing they have new clothes at Easter, Christmas, etc., even if it means wearing your old clothes so they may have new. Love is working along side your kids and never expecting them to do jobs you wouldn't. Love is being so darn tired from work but yet seeing they have a warm meal and a warm house. I could go on and on but all I'm trying to tell you is how deep our love for you kids was and is. Although it may be hard for them as children to realize this, I feel this should become easier as they grow older. Each of us expresses our love in different ways and maybe it will help you to know how we expressed ours. I know I made lots of mistakes and I sure wish I could have another chance but I know that's impossible and who knows what other mistakes I would make. God knows we're human and will always make errors, and all we can do is keep trying. I think you know how much we think of you kids. We believe we've got the greatest and no one could ask for anymore in a daughter than you. I know I'm no psychiatrist so all I can give you is my simple advice.*

Put the past behind you. Do you realize how much precious time we waste by dwelling on it? Maybe that little child in you is telling you to accept things as they are. Although I'm not going to let the little child in me ever go away completely—she keeps me thinking young. She made me climb to the top of the hay bales in the barn a couple of weeks ago and pretend I was King of the Mountain. I think every now and then everyone should revert to their childhood—do things that are kiddish and fun. Some people may think you're off your rocker but it sure can smooth over bad times. Accept your past. Know that there had to be good and bad. Live in the present. When things are rough, always look to someone who has it worse and thank God. Remember God is always there for you. Ask and ask and ask. I don't think I could have lived or live without doing that. Keep your sense of humor and guts which you've always done. You always picked yourself up and bounded right back and I know you'll keep right on. You've got a lot to be thankful for in yourself. Be who you are. Nobody wants you to change. You're somebody. If my genes passed on to you my bad faults—stubbornness, moodiness (I can't think of any more ☺) you may blame them on heredity.

I think I've put down enough of this. Read it and throw it away. The bottom line is—we love you. Use that if you can. Well I'm going to send this. I'll probably never write another like this.

Love, Mom

Suzane Piela's mother, shortly before she died

Suzane Piela's parents, Edna and John Piela